THE LIFE AND TIMES OF

Arthur Hildersham

PRINCE AMONG PURITANS

THE LIFE AND TIMES OF

Arthur Hildersham

PRINCE AMONG PURITANS

Lesley A. Rowe

Happy Christmas,
Paula,
with best wishes,
Lesley A. Rowe
Dec. 2013

Reformation Heritage Books

Grand Rapids, Michigan

Reformation Heritage Books
2965 Leonard St. NE
Grand Rapids, MI 49525
616-977-0889 / Fax 616-285-3246
orders@heritagebooks.org
www.heritagebooks.org

Printed in the United States of America
13 14 15 16 17 18/10 9 8 7 6 5 4 3 2 1

Library of Congress Cataloging-in-Publication Data

Rowe, Lesley Ann.
  The life and times of Arthur Hildersham : prince among Puritans / Lesley A. Rowe.
    pages cm
  Includes bibliographical references.
  ISBN 978-1-60178-222-9 (hardcover : alk. paper) 1. Hildersam, Arthur, 1563-1632. 2. Puritans—England—Clergy—Biography. I. Title.
  BX9339.H55R69 2013
  285'.9092—dc23
  [B]
                                        2013002590

For additional Reformed literature, request a free book list from Reformation Heritage Books at the above regular or e-mail address.

Contents

Acknowledgments

I have spent the best part of a decade researching and writing about Arthur Hildersham. I owe a great debt of gratitude to the many people who have helped me along the way. I am enormously grateful for the generous assistance and guidance of the early modern historians at Warwick University, especially my PhD supervisors, Professor Bernard Capp and Professor Peter Marshall. Robert Jones and Kenneth Hillier (local historians in Ashby-de-la-Zouch) and staff at the various archive offices also have been most helpful. Any remaining faults in the book are, of course, my own. I have Kathy Sedar to thank for the family trees and maps, and Diane and Alan Skelton for the photographs. My family has been extremely long-suffering and supportive throughout this project, and I will always be indebted to them.

This book is dedicated to Victor, Imogen, Oliver, and Joshua, and to the memory of my parents.

Notes on the Text

In most instances, unless indicated, I have modernized the spelling and the grammar of quotations from the original sixteenth- and seventeenth-century sources. Hildersham's last name was often written as "Hildersam" at the time, and I have left this spelling in the title of Clarke's biography. Titles of books generally have been left unaltered, except for modern capitalization and occasional changes from Roman to Arabic numerals. Dates are rendered according to the Gregorian calendar, which was introduced in 1752, with the year beginning on January 1—not on March 25, as in the old Julian calendar. Thus Hildersham's death is given as March 4, 1632, not 1631, as his monument indicates. All quotations from Hildersham's *Lectures upon John* have been taken from the second edition of 1632.

Why Bother with Arthur Hildersham?

Arthur Hildersham is, to a large extent, a forgotten Puritan. Since Samuel Clarke compiled a thirteen-page account of his life in the seventeenth century, there has been no biography of Hildersham.[1] Although his name appears in many collections of godly lives, the entry is usually brief and based solely on information derived from Clarke. No longer in print, except for short extracts, Hildersham's sermons do not have a place on our bookshelves alongside those of his contemporaries. Ask people in our churches to name leading lights of the Puritan movement, and few would include Hildersham in their list. In fact, most present-day Christians have probably never heard of him.

But this certainly was not the case in the late sixteenth century and the first half of the seventeenth century. During his lifetime, Hildersham was one of the most revered and prominent Puritan figures. He was related to royalty and many of the highest noble families in the land. His leadership of the Puritan Millenary Petition, presented to King James I on his accession to the English throne in 1603, reflected the esteem Hildersham's brethren had for him. Among his closest friends he counted men like Thomas Cartwright, Richard Greenham, John Dod, John Preston, John Cotton, William Gouge, and William Bradshaw. Ashby-de-la Zouch, the town in which he ministered for over forty years,

---

1. Samuel Clarke's "Life of Master Arthur Hildersam" appeared in his *The Lives of Two and Twenty English Divines* (London, 1660) and also in his *A General Martyrologie* (London, 1677). Citations refer to the former, unless otherwise stated.

was regarded as a beacon of the Reformed faith. Even after his death in 1632, Hildersham's opinions and example continued to be influential for the next generation of spiritual leaders, including the New England settlers, the Westminster divines, and Richard Baxter.

Why, then, have we neglected Hildersham, despite the renewed interest in our Puritan forefathers that occurred in the second half of the twentieth century? The answer lies in the fact that this revived appreciation has been print-driven: we have rediscovered the Puritans primarily through reprinted sermon collections. We delight in sermons that are pithy, full of striking quotes and metaphors drawn from every-day life that lodge in the memory and the heart. And here we find the difficulty with Hildersham, for he is less accessible to the modern reader. By the standards of his age, Hildersham published relatively little anyway—two large sermon series, one shorter volume, and a small treatise on the Lord's Supper—and his style can be off-putting initially for someone seeking a spiritual "quick fix." Although the thorough and rigorous nature of Hildersham's sermons richly repays the patient student, even C. H. Spurgeon, who highly valued Hildersham's works, was forced to admit, "he is copious and discursive, we had almost said long-winded."[2]

However, his story, combined with a study of his printed works, is rewarding in a number of ways. Hildersham is a guide who can help us better understand the rapidly changing and often confusing religious scene of the later Elizabethan and early Stuart period. He faced challenges and big questions that are still relevant, such as the following: What is a true church? What is the nature of true worship? When is it right to separate from a church? How should we relate to other believers who hold different opinions? How far are we bound to obey our consciences, even when it brings us into conflict with the state? Although we may not agree with all of Hildersham's conclusions, his way of thinking through issues according to biblical principles is instructive. Hildersham's response to his frequent suspensions from the Church of England (he was prohibited from preaching and, on occasion, even imprisoned)

---

2. C. H. Spurgeon, *Commenting and Commentaries* (London, 1890), 99.

provides valuable lessons on enduring persecution and inspires us to greater Christian commitment. In Hildersham's view, preaching was the highest calling; but when the pulpit was closed to him, his pastoral heart made him seek other means, such as education and charity work, to continue to serve his people. His example of faithfulness in godly living despite restricted circumstances reminds us that he was "doing what he could when he might not do what he would."[3]

There is often a temptation to spiritualize heroes of the past by concentrating solely on their preaching. The exclusion of their ordinary lives, mundane domestic routines, and business affairs can sometimes leave us feeling inadequate and guilty by comparison. This study of Hildersham will attempt to redress that imbalance by painting a well-rounded portrait of a man who lived for his Master not only in the pulpit but also in daily life, in "secular" activities, in friendships, and in trials.

A Note on the Title

Hildersham undoubtedly would take issue with the title *"Prince among Puritans"* on both counts: "prince" and "Puritan." His self-effacing nature is one reason so little has been written about him. A serious and humble man, his aim was always to direct others to Christ, not to himself. It was his second birth, rather than his first, that gave him cause to rejoice. Like many other godly men of his time, Hildersham requested that no sermon praising or elevating him should be preached at his funeral. Nevertheless, the high regard in which his brethren held him, as well as his noble birth and royal blood, make the appellation "prince" a fitting one.

As far as the name "Puritan" is concerned, it was originally a term of abuse coined by opponents of the godly cause. Hildersham himself called it an "odious" name. But he was prepared to accept another derisive label used by his enemies, that of "Precisian." This referred to his desire to adhere to the Word of God in every precise detail, both in

---

3. Cited in Matthew Henry, *The Lives of Philip and Matthew Henry*, ed. J. B. Williams (Edinburgh: Banner of Truth, 1974), 271. This was written of the ejected minister Rowland Nevet of Oswestry, who continued to live among his people even after he was silenced.

his theology and in all aspects of daily living. Just as the early church eventually adopted the scornful label "Christian" as a badge of honor, "Puritan" now has been purged of offense and invested with esteem. Surely Hildersham would forgive us.

Chapter 1

Beginnings
(1563–1576)

Elizabeth I had been on the English throne for five years when the man she would refer to as "cousin Hildersham" was born in 1563. It was a time of considerable religious uncertainty. Although the Elizabethan Settlement had clearly pronounced England to be a Protestant country, many were unsure how this would work out in practice. The previous two reigns of Elizabeth's half-siblings, Edward and Mary, had witnessed great spiritual upheaval: first a radical Protestantism had been declared the official religion of the state, then Catholicism was reintroduced. Elizabeth herself was a young, unmarried woman when she became queen, and who could say that her reign would not be just as short-lived or tumultuous as the ones before? Despite the increasing number of ordinary people who had embraced Reformation doctrines, many others remained confused or uncommitted. In large areas of the country, preaching ministries were scarce (sermons were as rare as black swans, a contemporary declared), and ignorance about the Bible and the gospel prevailed. Some people retained their loyalty to the old ways of the Catholic faith and traditional practice, while others saw hope of further reformation in the new regime. In 1563, England was a land divided in terms of religion and unsure what the future might hold.

Into this unsettled and ambivalent world, Arthur Hildersham was born on October 6, 1563, at Stetchworth, near Ely, in Cambridgeshire. Subsequently renowned for its association with horse racing, the area is green and rural, with swooping valleys and stretches of springy heathland. A deep track known as the Devil's Ditch cuts through the adjacent land. In Hildersham's time, Stetchworth itself was a small village, with forty-six householders recorded in the parish in the year of his birth. He was born at Patmers manor, for Arthur's father, Thomas Hildersham, was a gentleman of some standing in the community, and he also owned another estate in the adjoining Dullingham parish. (The lands of Patmers later became known as Place Farm, but by 1814 the farmhouse, which had stood at the northern edge of the village in 1770, was gone.) In 1483, the old manor of Patmers comprised 140 acres of arable land, four acres of meadow, and ten acres of underwood. These two Cambridgeshire manors, Patmers and Madfreys, had been settled on Thomas Hildersham in 1544 and previously had been held by his father, John, in 1536. They were in the possession of John's father, another Thomas (Arthur's paternal great-grandfather), at his death in 1525.[1] Clearly, on his father's side Hildersham came from solid and prosperous gentry stock, with roots stretching back some way in the soil of East Anglia. It seems likely that the family much earlier had some connection with the settlement called "Hildersham" eight miles southeast of Cambridge, but this link has not been proved. A heraldic visitation of Cambridgeshire that took place in the late sixteenth century further corroborates Thomas Hildersham's status as a "gentleman of an ancient family." The report of this visitation supplies details of a Hildersham coat of arms ("a chevron between three crosses flory") and a family crest ("a tiger [leopard] couchant argent, collared and lined or [gold]").[2]

Nothing is known about Thomas Hildersham's first wife, but his second, Anne Pole, Arthur's mother, could boast an even more distinguished and famous lineage. Anne was a direct descendant of the Yorkist royal line: her great-great grandfather was Richard, third Duke of York, who had been heir to the throne before his untimely death in battle, in 1460. His son, Edward IV, became king in his place, but the Plantagenet

---

1. A. P. M. Wright, ed., *The Victoria County History of the County of Cambridge and the Isle of Ely*, (Oxford: Oxford University Press, 1978), 6:172–74. See also Cambridgeshire Record Office, R59/281/2, Stetchworth Court Rolls, 1548–58.

2. John W. Clay, ed., *The Visitation of Cambridge Made in AD 1575 Continued and Enlarged with the Visitation of the Same County Made by Henery St. George Richmond—Herald, Marshall and Deputy to William Camden, Clarenceulx, in AD 1619* (London, 1897), 115–16.

hold on the crown of England had ended with the death of Edward's brother, Richard III, in 1485 on Bosworth battlefield, the last significant engagement of the War of the Roses. Plantagenet blood flowed in Anne's veins, and she was also related to the Tudors and many of the highest families in the land. Her cousins Katherine and Winifred Pole were, respectively, married to Francis, second Earl of Huntingdon, and Sir Thomas Barrington, of Hatfield Broad Oak. By naming her son Arthur, Anne was honoring not only her own brother, Arthur Pole, but reminding others of her royal connections: princes of both the Plantagenet and Tudor dynasties bore the name, as did the ancient, mythical King Arthur himself. The only known oil portrait of Arthur Hildersham, painted in 1619 when he was fifty-six years old, reveals recognizable Plantagenet features (which their Tudor successors inherited)—pale, red-gold hair and an aquiline nose set in a long, thin face—that seem to have descended to him through his mother.

Although Hildersham was very much a gentleman, he knew that, spiritually speaking, these social advantages ultimately counted for nothing. "None of us," he warned many years later, "have cause to glory in or be proud of our parentage and birth," for such titles had no lasting value. Indeed, pride in human distinction could be a great stumbling block to salvation. "Oh then," he lamented, "the madness of them that rest and glory in their first birth…and never seek to be born again, to be born of God."[3]

Because of these family connections, Elizabeth I was prepared to recognize Arthur Hildersham as a "cousin" and refer to him as such at her court. Those links may have been rather distant, but the more recent family tree also boasted a very prominent branch. Anne Pole's uncle, the older brother of her father, Geoffrey, was Cardinal Reginald Pole, Queen Mary's archbishop of Canterbury. Educated in Rome, and at one time a possible candidate for the papacy as well as a potential successor to the English throne, Reginald Pole died on the same day as his royal mistress, in 1558. Despite recent attempts to rehabilitate his reputation by emphasizing his humanism and commitment to Catholic reform, his

---

3. Hildersham, *CLII Lectures upon Psalm 51* (London, 1635), 286.

name will always be associated with the terrible campaign of Protestant burnings that took place in England between 1555 and 1557.

Reginald Pole's staunch Catholicism lived on in his niece, for Anne Pole and her husband, Thomas Hildersham, remained devout Catholics even after Elizabeth ascended the throne and outlawed their religion. It was probably their shared faith that had drawn them together in the first place. Gentry families like the Hildershams were able to sustain their Catholicism within the privacy of their households, procuring the services of priests to perform the Mass when they could. Some were prepared to put in an appearance at the local parish church in order to keep the authorities off their backs or even have their children baptized there if a Catholic priest was not available. We do not know whether Thomas and Anne Hildersham did this with their children, for the relevant parish registers of Stetchworth St. Peter's have not survived. In any case, if they did attend their local parish church, it is unlikely that they would have heard anything to challenge their spiritual convictions; in 1561 (two years before Arthur's birth), the vicar of St. Peter's was recorded as being a non-graduate and not licensed to preach. We do know that the Hildershams were zealous in their family devotions and in their determination to bring up their children as Catholics. The young Hildershams were taught to say their prayers in Latin, according to the Roman rite.

It was the custom for sons of the gentry to be sent away to school at a young age, perhaps six or seven. Social considerations ultimately governed Thomas Hildersham's decision about an appropriate education for Arthur; his aim was to "find a good school, where many gentlemans sons were taught."[4] The establishment he settled on was Saffron Walden School in Essex.[5] This school, which could trace its original foundation back to the fourteenth century, had a fine reputation for educating its pupils in a manner based on that operating at Winchester and Eton. It had been refounded in 1549 as one of the first of the eigh-

---

4. Clarke, "Life of Hildersam," 144.
5. See W. R. Powell, ed., *The Victoria County History of the County of Essex* (London, 1956), 2:518–25, and the anonymous *A Short History of Saffron Walden School 1317–1928* (available in Saffron Walden library).

teen King Edward VI grammar schools, when a connection with Queen's College, Cambridge, had also been established. Among its pupils in the late sixteenth century were the three renowned Harvey brothers, Gabriel, Thomas, and Richard, who became famous, respectively, as poet, satirist, and astrologer. Saffron Walden itself was a bustling market town in the late sixteenth century, taking its name from the cultivation of the saffron crocus, which supplied the dye for the wool upon which the prosperity of the town was based. It was also used as a medicine and in cooking. It is easy to imagine the young Hildersham riding into the town from his home further north, through purple fields ablaze with crocuses and the church of St. Mary the Virgin, a prominent landmark close to the school, on the hill ahead of him.

Thomas Hildersham found the social and educational credentials of the school impressive. Perhaps he was unaware of the spiritual convictions of the master, John Disborow, who was a godly man and a committed Protestant, or perhaps Disborow, a graduate of Trinity College, Cambridge, who took up his post at Saffron Walden in 1573, did so after Arthur Hildersham had already started as a pupil.[6] Whatever the case, in the providence of God, the boy was brought under the influence of gospel truth for the first time. Disborow ensured that the "grounds of the Protestant religion" were clearly taught within the school's curriculum. Prayers, sermons, and catechism all formed an integral part of school life.[7] Challenged by the biblical message, Hildersham put his faith in Christ's saving death and was converted. Later, he was to reflect that "childhood is the fittest age to be wrought upon" by the means of grace. Indeed, as the example of John the Baptist showed, "the youngest infant is not so incapable of saving grace, but that God is able to work it even in them."[8] Many other young men were experiencing a similar change at various schools throughout the land. Two prominent laymen, Sir Nathaniel Barnardiston and Sir Henry Vane, for example, were

---

6. For details of Disborow's life, see J. Venn and J. A. Venn, *Alumni Cantabrigienses: A Biographical List of All Known Students, Graduates and Holders of Office at the University of Cambridge, Part I: From the Earliest Times to 1751* (Cambridge: Cambridge University Press, 1922–1927), 2:44.

7. Clarke, "Life of Hildersam," 144.

8. Hildersham, *Lectures upon Psalm 51*, 296–97.

reported to have been converted during their school days, and they went on to become strong supporters of the godly cause.[9] William Gouge, who subsequently preached for many years at Blackfriars in London, was said to have been "possessed with an holy fear of God" while a scholar at Eton.[10] It is possible that Arthur Hildersham's brother, Richard, also attended Saffron Walden School and was equally challenged by the gospel, for he espoused Reformed convictions as well. At school, boys who shared a common love for Christ forged friendships that, in many cases, proved to be lifelong. Joseph Hall, the godly future bishop of Exeter and Norwich, developed a close spiritual bond with his classmates Hugh Chomeley and William Bradshaw at Ashby school in the 1580s, and their friendship lasted as long as they all lived.[11]

It is apparent that John Disborow took a special interest in his keen and able young pupil. Disborow encouraged Hildersham not only in his academic studies but also in his spiritual development. He felt a real affection for Hildersham, enjoyed his company and conversation, and took great care of him. With the majority of their pupils being such young boys, schoolmasters had both tremendous responsibility and great opportunity concerning the boys' physical and moral welfare. In many cases, the influence of teachers in these formative years seems to have been more important even than that of the child's parents. It is unknown whether Thomas and Anne Hildersham were aware at this early stage of the radical change in their son's beliefs. However, it seems likely that if they were, they did not consider it lasting or deep; otherwise, they would surely have removed him from the school. Of their other children we know frustratingly little. We have already noted that Arthur's brother Richard also renounced Catholicism, but we do not know if there were any other siblings. A Winifred Hildersham, who will appear later in the story, may have been a sister, but it is also possible that she was Richard's daughter.

---

9. J. T. Cliffe, *The Puritan Gentry: The Great Puritan Families of Early Stuart England* (London: Routledge and Kegan, 1984), 16.

10. Clarke, "The Life and Death of Doctor Gouge," in *A General Martyrologie*, 235.

11. Levi Fox, *A Country Grammar School: A History of Ashby-de-la-Zouch Grammar School through Four Centuries 1567–1967* (Oxford: Oxford University Press, 1967), 17–38.

By the time Hildersham was thirteen, he was ready to proceed to university. This means that he would have mastered the rudiments of the school curriculum—Latin, Greek, rhetoric, logic, and grammar—and was considered capable of coping with the next stage of his education. It was not unusual for boys of the time to go to university at such a young age, but Hildersham's accomplishments show that he was a bright and hard-working scholar.

Chapter 2

University Life
(1576–1587)

In the sixteenth century, Oxford and Cambridge were the only two universities in England, and both were exclusively male preserves. Hildersham was a native of East Anglia, and his school was connected to Cambridge, so it was natural that he should pursue his university education there.

What were the town and university of Cambridge like in 1576, when Hildersham commenced his studies?[1] Strong antagonism existed between the university and the town in the sixteenth and early seventeenth centuries. The university was expanding rapidly. Its fine, new buildings contrasted sharply with the shoddy hovels being built to house the increasing number of poor townspeople. Many of the Cambridge colleges had started as medieval religious houses and had become colleges before and after the monasteries were dissolved in the 1530s. Hildersham would have been familiar with the Cambridge sights that still captivate tourists today—the academic quarter centered on the church of Great St. Mary's, the Old Schools, and the line of mellow stone colleges strung out along the River Cam. University life revolved around the individual colleges, where the students lived. They came together for common meals in the college hall and for worship in the college chapel. Students shared chambers, often with a boy from the same county or part of the country, and all were assigned tutors responsible for their

---

1. For this and more information, see Victor Morgan, *A History of the University of Cambridge*, vol. 2, *1546–1750* (Cambridge: Cambridge University Press, 2004).

learning and moral welfare. The student-tutor relationship was vital, and celebrated "pupil-mongers" who attracted large numbers of students—such as Laurence Chaderton at Christ's College and later Emmanuel College, and John Preston at Queen's—influenced many.

For the most part, the university was a place where young men came to study for ministry in the Church of England, although some proceeded to the Inns of Court to make a career in law. Most were sons of the aristocracy and the gentry whose families paid for their education, but bright boys from poorer backgrounds also were able to attend if they could obtain the support of wealthy benefactors. The university admitted them as sizars and expected them to perform various menial tasks, such as lighting fires, copying notes, or running errands for their social superiors.

For many young men, university was a time of conversion and excitement as they discovered the great truths of the Reformation for the first time. They hungrily devoured the sermons of preachers like Chaderton at St. Clement's and William Perkins at Great St. Andrew's. In the late 1570s, when Hildersham arrived, the influence and ideas of the late Lady Margaret Professor of Divinity, Thomas Cartwright, were still evident. Cartwright, who spent two years in Geneva after having been dismissed from his university chair in 1570, was a principal leader of the Elizabethan Puritan movement and author of the *Second Admonition to the Parliament*, which argued the case for further church reform. In the spring of 1570, it was reported that men ran like boys to ensure a place at Cartwright's sermons at Great St. Mary's and that the sexton of the church was afraid of his windows being smashed in the crush.[2] Many students enthusiastically received Cartwright's series on the first two chapters of Acts, which set out the model of the primitive church, but some in authority frowned upon it as too radical. Division and conflict resulted. Cartwright's superiors finally silenced him, but his insistence on biblical principles continued to inspire a generation of young men. As a recent graduate, Arthur Hildersham wrote to Cartwright in 1583, seeking advice on his theological studies. The older man seems to have taken Hildersham to his heart,

---

2. Patrick Collinson, *The Elizabethan Puritan Movement* (Oxford: Clarendon Press, 1967), 112.

and this correspondence was the start of a friendship that was to last until Cartwright's death in 1603, when Hildersham was named as one of his literary executors, along with another friend, John Dod. Cartwright called Hildersham his "loving brother" and spoke of "the common love wherewith our Saviour Christ hath loved us both, and put us in trust with the mystery of his Word."[3] Samuel Clarke described Hildersham as "a great admirer, follower and friend of Master Thomas Cartwright."[4]

In reply to Hildersham's 1583 letter, Cartwright stressed the centrality of the Bible in any program of learning, writing that "the study of the Scripture itself...shall keep his pre-eminence still, that the study of no other writer, how fruitful [what]soever, shall shut forth some daily reading or meditation therein."[5] He went on to commend an equally balanced perusal of the Old and New Testaments, but admitted that some books required "more diligent study and attentive reading." On commentators Cartwright put forward the general principle that the new writers were to be read before the old. By new writers he meant Reformation scholars (in particular John Calvin), whose works were preferable to the older writings of the church fathers. In the wrong hands, these letters could have spelled danger for both men: Cartwright had advised Hildersham to keep the correspondence secret, or "else let it smell of the fire."[6] This is probably one of the main reasons why so few of Hildersham's letters survive.

The links between the two men were doubtless cemented in 1590 and 1591, when both were subjects of Archbishop Whitgift's purge of the Puritan leadership. Hildersham's connection with Cartwright linked him to the leadership and beginnings of the Elizabethan Puritan movement. His own influence, in turn, extended to a raft of younger disciples, forging a chain of continuing tradition that stretched from the time before Elizabeth's reign to the Civil War period and beyond.

---

3. Albert Peel and Leland H. Carlson, eds., *Cartwrightiana* (London: Allen and Unwin, 1951), 109. The margin apparently gives "ministery" for "mistery" in the body of the text.
4. Clarke, "Life of Hildersam," 151.
5. Peel and Carlson, *Cartwrightiana*, 108–15.
6. Peel and Carlson, *Cartwrightiana*, 115.

The Reformation in England gave rise to an acute need for educated and godly ministers, men who could preach God's Word with authority and understanding. So many English people had been brought up in the errors of Catholic teaching and continued to cling to false doctrine. Clear declaration of scriptural truth from the pulpit was the only antidote. In many parts of the country, ministers were unqualified to preach and merely read services from the Book of Common Prayer, frequently with little conviction or comprehension. Hildersham later referred to their ministry as "dumb and ignorant."[7] It is not surprising that the parishioners of such men remained in the dark about the Bible and its message.

The English Reformers appreciated the vital role of the universities as training grounds in their program of evangelizing the country. Consequently, the Elizabethan period witnessed the renewed endowment of existing colleges as well as the institution of new ones intended to educate men for this mission, like Emmanuel College in 1584 and Sidney Sussex College in 1596. Wealthy supporters of the godly cause often sponsored poor boys who demonstrated academic and spiritual potential, with the hope that they would enter the ministry upon completing their degrees. (William Bradshaw, who became a renowned preacher and writer, was sponsored in this manner.) Influential Protestants moved to promote sympathetic men to positions of authority within the university system. But, naturally, such initiatives provoked opposition and resistance from those who favored a more traditional or formal religion. These university power struggles merely reflected wider divisions in the English church and state as a whole.

Humanism and the liberal arts dominated the university curriculum.[8] Most teaching took place in Latin. With an eye to providing educated men for the ministry, reform-minded university leaders emphasized the subjects most useful to gospel preachers, especially the study of the biblical languages (Greek and Hebrew), logic, and rhetoric. At this time, the study of logic was greatly influenced by the work of Peter Ramus, who challenged the prevailing Aristotelian system. Ramism, as

---

7. Hildersham, *CVIII Lectures upon the Fourth of John*, 2nd ed. (London, 1632), 136.

8. See John Morgan, *Godly Learning: Puritan Attitudes towards Reason, Learning, and Education, 1560–1640* (Cambridge: Cambridge University Press, 1986).

it was called, became best known for its scheme of "method," which set out to organize various things from universal principles at the top, down through a series of divisions to the individual parts that constituted it. A series of diagrams called "Ramist trees" often illustrated this method: the trees became more and more branched as the process of subdivision was worked out. Ramist method helped Puritan preachers logically order their thinking and present their material in an easily understandable way, applicable to the experience of daily living. When we think of rhetoric, we tend to imagine flights of great oratory and linguistic fireworks, but the Puritans understood it differently. Above all, their aim was to deliver the Word of God to their congregations in a clear and unambiguous manner. Thus they developed the rhetoric of "plainness," presenting a methodical analysis of Scripture in a direct, unadorned, and natural style, with the purpose of inspiring repentance and faith in their hearers. Hildersham later declared that God chose "weak and simple" means to do His work, "a kind of preaching as is plain, and without all ostentation and show of human gifts."[9]

Thomas Hildersham chose the prestigious Christ's College as Arthur's place of study. It was a very large college, originally known as "God's House," with a reputation for being the "college of grammarians." Standing by the Barnwell Gate on the other side of town from the river, the entrance to Christ's College was an archway bearing the coat of arms of its benefactor, Queen Margaret of Anjou, supported by mythical beasts on either side. Arthur must have looked up and seen the heraldic crest each time he entered the ancient portals. Unbeknown to Thomas Hildersham, Christ's College also had an exceptionally strong Puritan presence. This choice of college once again testifies to God's overriding hand in Arthur Hildersham's life. His father was similarly unaware that the tutor he had selected for his son was, in fact, another godly Protestant. In the 1570s and 1580s, Christ's College was blessed with a succession of celebrated masters—Edward Dering, William Perkins, and Laurence Chaderton. The latter became a close friend of Hildersham and mentor to his "intimate friend" William Bradshaw. It

---

9. Hildersham, *Lectures upon John*, 251.

seems likely that Arthur was part of the group that met with Chaderton for weekly Bible study, prayer, and discussion in the master's rooms. Hildersham and Chaderton later worked together to organize the Millenary Petition and the Hampton Court Conference in 1603–1604.

By all accounts, Hildersham was a much-loved and respected student for his "piety, learning, ingenuity, affability and harmless inoffensive witty converse." His contemporaries recognized that he was serious about his faith and studies, but they also appreciated his good temper and conversation. With his warm manner and generous spirit, Hildersham made many friends at Cambridge. The bonds he forged there were truly important and helpful to him throughout his life and ministry. It is important to remember that the oft-mentioned "Puritan brotherhood" was nurtured and developed in the universities, especially at Cambridge, when the men discovered that there were others who thought and felt as they did. In their university years, the students formed many friendships that would later span the map of England and, in some cases, last as long as they lived. These associations allowed the men to discuss theology, seek and give advice on manuscripts, negotiate marriage alliances, witness business deals, and make recommendations for livings and lectureships. Perhaps most importantly, the men strengthened one another through prayer; this intercessory bond was a powerful connection, especially when times were hard. Influential men like John Cotton, John Preston, Samuel Fairclough, John Davenant, William Barlow, and Ezekiel Culverwell became friends at Christ's College and through wider university circles. In 1584, the Puritans founded the stronghold of Emmanuel College (of which Laurence Chaderton was the first master), which greatly encouraged these brotherly bonds.

Friendships between godly brethren continued as they left university and took up ministries in different parts of the country. Regular correspondence and mutual prayer helped to sustain fellowship, which was particularly important in times of difficulty and trial. Many of the scholars married the sisters or daughters of godly friends they had met at university, which added ties of blood to spiritual bonds. Hildersham's own wife, Ann, was the sister of a fellow student at Christ's, Edward Barfoot, who married a Winifred Hildersham. The Essex preacher Ezekiel Culverwell, whose sister was the wife of Chaderton, married Winifred

Hildersham as his second wife after both were widowed. Although the majority of these friends were nonconformists, not all were; rather, it was a living faith and a love for God's Word that brought them together. Hildersham, for example, counted William Barlow, future bishop of Lincoln, a true friend from university days. When Barlow was unable to protect Hildersham from further trouble with the church authorities in 1612, he wrote to the Earl of Huntingdon apologizing for his powerlessness, saying of Hildersham, "for in truth I love him" and affirming that Hildersham knew of his "heart and affection."[10] Hildersham also respected Andrew Willett, a conformist Puritan and successful rival in the election for a fellowship at Christ's. At the same time, Hildersham had university friends who later took the path to separatism. Francis Johnson, despite his subsequent ecclesiological disagreement with Hildersham, continued to refer to Hildersham as a "brother" and declared, "I do and shall always love him in the Lord."[11]

When he had been at Cambridge for two years (and thus was about fifteen years old), his father summoned him in order to reveal plans that would shatter Arthur's world and ruin his hopes for the future. Thomas Hildersham knew that his son was an able scholar who enjoyed theological study, and he declared that Arthur was to leave Cambridge to train for the Catholic priesthood in Rome. Thomas probably had in mind Rome's recently established English College, founded in 1576 as a center for English exiles awaiting the inevitable (or so they thought) return of their country to the Catholic fold. Under Jesuit influence, the College's final settlement in 1579 transformed it into a missionary college, poised for the reconversion of England. Of course, Arthur would be unable to return to his native land for some time, but his family connections through the late Cardinal Pole would ensure opportunity for advancement in the Catholic hierarchy abroad, if not at home. To a committed Catholic like Thomas Hildersham, it seemed the perfect plan for a younger son—one that would satisfy both religion and ambition. For

---

10. Historic Manuscripts Commission, *Hastings*, series 78 (London: His Majesty's Stationery Office, 1928 and 1930), 2:55.

11. Francis Johnson, *A Treatise of the Ministery of the Church of England* ([Low Countries?], 1595), 2.

Arthur, it posed a terrible choice. Either he must defy the father whom he loved and had been brought up to obey, or he must deny the biblical faith he now held so dear. With great sorrow, Arthur told his father that he could not agree to these plans. Thomas Hildersham grimly frog-marched his recalcitrant son off to London for a round of visits to various Catholic priests, hoping that they would be able to change his mind with their learned arguments. Despite the pressure, Arthur remained resolute. The exasperated Thomas finally realized he was not going to win and gave up the battle. Arthur's victory came with severe consequences, however; his father disinherited him and wanted nothing further to do with him. Not only did Arthur lose the care of a loving family, he also forfeited his only means of financial support. Faithfulness to the gospel had come at considerable personal cost. Alone, penniless, and rejected in London, with no prospect of resuming his university career, Arthur was in a dejected and forlorn condition. What would happen to him now—and to his hopes of serving the Lord as a preacher of the Word?

Over thirty years later, when Hildersham was preaching a series on John 4, the comments of the Samaritan woman about her forefathers' worship gave him opportunity to reflect on issues of family loyalty and tradition. Although he did not refer directly to his own experience, he was well aware that, for many, converting to the evangelical faith meant rejecting the Catholicism or formalism in which they had been raised. To those who agonized over whether it was right to disobey their parents in this way, Hildersham advised, "It is no undutifulness in a child, to swerve from his father's example in anything, wherein his father hath swerved from the Word of God."[12] Although the Bible commanded us to obey our parents, he argued, this did not extend to matters in which they themselves had departed from God's instructions: "There are certain fathers whose example ought to be of great authority with us in matters of religion," Hildersham continued, but only those who "followed the direction of the Word" and walked in the ways of the Lord.[13] Hildersham reminded his hearers of Christ's words to the disciples, "He

---

12. Hildersham, *Lectures upon John*, 144.
13. Hildersham, *Lectures upon John*, 143.

that loveth father or mother more than me, is not worthy of me."[14] Of course, it is a great blessing and a "bond for a Christian to keep him in the love of the truth" when "his own parents and ancestors have been lovers and professors of the true religion." But when this was not the case, a person should not feel guilty or bereft, since he had an infinitely more precious spiritual heritage: "And though…we did know none of our own ancestors that professed the religion that we do; yet so long as we profess no other religion than the patriarchs, prophets and apostles did…we cannot justly be said to have forsaken the God of our fathers, or to be of any other religion than our forefathers were of."[15] The church historian Thomas Fuller declared that Hildersham's experience was a living illustration of Psalm 27:10, "When my father and my mother forsake me, then the LORD will take me up."[16]

When at his lowest ebb after his father's departure, Hildersham had a visitor in London, who, in God's providence, was to prove the means of his deliverance. John Ireton, a fellow of Hildersham's own Cambridge College, Christ's, came up to the capital and was surprised to discover his young friend spending so much time away from his studies.

"Arthur," Ireton asked, "why art thou so long from thy book, and losest so much time?"

"Alas," Hildersham responded sadly, "I shall go no more to Cambridge." Hildersham then went on to explain what had happened, and how he had no money to pay for his fees and upkeep at university. Faced with this apparently hopeless situation, Ireton had a sudden inspiration.

"Be not discouraged," he told Hildersham. "Thou hast a noble kinsman, whom I will acquaint with thy case: and I doubt not but he will provide for thee."[17]

Ireton was referring to Henry, third Earl of Huntingdon, a man renowned for his support of gospel preachers and often dubbed "the Puritan Earl." The earl's mother and Hildersham's mother were cousins,

---

14. Hildersham, *Lectures upon John*, 275.

15. Hildersham, *Lectures upon John*, 143.

16. Thomas Fuller, *The Church History of Britain from the Birth of Jesus Christ until the Year 1648* (London, 1655), 142.

17. Clarke, "Life of Hildersam," 144.

so family loyalty as well as shared faith drew the two men together. Ireton himself was from Leicestershire, the earl's county, and was ideally placed to approach him on Hildersham's behalf. When presented with the tale of his young cousin's predicament, the earl was only too glad to help. He summoned Hildersham, encouraged him, and promised him maintenance. He sent Hildersham back to Cambridge to complete his studies and instructed Ireton to make sure Hildersham was placed with a good tutor. The earl, knowing Thomas Hildersham's zealous Catholicism, imagined that previously Arthur must have been under the care of a coreligionist. When he learned that his tutor had, in fact, been a sound Protestant who cared greatly for his pupil, he was more than happy for his new protégé to continue with the same man.

Soon after Hildersham gained his master of arts degree in 1584, he was required for the first time to undertake a college exercise known as "common-place." This was really a sermon in all but name and length, delivered to fellow students and college officers. Doubting his own gifts and fearful of such an undertaking, Hildersham begged one of his close friends to take his place. However, the friend realized that if he agreed to such a request, Hildersham probably would never have the courage to preach again. And so, out of love, his friend turned him down and reminded him of a man called Sidney Zouch—like them, a student of Christ's College—who had obtained another fellow to speak in his place. When Zouch listened to the stand-in preach, and to other students who (he felt) performed their task so well, Zouch was completely disheartened and was never persuaded to preach again, despite his being a gifted scholar. So, with no alternative and in great trepidation, Hildersham commenced his first sermon. His friend sat on the other side of the college chapel, and Hildersham drew encouragement from the knowledge that he was praying all the while.

Hildersham continued with his university career. His reputation for learning and piety prompted a majority of the college fellows to nominate him for a fellowship at Christ's College. However, even at this early stage, he met with opposition: the master of the college, Edmund Barwell, stepped in and blocked Hildersham's appointment. Instead, another candidate, Andrew Willet, was chosen. Although Hildersham protested to Lord Burghley, the university chancellor, about how the election had been carried out, there seem to have been no ill feelings between the two rivals for the post. Willet, who became a notable conformist Puritan, later praised Hildersham in the dedicatory epistle to his volume of sermons on 2 Samuel, calling him "the hammer of the schismatics, whom they commonly call Brownists."[18] Hildersham valued Willet's writings as well, for Willet's *Synopsis Papismi* was one of only three books specifically named and bequeathed in Hildersham's will.[19] The protest to Burghley bore fruit—he ensured that Hildersham was successful in another fellowship election, this time at the smaller college of Trinity Hall.

During his Cambridge years, Hildersham became closely acquainted with another great figure of Elizabethan Puritanism, Richard Greenham. Greenham was famous both for his literary works and his example of pastoral ministry. His parish of Dry Drayton was located just outside Cambridge, and he established a household seminary for ministerial students there. Young men like Hildersham thus were able to spend time in a parish environment and gain practical experience of pastoral service. Within Greenham's home, the students, notebooks in hand, plied him with all manner of questions, especially those concerning difficult cases of conscience and thorny theological issues. Greenham's answers were written down and later collected. Some of these survive in manuscript form at the John Rylands University Library in Manchester and provide fascinating insight into Greenham's wisdom, as well as to the issues that concerned ministerial candidates at the time. It has been thought that Hildersham, as one of Greenham's disciples in the early 1580s, may have been the one who wrote down all this material, but others have suggested John Hopkins as a more likely scribe.[20] Whatever the case, the manuscript contains folios Hildersham himself authored, which shows that he was a receptive student of Greenham. Hildersham's exhortation to two parties contracting together before marriage, his treatise concerning

---

18. Andrew Willet, "Dedicatory Epistle," in *An Harmonie upon the Second Book of Samuel* (Cambridge, 1614).

19. Leicestershire Record Office, Leicestershire Wills, Ashby no. 77 (1632).

20. John Rylands University Library (Manchester), Rylands English Manuscript 524. This has been reproduced and edited by Kenneth L. Parker and Eric J. Carlson in *"Practical Divinity": The Works and Life of Revd Richard Greenham* (Ashgate: Aldershot, UK, 1998), 129–259. They suggest Hopkins as a possible scribe; see 34–35.

preparation for prayer and its ordering, and his two works on preparation for the Lord's Supper all reflect an emphasis on practical divinity that owed much to his mentor, Greenham.[21] As we will see, this training at Dry Drayton was tremendously helpful to Hildersham, especially as he embarked on his own ministry in Ashby.

Through Richard Greenham and his seminary came opportunities to fellowship with another circle of godly brethren. Many would later take younger men into their own homes and provide them with a similar experience of pastoral work. There is no direct evidence to show that Hildersham ran any kind of formal seminary in Ashby, but it is clear that many junior figures, such as Francis Higginson, Thomas Hooker, and Simeon Ashe, spent time in his home and came under his influence during the course of their careers.

By the age of twenty, then, Hildersham, with no family background of Reformed religion, already was a part of these networks of godly fellowship. The influence of older saints like Cartwright and Greenham had formed his ideas on church government and pastoral ministry. He also drew upon a large group of similarly minded peers for mutual encouragement, support, and advice once he entered the ministry. Arthur continued in his duties at Trinity Hall until September 1587, when a momentous change in his life occurred.

---

21. John Rylands University Library, Rylands Eng. MS 524 (1581–1584): "The effect of an exhortation in private to two parties at their contracting before the witnesses, by Maister Hildersam" (f. 75); "Concerning private reading of the word. Arthur Hildersham" (f. 96b); "A preparation to the Lords Supper. A. H." (f. 100); "A larger preparation to the Lords Supper in form of a Catechism. A. H." (f. 103).

Chapter 3

Lecturer at Ashby-de-la-Zouch
(1587–1593)

Hildersham's patron, the third Earl of Huntingdon, had been following the progress of his young relative's career from the family seat at
Ashby-de-la-Zouch in Leicestershire. In the second half of the sixteenth
century, Ashby castle was the main residence of the earl and his family.
Edward IV had granted the manor of Ashby to the Hastings family
in 1462, and in 1472 permission was given to erect a fortified manor
house. Over the years much building work was undertaken until a mag-
nificent castle took shape, the ruins of which still dominate the town of
Ashby to this day.

Henry Hastings, third Earl of Huntingdon, was a very interesting
and powerful figure.[1] Brought up and educated at court with the young
Prince Edward, later to become King Edward VI, he too became pas-
sionately committed to the Reformed faith and was known as "The
Puritan Earl." Some who were impatient with the slow pace of religious reform under Elizabeth wanted to replace her with her cousin
Huntingdon, or at least have him named as her heir. He, however, was
deeply loyal to the queen and spent many years endeavoring to convince
her of that loyalty. For a time he was the temporary guardian of Mary
Queen of Scots during her imprisonment in England, which finally may
have helped to persuade Elizabeth that he was faithful to her cause.

---

1. For a biography of the third earl, see Claire Cross, *The Puritan Earl: The Life of Henry Hastings Third Earl of Huntingdon 1536–1595* (London: Macmillan, 1966).

Eventually, she overcame her suspicion of Huntingdon and appointed him President of the Council in the North in 1572. Based in York, the earl was responsible for the administration of the five counties north of the river Trent (Yorkshire, Durham, Northumberland, Cumberland, and Westmorland). It was a position of serious responsibility. The earl expended great effort and large sums of his own money in the queen's service. In addition, he served as Lord Lieutenant of Leicestershire. All in all, he was among the leading handful of nobles in the country.

The cause of promoting biblical preaching always was near to the earl's heart. This was evident in his role as Lord President of the North—an area where Protestantism often had been slower to take root—and closer to his home in Leicestershire. A contemporary chronicler, Camden, had initiated the rumor that the dire state of Huntingdon's finances was due to his wasting his fortune "by relieving (at his great cost) the hotter spirited ministers."[2] In fact, as the earl's biographer has shown, many other factors (including costly legal disputes over land and expenses that arose out of his duties to the queen) had contributed to his financial difficulties. Hildersham recognized this as he defended his patron and others against the aspersions of critics like Camden in 1610, when he declared, "I have heard it oft said of some, that their bounty unto ministers did undo them; but I could never hear it proved. I doubt not, but such might fall into decay (for God's promises for earthly blessings are all with this condition, 'so far as shall be good for them'), but this, doubtless, was not the cause of it."[3]

Like many of his rank, the earl owned the advowsons (the right to recommend clergy to fill vacant benefices) of a number of parish churches. Wherever he could, he made sure that godly, educated men were selected to be vicars and rectors. Of course, such a system was open to abuse, and in many parishes the course of reform was frustrated because the patron chose unworthy incumbents who could neither preach nor care for their flock. In many instances, if the patron disapproved of biblical preaching or reform, he would deliberately appoint a traditionalist candidate. Only ministers ordained by the bishop and licensed to preach in a particular

---

2. Cited in Cross, *Puritan Earl*, 98.
3. Hildersham, *Lectures upon John*, 318.

area were legally able to do so, which made it almost impossible for scriptural truth to be expounded in some places.

However, there was a means for circumventing such difficulties, and the earl took advantage of his opportunity. Towns and parishes were able to establish lectureships, paying a minister to deliver lectures either on weekdays or Sunday afternoons. These "lectures" actually were a series of sermons; and, as lecturers were less bound by ecclesiastical regulations than parish ministers were, they had more freedom to preach the gospel. In London, especially, the Puritan lectureships became renowned as centers of powerful evangelical preaching. Sometimes, of course, friction existed between the parish minister and the lecturer, if they did not agree on the contents of each other's sermons. Although the Earl of Huntingdon was the patron of the parish church of St. Helen's in Ashby and thus able to appoint its vicar, he also established a lectureship in the town so that another godly preacher was available to serve the local people. The earl regarded Ashby as a missionary center, for loyalty to Catholicism and old traditions remained strong in the surrounding area.

The reformation in Ashby had flourished under the earl's strong leadership and through the ministers he appointed to serve there. Foremost among them was Anthony Gilby. He was a man of great integrity, deeply committed to the Protestant cause, and as a result had gone into exile in Geneva during Queen Mary's reign. Gilby played an important part in the production of the English Geneva Bible. He had rubbed shoulders with many of the Continent's leading Reformers while in Geneva, and on his return to England after Elizabeth's accession his influence upon many of the newly appointed church leaders was considerable. If he had wanted, he could have accepted a bishopric himself, but he was critical of the flaws in the episcopal system and declined any such overtures. As it was, Bishop Aylmer commented wryly that Gilby ruled like a bishop from Ashby, such was the respect the godly people had for him.

The earl invited Gilby to be his preacher in Ashby, and Gilby spent the last twenty-five years of his life in the town. Using Ashby as a base, Gilby continued to urge and strive for further reformation of the church in England. It does not seem that he ever served as vicar of Ashby, but rather as town lecturer and household chaplain to the earl's family. Under Gilby's ministry, and that of the quiet but faithful Thomas Widdowes, the vicar of St. Helen's who worked alongside him, Ashby became renowned as a place where ministers clearly proclaimed the gospel. People traveled from miles around to hear them expound the Scriptures, especially during the weekday exercises and lectures. Local ministers, too, met regularly to hear each other preach in "prophesyings" (based on the model of I Corinthians 14:29–31) and for discussion afterwards. According to John Udall, these prophesyings in Leicestershire were particularly strong, and "furthered knowledge greatly."[4] To the alarm of the authorities, laypeople also began to attend. In Ashby the doors of the church were left open to avoid accusations of secrecy, and in 1576 Gilby reported that the people "did of themselves quietly come to pray with us, and to learn some good lessons in God's schoolhouse."[5] In such an atmosphere, and with the earl's protection, Ashby became a refuge for those of tender conscience, seeking a place to worship that did not bring them into conflict with those who thought differently. Looking back to these heady days of the 1570s and early 1580s, Hildersham later commented, "Of this town myself can say that I have known the time, when it did shine as a light to all the country, and was famous among the churches of Christ for the religious observance of the Sabbath day."[6]

Anthony Gilby died and was buried in Ashby on December 31, 1584. The parish register recorded that he was "a detestor of popery from his youth and a preacher of the gospel."[7] Gilby's death left vacant the lectureship in Ashby, which prompted the earl to invite his young protégé, Hildersham, to take up the position on September 14, 1587. No doubt the earl had heard good things about Hildersham's progress at Cambridge, his dedication to his studies, his preaching, and his commitment to reform. For Hildersham, a young man of twenty-four, the summons to Ashby must have brought mixed emotions. When we

---

4. John Udall, *The State of the Church of England Laid open in a Conference*, 29; cited in C. D. Chalmers, "Puritanism in Leicestershire, 1566–1633" (MA thesis, University of Leeds, 1962), 43, 63.

5. "The Ashby Remonstrance," 1576; cited in Chalmers, "Puritanism in Leicestershire," 67.

6. Hildersham, *Lectures upon Psalm 51*, 708.

7. Parish register for St. Helen's Church, Ashby-de-la-Zouch, Leicestershire Record Office DE1013/1.

remember that Hildersham was fresh out of university and had lacked confidence when he first began to preach, it seems this call to replace the famously eloquent Gilby would have been daunting. And yet here was the opportunity he had prayed and prepared for—a chance to engage in the ministry to which God had called him. Hildersham would be associated with Ashby for the next forty years of his life.

What would Hildersham have found when he moved to Ashby in the autumn of 1587? It was a small Leicestershire market town with a population of about 800 in 1570, and between 1,000 and 1,400 in the first forty years of the seventeenth century.[8] The great castle of the earls of Huntingdon physically overshadowed the town and stood at its heart, with the old stone church of St. Helen's nestled beneath its walls. The earls dominated Ashby economically and socially, too; nearly all the residents were their tenants, and they controlled the manorial courts that governed the town. The presence of the earl at the castle brought considerable trade into the area and gave Ashby the importance of a much larger town. But Ashby was not a wealthy place, on the whole, for the soil was poor and acidic, which meant the land was largely turned over to cattle rearing, horse breeding, and growing basic crops such as oats and barley. Later the area became famous for its coal mining. In Hildersham's time, some mines were already operating on the 300-acre barren heathland to the west of Ashby known as the Wolds and at nearby Coleorton, but the mineral reserves were not fully exploited until after the industrial revolution. In the town itself, most inhabitants would have kept a few animals, cultivated a bit of land, and engaged in trade. People from all around flocked to Ashby for its twice-weekly markets and annual livestock fairs. Indeed, Ashby became well known for its horses and leather dressing. As in similar towns, bear- and bull-baiting would have been a regular spectacle. Over forty alehouses and inns existed in the town by the 1620s, a large number for a relatively small place, and the preachers regularly had to address the drunkenness and gambling they fostered.

One reason for the preponderance of alehouses was Ashby's location at the center of a network of road systems, for these establishments

---

8. For information on Ashby, see C. J. M. Moxon, "Ashby-de-la-Zouch—A Social and Economic Survey of a Market Town, 1570–1720" (DPhil thesis, University of Oxford, 1971).

would have provided food and refreshment to weary travelers. Some 120 miles from London, Ashby lay on the main roads between Leicester and Burton-on-Trent, Nottingham and Tamworth, and Derby and Coventry. As we will see, this relative ease of mobility enabled Hildersham to minister to a wide area, traveling many miles by horseback. It was also significant that Ashby was a border town, lying on the boundaries of Leicestershire, Staffordshire, and Derbyshire, which meant that if someone was having problems in one county he could escape into the adjoining one. Hildersham later encountered difficulties with his bishop, based in Lincoln, but he only had to travel a few miles from Ashby to enter the jurisdiction of the bishop of Coventry and Lichfield or that of the archdeaconry of Nottingham, which was part of the northern province of York. As we will discover, when officials in these areas were sympathetic to Hildersham's views, they allowed him to continue preaching even after his own bishop had banned him.

So, in 1587, Hildersham entered a town that had already gained a reputation as a center of Puritanism for more than twenty years, but a place where godlessness and social problems were still very evident. Perhaps surprisingly, Hildersham encountered a good deal of ignorance about the Bible and Christian teaching even in this community that had had the benefit of gospel preaching for such a long period. We do not know much about Arthur's ministry in these early years, as no copies of his sermons or lectures survive, but we know that he set about his task of teaching and catechizing the people faithfully and thoroughly. The old minister of Ashby, Thomas Widdowes (who had married Gilby's daughter Esther in 1570), continued to serve his flock and surely would have helped and guided his younger colleague in the early days. Hildersham and Widdowes shared a commitment to the doctrines of grace and evangelical priorities, as well as similar temperaments. After his death, the earl was to praise Widdowes as "faithful, careful, and diligent in his function, according to his talent."[9] It seems as if Widdowes was one of those unsung heroes of the faith, quietly pursuing his calling and content to let those with greater gifts, such as Gilby and Hildersham, take the limelight.

---

9. Cited in Cross, *Puritan Earl*, 141.

Hildersham came on the scene when the prophesyings had been suppressed officially, but their legacy of fellowship continued. Many of the longer-serving local ministers knew each other very well and had become accustomed to seeking each other's advice and accepting one another's judgments. Often we hear about only the famous preachers of the Puritan era, but in the Ashby area a group of little-known but faithful ministers supported and encouraged each other through regular fellowship. In addition to Thomas Widdowes there were Henry Presbury, vicar of nearby Packington from 1558 to 1593, who came to the Ashby lectures regularly and often consulted with Widdowes at the same time; Gabriel Rosse, Presbury's successor at Packington, who allowed his nonconformist parishioners to travel to Ashby to receive Communion according to their consciences; Hugh Blithe, minister of the village of Appleby, who left some of his theological books to Timothy Hildersham in his will of 1608; George More, who ministered at Calke and was to share in John Darrell's exorcism activities; and Hildersham's old friend John Ireton, who had been rector of Kegworth since 1581. To this number were added men like Henry Aberly, formerly curate of Burton; John Brinsley, curate and schoolmaster of Ashby; and Julines Herring, More's successor at Calke. Also included was Anthony Nutter, nonconformist rector of Fenny Drayton. In a diocesan commission enquiry of 1599, when Nutter was accused of denying Communion to a parishioner, Hildersham was called on to examine witnesses.[10] Perhaps the bishop thought that Hildersham's participation would help ensure fairness. Whatever the case, both Hildersham and Nutter later were suspended for their nonconformity. Hildersham became the acknowledged leader of this group of ministers because of his spiritual maturity and learning.

From the start of his ministry, Hildersham began teaching the parishioners of Ashby about the meaning of the Lord's Supper and how they should approach it in a worthy manner. According to the Church of England's regulations, only notoriously loose-living individuals could lawfully be excluded from Communion, and most people considered it their "right" to receive it. Some would even take their minister to court if

---

10. Leicestershire Record Office ID41/4/174. See also Chalmers, "Puritanism in Leicestershire," 100–102.

they were denied, especially at Easter, the one big occasion in the church calendar when, traditionally, everyone partook. Many of these people, of course, were not true believers and felt that receiving the bread and wine somehow made them Christians. In addition, the Catholic teaching that the elements became the physical body and blood of Christ in the priest's hands during the Mass still had a place in many people's minds, even after the Reformation in England. Hildersham countered these problems primarily with education rather than confrontation. Hildersham hoped his flock would come to a true biblical understanding through his clear and simple explanation about the Lord's Supper and how it was intended for those who were already believers—"not to begin, but to confirm faith where it is already begun."[11] From the start he prepared a book of questions and answers on the Lord's Supper that he used to dispel ignorance and superstition. This little treatise, which existed in manuscript form for many years prior to its publication in 1609 as *The Doctrine of Communicating Worthily in the Lord's Supper*, eventually became an early modern best seller and ran through eleven editions by 1643.[12] John Cotton described the questions and answers in the book as having been "of singular good use to many poor souls, for their worthy preparation to that ordinance. And in very deed they do more fully furnish a Christian to that whole spiritual duty, than any other, in any language (that I know) in so small a compass."[13] In the book, Hildersham took his readers through six graces that were necessary before participating in the Lord's Supper—a sincere and right desire of it, knowledge, faith, repentance, newness of life, and charity (love)—explained the proper manner in which believers should receive the Supper, and concluded by showing how the sacrament should affect a person afterwards. Following the example of his mentor, Richard Greenham, rector of Dry Drayton, whom he had observed at work during his Cambridge days, Hildersham recommended that the first administration of the sacrament should be

---

11. Hildersham, *The Doctrine of Communicating Worthily in the Lords Supper* (London, 1609), 86.

12. Hildersham's treatise, published anonymously, was appended to one by William Bradshaw, titled *A Direction for the Weaker Sort of Christians; Shewing in What Manner They May Be Prepared to the Worthy Receiving of the Sacrament of the Bodie and Bloud of Christ*. An earlier manuscript copy of Hildersham's treatise exists in the John Rylands University Library, Eng. MS 524, fos. 103–11.

13. John Cotton, "To the Godly Reader," in Hildersham, *Lectures upon John*, sig. A4.

delayed until the people had a good understanding of its meaning and what they were doing. He also advised that each time the Lord's Supper took place, a preparatory sermon should be preached beforehand, both to ensure that everyone was fully aware of what was going to happen and to stir up faith and repentance in the hearts of the congregation.

In addition to instructing and catechizing, Hildersham's main task as lecturer was to deliver a weekly sermon every Tuesday morning to a congregation gathered in the church. Again, no copies of these early lectures have survived, but his later series on John 4 (delivered between 1609 and 1611) and Psalm 51 (delivered between 1625 and 1631) subsequently found their way into print. These lectures give us some idea of Hildersham's subject matter and style, as well as the sort of people he was addressing. It is obvious that the lectures attracted large congregations and that sometimes more than twenty fellow ministers from nearby towns and villages also were present. We know that the fifth earl, great-nephew of the third earl, frequently attended the lectures on John, and his example no doubt prompted many others to come along. Hildersham himself commended the earl for "that encouragement I did receive from your lordship in the preaching of them…by that worthy example also you gave unto all my auditory in your constant and diligent frequenting of them."[14] Hildersham did not want the townspeople to have the idea that attendance at the weekday lectures was an optional "extra" compared to the services on Sunday, which were compulsory, but he did admit that those who were better off or could arrange their own affairs were more obligated to attend on Tuesday mornings than poorer people who might find it almost impossible. A servant whose master required his services, or a day laborer who would forfeit a whole day's wages if he took time off to attend a weekday service, might not have had any choice but to be absent. Hildersham put it like this: "Such as are of wealth and ability to live of themselves, are more bound to frequent the public exercises on the week day, than poorer men. Such as by their callings have more leisure and freedom from worldly employment, than such as have more necessary and important business."[15] However, during his lectures

---

14. "Epistle Dedicatory," in Hildersham, *Lectures upon John*, sig. A2.
15. Hildersham, *Lectures upon John*, 241.

Hildersham occasionally addressed poor people and servants, so it is obvious that some, at least, did manage to get there. Parishioners who were believers, of course, were more motivated to attend the Tuesday services in order to hear expository preaching than others who did not possess a personal faith. Perhaps, then, we might expect the lectures to contain more teaching directed to the faithful, and Sunday sermons to contain words for a wider, mixed congregation. It is true that Hildersham's lectures comprised a mass of godly instruction for God's people, as we will discover, but they were also evangelistic in content. Recognizing that there were unconverted people and mere "formal professors" in the pews before him, Hildersham often directed a challenge to them.

But Hildersham was in demand as a preacher elsewhere in the area, not only in Ashby itself. Weekday sermons, or "exercises," had also been established in a number of other centers in the vicinity, and Hildersham traveled to preach at several. Most notable among these were the exercises at Repton in Derbyshire (seven miles away) and Burton-on-Trent in Staffordshire (eight miles away), to which many people flocked to hear the Bible expounded. It was recorded that Hildersham was "the main upholder of these two exercises for many years," which "were the means of great good to the souls of many, both ministers and private Christians in the parts adjacent."[16] Hildersham enlisted William Bradshaw to help with preaching at Burton and Repton, and his biographer describes how proceedings were conducted: "Some one of them preached his hour upon the Scripture propounded the meeting before, and the rest or a certain number of them spent afterward, each one his half hour or thereabout on some other portion of Scripture, one being appointed to moderate, by minding that each spake, if occasion were, of the time, and to close up all with some succinct rehearsal of what had been delivered, together with an additament [addition], if it seemed good, of somewhat of his own."[17] When Bradshaw, a diffident man, could be persuaded to take the chair at these meetings, he was known as the "weighing Divine" for his gracious dexterity in balancing different opinions.

---

16. Clarke, "Life of Hildersam," 147.

17. Thomas Gataker, "The Life of Master William Bradshaw," in Clarke, *A General Martyrologie*, 51–52.

To fulfill these preaching commitments, Hildersham would have required a stable with a few horses; we know that he bequeathed his "best mare" to one of his sons in his will. No doubt he experienced many difficulties on the rough sixteenth-century roads, riding in all sorts of weather conditions, but it seems he knew God's traveling mercies. Hildersham's friend Bradshaw experienced a real "miracle of mercy" on one of his journeys when he was plunged into a deep mill pond by his horse. Bradshaw was saved from drowning by a passerby who noticed Bradshaw's floating body and urgently shouted to the miller to close the floodgates, which stopped the rapid current of water and allowed him to be rescued just in time.[18]

For six years Hildersham labored among the residents of Ashby as their lecturer, teaching them faithfully, getting to know them, and becoming involved with their daily lives. He lived in the town near the church and the market place, the hub of town business and interaction. He was available for spiritual counsel and practical assistance. With his marriage and the beginnings of his own family, he put down roots in Ashby, and the people began to regard him as one of their own.

---

18. Gataker, "Life of Master William Bradshaw," in Clarke, *A General Martyrologie*, 29–30.

Chapter 4

At Home in Ashby

When Hildersham moved to Ashby in 1587, he was twenty-four years old and unmarried. We cannot be sure where he was living at this stage, although we know it could not have been the vicarage next to the church because Thomas Widdowes, the current vicar, would have been occupying it. It seems likely that he would have taken over the tenancy of the large house in which the previous lecturer, Anthony Gilby, had resided. There were only a few dwellings of any size (more than eight rooms) in the town during this period, of which Gilby's was one. So it seems logical to suggest that this was the same house where it is known that Hildersham lived from 1605 onward. Sadly, this house, on Wood Street, was demolished in 1643 during the Civil War, but for nearly forty years after Hildersham's death, the local people knew the adjoining gate and lane as "Hildersham's gate." Even at the beginning of the twentieth century, folk memory in the town recalled the existence of what must have been a fine residence in Tudor times: "According to tradition there were at one time four houses of importance in [Wood] Street. One, called the Hall, an Elizabethan mansion, stood at the top of Field Lane; it was a large house, made of stone, some of which probably form the wall by the roadside. The interior, with its wide staircase, carved oak, ornamental ceilings, and large lofty rooms, showed that it had been occupied by persons of consequence. It had a terraced garden, with steps from one level to another."[1] Positioned within the

---

1. W. Scott, *The Story of Ashby-de-la-Zouch* (Ashby-de-la-Zouch: George Brown, 1907), 241.

rectangle of church, castle, and Wood Street, which formed the basis of the ancient town settlement, Hildersham's house was thus at the heart of community life. It also controlled, via its gate, access to the extensive pastureland of the Near Commons, and, in addition, its location on the main road to Nottingham would have facilitated Hildersham's preaching trips to other places. Everybody in the town knew where Hildersham lived, and his house became a symbol of his commitment to the town. Even when he was suspended and banned from preaching, he and his family continued to live in the house, and people knew that they could go there for spiritual advice, hospitality, and "poor relief," welfare support for the impoverished of Hildersham's day. Even today, the site is a prominent one, now occupied by a substantial eighteenth-century property known as Lorne Hill House, and ancient stones in the wall that runs along the adjoining lane may well date from the time when Hildersham was living there.

In contemporary society we sometimes get uneasy when we hear of pastors or preachers being well off and living in big houses. Rightly, we are concerned if we feel they are becoming too worldly or affluent, for they may be drawn away from sacrificial service to God. However, when we go back to the sixteenth and seventeenth centuries attitudes in society were slightly different. Anticlericalism was common at the time of the Reformation, and people criticized Catholic priests for their immorality, ignorance, and self-indulgence. After the Reformation in England, there was uncertainty about the status of the newly married Protestant clergy. Were they of the lower sort, with a smattering of book learning, or were they actually of the class of gentlemen, to be respected and honored? Faithful ministers did not seek glory or power, but they realized it was important for society to respect their office so that people could receive the gospel message with reverence. Ministers who lived in poverty were often looked down on and their teaching scorned. That is not to say that ministers sought after wealth, or felt that it was an indication of God's blessing on their ministry—they were well aware of the dangers of trusting in riches and earthly things—but they believed God's messengers should be treated with the respect due to their calling. They sought to be, in Christ's words of Luke 10:7, "labourer[s] worthy of their hire." In an age with no welfare state, there were also significant obligations that ministers had to fulfill: they were expected to keep an "open table," supplying food to deserving poor people who came to their doors each day and giving generously to relieve the poor in their hardships.

Hildersham, as we have seen, had many social advantages. He was born a gentleman and educated as such. The fact that his patron, the earl, was also his cousin, significantly smoothed his way in local society. The townspeople would no doubt think twice about opposing or criticizing someone who had the wholehearted support of their landlord and temporal master. But Hildersham himself was a very humble man who regarded himself only as God's instrument. He never presumed upon his high birth, and, as previously mentioned, he warned others not to trust in earthly rank or ancestry. Hildersham had been made penniless when his father disinherited him as a youth, and he always was aware of his indebtedness for the earl's generous provision (which his heirs, the fourth and fifth earls, continued). This Hildersham acknowledged with gratitude in the preface to his *Lectures upon John*, which he dedicated to the fifth earl:

> To give public testimony to the world, of my duty and thankfulness unto your honour, and unto your noble house; unto whom (next under God) I do owe whatsoever poor abilities He hath been pleased to give unto me, for the service of His church. For as that noble uncle of yours [the third earl]...did first maintain me in the university, and after brought me to the exercise of my ministry in this place; so have I been by the favour and bounty of your noble grandfather [the fourth earl], and of your honour continued here, for more than forty years.[2]

Hildersham was referring in particular to the generous financial settlement the third earl had made on him when he was appointed lecturer in Ashby. The earl was the lay rector of the benefice, which meant that all the tithes from the parishioners went to him, and out of them he paid the vicar of St. Helen's. When Hildersham was called as lecturer, the earl settled the income from what was known as the "greater tithes" on Hildersham for life. This gave Hildersham considerable financial security and spared him from the kind of demeaning tithe disputes that many of his clerical brethren had to undergo in order to get the money

2. Hildersham, "Dedicatory Epistle," in *Lectures upon John*, sig. A3.

that they had been promised. Although this made Hildersham a wealthy man by Ashby standards (he left an estate valued at 525 pounds, ten shillings, and four pence—about fifty thousand pounds in today's money) and gave him the ability to live in some comfort, his fortune was nothing compared to that of the great merchants and courtiers of his age. He was also renowned for his generosity and concern for the poor. He stewarded the resources entrusted to him with diligence and faithfulness. Hildersham often was described as "the patron of the poor," and on his death he left a considerable legacy to be used for Ashby's impoverished citizens. His library accounted for a significant proportion of his assets and was valued at sixty-six pounds, six shillings, and eight pence. It must have comprised over two hundred books,[3] many of which would have been theological works, but Hildersham's interest in the natural world and cosmology, encouraged by a liberal humanist education, was demonstrated in his collection of maps and his copy of Petrus de Alliaco's *Imago Mundi* (A picture of the world). This volume he inscribed with the Latin motto *nosce teipsum*, "know thyself."[4]

In early modern times, a man was not considered fit for marriage until he was financially established enough to provide properly for a wife and family. To marry sooner would have been viewed as highly irresponsible, and most fathers would not have consented to their daughters' marrying someone in such circumstances. Christians did not undertake marriage lightly, but only after a good deal of thought and prayer about the suitability of the prospective partner. Parents or respected friends usually played a major part in advising and bringing about a match. Hildersham supported the practice of a couple making binding contracts before witnesses prior to marriage itself (citing the example of Mary and Joseph), so that the pair could examine their hearts to see if they were able to supply the mutual help and comfort required in such an undertaking. For, he declared, "there is no action of this life should be undertaken with

---

3. Leicestershire Record Office PR/I/34 f. 29 contains the probate inventory of Hildersham's goods, compiled at his death in 1632.

4. This volume is now held in Cambridge University Library, as it was part of the bequest of Richard Holdsworth, Master of Emmanuel College, in 1649. De Alliaco's book was one of the earliest scientific books, containing a map of the world, and it greatly influenced Christopher Columbus.

more religious care than the action of knitting in wedlock because it is the covenant of God, Proverbs 2 [v. 17] and the parties are knit by God, Matthew 19."[5] To the modern Western mind, colored by Hollywood's notions of romantic love, it might all seem a little cold and calculating, but these marriages were often long-lasting, with real affection and companionship frequently blossoming after the wedding.

Hildersham's advice to others had been that they should first consider whether "the Lord have fitted them to the duties and works of marriage," so that in the future they would "be able to bear all the crosses and burdens of it with comfort," assured of God's calling to that estate.[6] By the age of twenty-seven, Arthur was in a position to think of taking a bride and certainly would have examined his heart before God in this matter. He was settled in Ashby and was mindful of the importance of having a helpmeet who could assist him in his work. In the normal course of events, his parents would have identified some possible candidates for him to consider, but they had disowned him and did not share his faith anyway. So it is likely that the earl and some other relatives, the Barrington family of Essex, acted *in loco parentis* in Hildersham's marriage arrangements. Another cousin of Hildersham's mother, Winifred Pole (sister to Katherine, Countess of Huntingdon) had married into the Barringtons of Hatfield Broad Oak, and the family had become one of the leading supporters of religious reform in that county. Hildersham's bride, Ann Barfoot, whom he married on January 5, 1591, was an Essex girl, and it is quite possible that they were married at Hatfield Broad Oak.

Ann Barfoot was the daughter of Thomas Barfoot of Lambourne Hall in Essex. The Barfoot family had made their money as cloth merchants in the city of London; Ann's grandfather Robert Barfoot was a leading member of the Mercer's Company. He owned the manor of Lambourne at his death in 1547, but it was Ann's father, Thomas, who built Lambourne Hall in 1571. Little is known of Thomas's spiritual beliefs, but he cannot have been hostile to the Reformed faith since he allowed his daughter to marry a godly minister. As someone with a

---

5. John Rylands University Library, Rylands Eng. MS 524, fol. 75, "The effect of an exhortation in private to two parties at their contracting before the witnesses by Master Hildersam."

6. John Rylands University Library, Rylands Eng. MS 524, fol. 75.

background of "new money" made in trade, he no doubt also thought it socially advantageous for Ann to become allied to someone of Hildersham's ancient pedigree and name. Ann was one of a family of nine—she had six brothers and two sisters—and her brother Edward, a graduate of Arthur's old Cambridge College, married a Winifred Hildersham. This lady may have been Arthur's sister or more likely his niece, the daughter of his brother Richard. Edward Barfoot was dead by 1592, and his widow, Winifred, went on to marry Arthur's friend, the prominent Essex Puritan preacher Ezekiel Culverwell, in October 1598.

As is often the case with ministers' spouses in the past, we do not know very much about Ann Hildersham. It was recorded that she was "a very loving and careful wife of him, and the like mother of his children."[7] In his sermons, perhaps with his own wife's example in mind, Hildersham sometimes used the illustration of a mother's loving care for her children as a way of understanding God's even greater care for His children: "As you that are tender mothers are more moved with the groans, and tears of your children, than with their words," Hildersham wrote, "so it is with the Lord; the sighs and tears of his children prevail with him in this case much more, and give more efficacy to our prayers than any method or words we can use."[8] However, a few episodes indicate that Ann Hildersham was a strong-minded woman who involved herself very closely with her husband's ministry. One of these occurred around 1616 or 1617, when Hildersham had been removed from the ministry and forced to go into hiding. Presented with the offer of a pastorate at the English congregation in Leiden, Holland, Hildersham would have accepted, we are told, "had not his wife's unwillingness to go over the seas, retained him here."[9] Unlike the missionary William Carey, who, 180 years or so later, was prepared to contemplate sailing for India without his wife, Hildersham would not take such a major step without the full agreement of his spouse. The other incident occurred after a fire in Ashby in 1604 when Ann Hildersham was to be found

---

7. Clarke, "Life of Hildersam," 146.
8. Hildersham, *Lectures upon Psalm 51*, 67.
9. Clarke, "Life of Hildersam," 150.

giving her opinion of events in a very forthright manner—but more of that in due course.

Within two years of their wedding, Arthur and Ann had become the parents of two little daughters, both of whom died in infancy and were buried in the Ashby churchyard. Sarah was baptized on October 30, 1591, and was buried eight days later on November 7, 1591. Mary, who was baptized in October or November 1592, went to the grave on November 28, 1592. A third daughter, another Mary, baptized on June 28, 1598, died at four-and-a-half years old and was buried on January 5, 1603. Infant and child mortality was, of course, very high at that time, and most families experienced the loss of children. Nevertheless, parents loved their offspring very much and grieved not a whit less because of the frequency of their bereavements. Hildersham assured his congregation that it was natural for parents to feel a "great affection and love" for their children and that the loss of a child "went nearer the heart" than any other affliction. He gave the biblical examples of Abraham, David, and the widow of Zarephath to illustrate how parents showed "natural affection" to their children and felt great sorrow when they suffered.[10] The deaths of his own daughters must have given Hildersham real insight and sympathy as he counseled and comforted others going through similar grief. However, he also warned people of "over-loving" their children, and of "loving them more than God." When Hildersham preached on the nobleman who came to Jesus, afraid that his son was dying (John 4:49–50), he stressed that "the extremity of worldly grief, will make the mind and heart of man uncapable of heavenly things." This would prevent one from praying and from gaining any consolation from the gospel, while giving "great advantage to Satan."[11]

The other five Hildersham children, however, lived into adulthood: Anna (baptized January 6, 1594), Samuel (baptized August 19, 1595), Timothy (baptized at the end of May in 1600), Nathanael (baptized September 9, 1602), and Sarah (baptized December 9, 1604). Like other Puritans, Hildersham advocated biblical names for children, to express "the desire we have our child may imitate the worthy example of

---

10. Hildersham, *Lectures upon John*, 390–91.
11. Hildersham, *Lectures upon John*, 433.

that person, whose name he beareth." For, he explained, "to those names which the Holy Ghost has sanctified with His own pen, there is greater reverence and respect due, than to others."[12] It is not fanciful, then, to suppose that after the deaths of their baby daughters, the Hildershams, similarly to Hannah in the Old Testament, had been praying for the gift of a son and that Samuel Hildersham, like his biblical namesake, had been dedicated to God from his birth. Indeed, Samuel went on to become a faithful gospel preacher, following his father into the ministry.

For Hildersham and his wife, bringing up children and establishing a godly home was of the utmost importance, and he had a great deal to say on the subject in his sermons. As a starting point, Hildersham clearly taught the biblical doctrine of original sin, "that every infant so soon as it is born and conceived standeth guilty of sin before God, and is by nature the child of wrath."[13] God entrusted parents with the serious responsibility of their children's spiritual welfare: "Every parent is as deeply charged by God, with the souls of his children, as any pastor is with the souls of his flock, and more deeply too." Hildersham's aim was "to exhort, and stir us up that are parents, to do the uttermost of our endeavour to work grace in our children, and so to cure that deadly wound, that we have given them, and to preserve them from perishing by that poison, and infection that we have conveyed into them." How crucial then that "parents must be earnest with God, in prayer, for their children" and that "they should pray earnestly to God to give them wisdom, to know what they may do to destroy corruption, and breed grace in their children." Arthur explained the need for parents to set an example of godliness for their children to follow, saying, "You that are parents must be careful to give good example unto your children; cause it to appear unto them in your whole conversation, that you yourselves do unfainedly fear God, and love good things." For "without this neither your commandments, nor correction, nor instruction, will do them any good."

As well as emphasizing the tender love and care that parents should display to their offspring, Hildersham stressed that discipline, correction,

---

12. Hildersham, *Lectures upon John*, 202.

13. These quotations on bringing up children are taken from Hildersham, *Lectures upon Psalm 51*, 275–303.

and instruction were necessary and not to be neglected. In order to do these tasks effectively, parents should maintain their authority over their children: "Every father must be a ruler in his own house, every child must be kept in subjection." If this biblical model was not followed and parents tried to be "friends" to their children (or, as Hildersham described it, "hail fellow well met"), then children would lose respect and dishonor God. We tend to regard the breakdown of family discipline as a modern phenomenon, but it is evident that Hildersham saw it as a common problem in his own era. Parents should never administer discipline in a harsh or unloving manner, for Hildersham granted that "those parents govern best, that can maintain their authority, and keep their children in awe with little or no sharpness and severity; and many parents are too apt to offend in too much rigour this way." But, on the other hand, "no parent may hope to weaken and destroy the corruption that is in his child's heart, though he teach him never so well, and use all the allurements he can, to draw him to goodness, if he do not also correct him, and use the rod sometimes." For, he reminded his hearers, "we love not our children, we hate them, if we correct them not."

Instruction, too, was vital and should begin at an early age: "Betimes, while they are very young, as soon as they discover any capacity or understanding...teach them to know God, to know what is good, and what is evil, teach them some few of the first and easiest principles of religion." Hildersham continued, "You must betimes [early] acquaint them with the practice of religion, as reading of the Word and prayer and giving of thanks at their meat and singing of psalms." In addition, he exhorted, "You must bring them with you to the church to the public worship of God, betimes even while they are very young, even so soon as they can come, and be there without disturbance to the congregation, that they may become acquainted with God's worship and ordinances betimes." Arthur's final piece of advice on this subject was, "You that are parents must examine your children how they profit by the means of grace, try how they understand what they hear, repeat it, and make it plainer to them; and in repeating it, apply it also." Daily family devotions and catechizing were important means of instruction. Whether sending their children to school, placing them in other households for service, or arranging marriages for them, parents should ensure that their children were entering situations in which God was honored and the means of grace were available.

Hildersham thus summed up his wealth of practical advice to parents: "The interest they have in their children's love and affection, is a great matter; and so is the advantage they may take of their children's tender years; and so is their continual conversing with them; and so is their authority also. None have such opportunities to instruct, and bring others to goodness, as parents have." He concluded, "If either we respect our children, or our own comfort or the glory of God, we must be careful to do our best endeavour that the corruption of nature, that we have conveyed into them may be healed, and that saving grace may be wrought in their hearts."

All of this advice and instruction takes on a poignant personal note when we consider Arthur's own family situation. Although there is no concrete proof, evidence suggests that his middle son, Timothy, may have been physically disabled in some way. He never left home for the typical pursuits of university or marriage, and Arthur made particular provision for Timothy in his will. His older brother, Samuel, was to ensure that Timothy received a generous, regular allowance as well as his father's best horse or mare. Perhaps Timothy, like Mephibosheth in the Old Testament, was lame or unable to walk, so the horse would enable him to get about. In 1628, too, the Ashby Overseers of the Poor made a gift of sixpence to Timothy from a bequest they had received for the poor of the parish. It was only a gesture, but it demonstrated that Timothy was unable to provide for himself and was a mark of the love and respect the parishioners had for the Hildersham family. Hildersham left to Timothy "my best Bible [I] was wont to wear in my pocket," which shows that he felt a particular tenderness for this son. When preaching about God's fatherly tenderness to His children, Hildersham frequently illustrated his point with the example of human parents' feelings for their own imperfect offspring. Such references would have had a special resonance for his hearers if Timothy was indeed disabled in some way. For example, when affirming that God did not reject His servants for any of their infirmities, Arthur declared that "even we that are evil stand thus to our little ones, that we cannot loathe them, or neglect them for any out-breach, or looking asquint, or any other such like deformity;

yea many a thing which in another man's eye is a great blemish (as the pock holes in the face, or such like) to us seemeth none at all; yea the weaker and more feeble any of our children are, the more tender we are over them."[14] He also affirmed that "men may beget children that are defective...blind...cripples...fools. But our heavenly Father begets no such children, all His children are perfect, and have no such defect of parts in them."

After six years of serving as Ashby's town lecturer, a big change was about to happen for Arthur and his family. In October 1593, the third earl invited his protégé to become vicar of Ashby.

---

14. Hildersham, *Lectures upon John*, 454. Similar references can be found at 11, 97, 192–93, 218, 391–93, and in *Lectures upon Psalm 51*, at 61, 74, 80, 358, 660.

Chapter 5

Vicar of Ashby
(1593–1605)

On the death of Thomas Widdowes, vicar of Ashby, the Earl of Huntingdon offered the vacant incumbency to Arthur Hildersham, who had been serving as the town's lecturer. Obviously, the earl considered Arthur the best candidate to fulfill his great desire that "the supply of that place be continued and increased." In his letter inviting Arthur to become vicar, his cousin continued, "Let this be your care, to advance the glory of God by exercise of your ministry which you shall do best when you are in your pastoral charge."[1]

The chief aim of Hildersham's ministry was to advance the glory of God. Although no sermons survive from his time as vicar, Hildersham's later writings illuminate his attitude toward his ministerial calling. Like other Puritans of the period, he had a very high view of preaching: "The Word of God, and the Ministry thereof," he declared, "is the salvation of men." Indeed, "the only means of regeneration" was "the Word preached." To fulfill this divine calling was an arduous undertaking for which the minister was answerable to God. Hildersham listed a set of guidelines "out of God's Word" that he hoped would help others in the ministry, and which also demonstrated his own pastoral priorities:

> I. We must be diligent and painful [painstaking], both in study and in preaching...

I. Cross, *Puritan Earl*, 141.

2. When we teach we must labour to teach that (not wherein ourselves may show most learning or eloquence), but which may be most profitable and of use to them we teach...

3. Strive to teach in that manner, as may most profit thy hearers... that is, apply thy doctrine always to the present estate and condition of thy hearers...

4. Take heed to thy life, that thou do nothing to hinder the fruit of thy labours...

5. Be earnest in prayer, that He would make thy ministry fruitful...

6. Enquire for fruit, and deal with thy people in private, to see how they profit by thy labours.

Thus the model minister Hildersham set forth was a studious, hardworking man who led an irreproachable life, who was earnest in prayer, and who had a sensitive knowledge of the individual needs of his congregation. Every indication shows that Hildersham was just such a minister: the memorial Samuel Hildersham erected to his father in Ashby church declares that he was known for his "sweet and ingenuous disposition, his singular wisdom in settling peace, advising in secular affairs, and satisfying doubts, his abundant charity, and especially for his extraordinary knowledge and judgment in the holy Scriptures, his painful [painstaking] and zealous preaching, together with his firm and lasting constancy in the truth he professed." In other sermons, Hildersham taught that a minister should not be aloof or proud, but, emulating Christ's example, he should be accessible to those who wished to confer with him: "not to show himself stately, or austere, or churlish, or strange to any of his hearers, that shall be willing to make use of him that way." Ideally, a pastor should live near to the church itself so that people would know where to find him. To carry out his role properly he must love his flock.[2]

As far as the hearers of the Word were concerned, Hildersham told his listeners that they too had a number of responsibilities, both to the message itself and to the ministers that delivered it. He urged them to

---

2. All the above quotations on ministry are taken from Hildersham, *Lectures upon John*, 168, 280, 290, 228, 66.

listen to the sermon attentively, having prepared their hearts in advance. They were to accept reproof from the minister as if from God Himself and to love their reprover the more for making them aware of their sin. More generally, they were to love and esteem all faithful ministers of the gospel, recognizing their authority and giving them the honor due to their office. God's people should seek to live under a faithful ministry and be prepared to contribute financially to the upkeep of faithful pastors. To live holy lives, Hildersham pointed out, was the best way for Christians to demonstrate that they had truly profited by the teaching of their ministers.[3]

Hildersham's sheer popularity as a preacher put him in rather a difficult position. Because crowds flocked from miles around to hear him preach, often forsaking their own parish churches where the preaching was not so good, some of Hildersham's fellow ministers alleged that he encouraged the practice of "sermon-gadding." On two occasions he addressed this situation directly. "What are we to think," he asked, "of the people that go from their own pastors to hear others?" Answering that question, he upheld the general principle that preaching was God's gift to the church as a whole, so that "every Christian hath right and title to the gifts of all God's servants, and therefore it is no sin for them (when conveniently they may) to make their benefit of them." If their local church did not proclaim truth, then people clearly had a responsibility to seek out a church that did proclaim it. However, he warned his listeners against partiality and despising "the ministry of the meanest of God's servants" in favor of those with greater gifts. In normal circumstances a person should listen to the preaching of his own pastor, provided that he was "a man whose gift is approved by God's church, and who is conscionable [conscientious] in his place and of unblameable life." Such a minister should not be scorned, even if his gifts were inferior to another's. Hildersham advised fellow ministers to accept it with a generous, rather than a jealous, heart when their parishioners went to hear other men preach, if they did so for the right reasons. Ministers should rejoice to see spiritual fruit being produced in the lives of their flock.

---

3. All references to hearing the Word are taken from Hildersham, *Lectures upon John*, 125, 295, 105, 280, 247, 315–18.

What evidence there is indicates that Hildersham, day by day, served his people with diligence and a pastoral heart. The Ashby parish registers, containing details of all the births, marriages, and deaths in the town, were conscientiously and carefully maintained during Arthur's time as vicar. During his twelve-year incumbency, 410 baptisms of children, 259 burials, and 80 marriages were performed. Interestingly, the registers also show that Hildersham clearly preferred the title "minister" to that of "vicar"—this was how he always signed his name at the foot of each page of the register. It was another indication that he perceived himself as God's servant, ministering faithfully to the local inhabitants. He baptized six of his own children between 1594 and 1604, but, unlike some later vicars who announced the birth of their own offspring with an ostentatious flourish in the registers, Hildersham's children were recorded just like any other in the parish. We know that Arthur advocated a careful administration of the Lord's Supper, to be given only after a time of intensive teaching and preaching about its true meaning, but how frequently Ashby church celebrated it at this time is not certain. Accounts from 1627 to 1628 show that the Lord's Supper took place on four occasions during that year, with two services at Easter. Each time there was a collection for the poor as part of the service. This practice would certainly match the model Hildersham outlined in his treatise on the Lord's Supper, and he may well have instituted it as vicar.

Other records and accounts give us little glimpses of what it would have been like to live in Ashby during these years when Hildersham was vicar, loyally supported by the earl. It seems as if Ashby was a place renowned for the preaching of the gospel, and the powerful movement of the Spirit in conversion was very evident. Looking back, Hildersham recalled that the town had witnessed its greatest number of conversions at the beginning of his ministry. Residents of Ashby diligently observed the Sabbath, and the church was full. In fact, it seems that few churches in England could boast such large congregations. Ashby became known as a beacon of gospel light in an area of surrounding darkness, and people flocked from miles around, particularly to the midweek lectures and exercises. Spiritual fervor characterized the people of God in the town. The congregation held regular public fasts, seeking God's face and humbling themselves in prayer before Him. Local ministers gathered together under Hildersham's leadership for regular conferences. "Revival" was not a term in use at the time, but many features that characterized such periods of special blessing were evident in Ashby during the 1590s. It was this godly atmosphere that drew the Puritan minister John Darrell to settle in the town in 1592. He became one of Hildersham's closest associates and was at the center of a notorious controversy (of which more will follow later). Hildersham allowed John Darrell to preach from his pulpit in St. Helen's church on Sunday, November 17, 1594, when he delivered a sermon arguing against the ringing of church bells on the Sabbath. Darrell, John Ireton, and others shared times of fellowship over dinner at Hildersham's house. John Brinsley, a godly schoolmaster of similar mind to Hildersham, was appointed to Ashby Grammar School in 1599, and he later became church curate as well. Brinsley was a loyal ally of Hildersham's, who was to become well known in his own right as the author of a famous book of the time on education, titled *Ludus Literarius: or, The Grammar School* (1612). The town of Ashby drew believers from all ranks of local society, including the earl himself; the earl's bailiff, John Burrows, and his wife, Margery; the influential locksmith, William Cox, and his wife; and people like Robert Spencer, a man so needy as to be in regular receipt of poor relief.

But the very success of the gospel in Ashby during these years brought its own problems, not least what appeared to be an intensification of Satan's attacks. Hildersham declared that the increase of sexual immorality (in particular, incidents of fornication) in the town was due to a direct rejection of the gospel. He also spoke out against those who spent time drinking and gambling in the alehouses instead of attending church services. There were also suspected cases of demon possession in the 1590s. (One involved John Brinsley's servant, Phipps, although it was later judged not to be a case of demon possession.) Perhaps the greatest challenge to the gospel that Hildersham identified was a mere formality or outward observance of religion, where the heart remained untouched by true repentance and faith. This led to hypocrisy—a powerful enemy to the gospel in a place where it was socially advantageous to give at least lip service to a religious profession. Many attended church and appeared to be morally upright citizens, but, Hildersham stressed, this was not enough in itself to please God: "An unblameable and a virtuous life will not serve the turn without [saving] knowledge."[4] And so Hildersham continued to challenge the presumption and false hopes he encountered in those around him.

One facet of Puritan preaching that Hildersham strongly advocated, but that would be less acceptable today, was so-called "particular preaching" or "close dealing." Ordinary Christians as well as ordained ministers could deliver reproof for sin to their brethren; this could take place either in private or, if necessary, publicly, from the pulpit. Ministers and others could challenge the guilty party directly, in the way that the prophet Nathan challenged David after his sin with Bathsheba. The aim was always to bring the sinner to repentance and a restoration of his relationship with God. However, even at this time there was an acute awareness of the problems that could arise when such a practice was used insensitively, and many preachers shied away from naming names and sins in public. Hildersham, who devoted a whole sermon to the doctrine that "they that would win souls to God, must plainly and particularly discover to men their sins," was aware of this reticence.[5] His sermon was as much to encourage his reluctant ministerial colleagues to engage in particular preaching as it was to urge their hearers to receive such reproofs in the right spirit. In typical Hildersham fashion, he qualified his strong advocacy of the practice with a number of cautions about how to undertake it properly. He said that the reproof must be issued "particularly and plainly, that the party may feel himself and his own sin touched," and in public if the offenses themselves were "public and scandalous," but it might often be better done privately or discreetly, so that "the credit and estimation of the person that sinneth may be preserved as much as may be." Hildersham advised, "A minister is not always bound in plain terms, imperiously, sharply, and bitterly to reprove the sins he knoweth by his hearers," but should adopt the course most likely to prevail in each circumstance. He cited with approval Christ's use of a "holy craft and cunning" to win the Samaritan woman at the well. The party at fault should be aware of his pastor's love for him, Hildersham stressed, and that the reproof was issued for the sinner's spiritual benefit

---

4. Hildersham, *Lectures upon Psalm 51*, 481.
5. Hildersham, *Lectures upon John* (lecture 13, May 2, 1609).

rather than out of any kind of malevolence. If the guilty party rejected the rebuke, it was evidence of a lack of grace in the hearer's heart: "Many will object against the preacher thus, I know he meant me: and what call you this but malice? If he had loved me, he would have told me in private." Elsewhere, Hildersham explained that sometimes the application to an individual was unintended by the preacher, who knew nothing of that person's particular sin, so that it was purely the operation of the Holy Spirit working to bring him or her to conviction.

Some of these factors may have been relevant in the difficult case of Richard Spencer. A chandler by trade, Spencer came from a family that had been established for several generations, at least, in Ashby. In September 1604, a serious fire occurred in the town, and three houses were burned to the ground. One of these belonged to Spencer, and as a consequence he also lost all his earthly goods, which had been inside the property. Spencer claimed that money had been removed from his house during the course of the fire, and he approached John Brinsley, the curate, asking that he publicize these losses in the church, with the hope of recovering the money. According to Spencer, Brinsley refused in no uncertain terms, suggesting that the fire had been God's judgment on Spencer's desire to have his children baptized with the sign of the cross, a practice many Puritans rejected as unbiblical. Spencer asserted that he was only asking for what the king's law enshrined. But then Spencer's complaint widened to include not only John Brinsley but also other members of the Puritan group in Ashby. He accused Ann Hildersham of telling a local widow named Joan, in whose home the fire had begun, that although God would comfort her and cause her house to be rebuilt, Spencer's loss was due to God's judgment, and that he should beware of future judgments because he favored the surplice (the ceremonial garment many Puritans spurned as a Catholic symbol). Spencer also alleged that, in a sermon, Hildersham had said the occupants of two of the burned-down houses were Christians, but that he could not tell what to make of the third. Spencer clearly thought he was being singled out for criticism.

We know about this episode only because of a complaint letter the embittered Richard Spencer sent to one of the bishop of Lincoln's officials in 1606, so it is difficult to be sure of the true course of events.

At face value, it might appear that the Hildershams and John Brinsley were being unduly harsh to a man who had suffered a severe setback merely because they had different views about certain disputed church ceremonies. However, as we will see later, although Hildersham (and others like him) thought such ceremonies unscriptural, he respected that the consciences of other believers allowed them to accept these practices. He certainly did not reject these people as unbelievers or feel that differences on such secondary matters should cause division between brethren. And so it seems that there was more to this case than meets the eye. Although we cannot be sure, there is a strong possibility that Spencer was in fact an ungodly man who may have been trying to stir up trouble for Hildersham and his friends. Hildersham said in his 1609 sermon, "When a man's offence is known and scandalous to many, the minister is not bound to admonish him in private; but may (without malice) reprove it publicly." Surely Hildersham would not have administered such a public reproof without good reason and certainly would not have taken this step if Richard Spencer had been a decent man whose only fault was to prefer traditional prayer-book ways. Several of Richard Spencer's sons were later to be reported for gross immorality and drunken pranks, which suggests that a rowdy, careless atmosphere may have prevailed in their home.

Spencer may have been encouraged to write the letter by some in the diocese who were trying to find evidence to pin on nonconformists like Hildersham and Brinsley, who were already in deep trouble with their bishop. The fact that Spencer waited for nearly two years to make his complaint, until a vigorous campaign against nonconformity was being waged, tends to support such an argument. This episode demonstrates, however, that the gospel will always bring division and will be opposed by many in the world who reject its claims. Hildersham had his opponents within the town, despite his success and the high esteem in which the townspeople generally held him.

Hildersham was vicar of Ashby for a mere twelve years. In 1605 he was suspended, never again to have a pastoral charge. Times were changing. He was deprived of the support and protection of his beloved patron and cousin, the third earl, who had died in 1595. He was succeeded by his brother, George, who became the fourth earl. Although he was suspected of youthful Catholic sympathies, the fourth earl continued to support the godly preaching ministries his brother had established. By 1604, he too was dead, and his young grandson, Henry, succeeded him and became the fifth earl. Because Henry had been brought up in the devoutly Protestant household of his great-uncle (the third earl), the people of God had great hopes for him but also felt uncertain because of his youth. This local lack of security was echoed on a national scale when James I acceded to the English throne in 1603. What direction would the Church of England take under his rule? Evangelical and nonconformist ministers like Hildersham faced an uncertain future.

But how could such a godly man, who had served his people faithfully and humbly, be removed from his ministry at the height of his powers? Was he some kind of radical extremist, preaching division and heresy? Hildersham's enemies certainly alleged this to be the case, but to answer these charges we must first interrupt the narrative of his life to examine in greater detail the content of his message and his theological position. Then we will turn to the state of the Church of England and contemporary ecclesiastical politics.

Chapter 6

❦

Hildersham's Message

Arthur Hildersham was not an original or innovative theologian, like William Perkins or John Owen; nor, it seems, was he a particularly dramatic or charismatic preacher, like Richard Sibbes. Typically Puritan, his pulpit manner was described as "grave and authoritative," and his sermons were detailed and carefully balanced, dealing thoroughly with all aspects of a subject. After setting out the background to a biblical text (the reasons), he would go on to expound the doctrine, then give applications, usually split into several different categories for different types of hearers. Often there would be qualifications and cautions to his main premise, so listeners had to pay careful attention in order to follow the thread of his argument. This is perhaps why Spurgeon described Hildersham's works as "rather heavy reading."[1] Robert Harris (the successor to John Dod at Hanwell and sometime head of Trinity College, Cambridge), when advising young men about theological reading matter, recommended Hildersham as an example of "solid preachers."[2] Hildersham, then, was a faithful and thoughtful expositor of the Bible who, by his own estimation, was first and foremost a pastor and preacher. His overriding concern was for the spiritual welfare of his congregation. The message that he delivered to them, in sermons and lectures, was

---

1. Spurgeon, *Commenting and Commentaries*, 161.
2. Clarke, "The Life and Death of Dr. Harris," in *A Collection of the Lives of Ten Eminent Divines* (London, 1662), 315.

therefore of the utmost importance to him, for it involved the salvation of their eternal souls. It was a message from God Himself, through the Scriptures, and Hildersham was obeying a divine call in imparting it. He once described ministers as "both the Lord's mouth unto us to deliver us His Word and the Lord's hand unto us to deliver us His sacraments."[3]

More than 250 of Hildersham's sermons, preached between 1609 and 1631 in Ashby, survive in printed form. The two main series were *Lectures upon the Fourth of John* (108 lectures, from 1609 to 1611) and *CLII Lectures upon Psalm 51* (152 lectures, from 1625 to 1631). Although we cannot capture the full experience of actually hearing them preached, Arthur recorded that he wrote out each lecture beforehand, so that what we read on the page is a fair representation of what he said. From the printed page, it is still possible to hear Hildersham's authentic voice. It is clear that in his theology Hildersham was a mainstream and orthodox Calvinist. Throughout Elizabeth's reign, this was the prevailing theology of the Church of England, and it was not until the beginning of the seventeenth century that this consensus began to break down.

What, then, did this mean in practice? What kind of message was Hildersham delivering to the people of Ashby from his pulpit in St. Helen's Church? Like his other Puritan brethren, his preaching was rigorously doctrinal and wide-ranging, offering biblical teaching relevant to every aspect of life. It dealt with the big theological themes of God, His nature, and His purposes, as well as particular advice on, for example, bringing up children and wearing appropriate clothing. In his introduction to the series on John 4, Hildersham's friend John Cotton summed up the contents this way:

> The scornful vanity of corrupt nature, the loathsomeness and desperate nature of sin, the wonderful power of God's grace in the conversion of a sinner, the trial of a man's own deceitful heart, the amiable life of God's grace in the regenerate, the comfortable benefits of afflictions, sundry sweet consolations of a troubled spirit, the vanity of popery, the necessity of a faithful ministry, the

---

3. John Rylands University Library, Eng. MS 524, f. 105r.

beauty of God's ordinances holily administered, and the resolution
of sundry cases of conscience fitting these times.[4]

It would be impossible to cover adequately the depth and range of subjects Hildersham tackled, so a taste of some of his main and recurring
themes must suffice.

Conversion

From the earliest days of the Reformation, the necessity of conversion
had been central to Protestant preaching. Indeed, preaching was the
prime means that God had ordained for the conversion of His people.
"It is the only means the Lord hath sanctified to work saving grace in
His elect, and to bring them to eternal life," Hildersham insisted.[5] In
his series on John 4, the conversion of the Samaritan woman (vv. 1–30)
has a central place, so Hildersham explored the subject in some depth
in his preaching. He believed that conversion was entirely a work of
free and sovereign grace. As he declared, the "conversion of a sinner is
the greatest miracle that ever God wrought."[6] Conversion entailed the
"changing of our nature," which was intrinsically opposed to everything
in the gospel.[7] Because the natural man was dead in trespasses and sins,
"our conversion is called not the restoring of a sick man, nor the healing
of a lame man, but the *raising of a dead man*, Rev. 20:6. And how can a dead
man desire life, or use any means to attain it?"[8] Hildersham's works stress
"free grace" and the human inability to save oneself, often contrasted
with Catholic teaching on the subject. However, in his later *Lectures upon
Psalm 51*, delivered towards the end of the 1620s, it was the growing
threat from Protestant Arminian teaching on conversion (which emphasized free will) that caused Hildersham to stress again the importance of
God's free grace. Much of lecture 105, preached on December 9, 1628,
is devoted to explaining and refuting the "Pelagian" teaching of these
"most dangerous seducers" who, "whatsoever they pretend,...impeach

---

4. Cotton, "To the Godly Reader," sig. A3v.
5. Hildersham, *Lectures upon John*, 169.
6. Hildersham, *Lectures upon John*, 28.
7. Hildersham, *Lectures upon John*, 26.
8. Hildersham, *Lectures upon John*, 28.

the grace of God, and give either all, or almost all of the glory of this great work, unto man himself." Arminians taught, said Hildersham, that after God had done His part, "it lieth in the power of a man's own will, whether the grace of God shall be effectual to his conversion or no, he is able of himself either to accept of it, or to reject it." For a Calvinist like Hildersham, this ran counter to scriptural teaching that any person's conversion was entirely due to God, who not only gives the grace to enable men and women to repent but "doth also infuse, and work the grace of repentance in him, he doth so change his will, that he doth most willingly repent, and obey the call of God."[9]

Election

The biblical doctrine of election was central to classic Calvinist theology, along with the associated teaching on particular redemption (that the benefits of Christ's death were limited to His chosen people). It is evident throughout his writings that Hildersham was an unwavering and orthodox predestinarian. He subscribed both to a divine election and a corresponding reprobation in the same way that William Perkins did. The doctrine of election served as "an unspeakable comfort" to the elect themselves, but it was "a fearful sign of reprobation" among those who exploited the doctrine to do more wickedness.[10]

Hildersham described the predestinating decree of God as "the secret of all secrets," and yet he declared it would be revealed to each of those who, with "an honest heart desire to be taught of God."[11] Perseverance of the elect was due not to their own faithfulness, but because of "the unchangeableness of God's love and decree. No man hath received the Spirit, but only such as God hath elected to salvation, and loved in Christ before all worlds."[12] As a pastor, Hildersham was well aware that the doctrine of predestination raised many questions for his congregation, and in his *Lectures upon John*, he dealt openly with such queries:

---

9. Quotations on conversion taken from Hildersham, *Lectures upon John*, 29, 26, 28, and *Lectures upon Psalm 51*, 523, 524, 511.

10. Hildersham, *Lectures upon John*, 99.

11. Hildersham, *Lectures upon John*, 212.

12. Hildersham, *Lectures upon John*, 52.

If any man shall demand of me the reasons of this doctrine: the cause why the Lord should thus love His elect, and be so partial towards them: that though He hates sin in all, and hates the reprobate, and damns them for their sin, yet He hates not His elect for their sins, but loves them even before there is any grace in them at all, even before they have repented of their sins, I can give no other reason of it, but His own good will and pleasure only, *he hath mercy on whom he will have mercy*, saith the apostle, Rom. 9:18 and Ephes. 1:11. *He worketh all things after the counsel of his own will.* And in this it becometh every mortal man to rest without enquiry any further, and to say with the holy apostle, Rom. 9:21–22: *Hath not the potter power over the clay? What if God will* do *thus.*[13]

As well as challenging the presumption of the ungodly who falsely assumed they were among the elect, Hildersham also wanted to encourage the trembling sinner who feared that God's "special mercy belongeth to none but to His elect, and they are but a few.... And I have so lived as I see cause to fear...at least I cannot be sure that I shall find mercy with God, though I should turn unto Him."[14] Hildersham reassures the latter that although the number of the elect was indeed small compared to the number of the reprobate, "yet hath no poor sinner that desireth to turn to God, any just cause given him to be discouraged from it by this doctrine."[15] All those who earnestly desired grace would be sure to find it. While the elect might not respond immediately to God's offer of salvation, it was certain that in due time they would be converted. Indeed, in the ordinary course of things, all those whom God intended to save should "have the means of grace vouchsafed unto them, at one time or another."[16] And ministers were to be encouraged, since "the Lord of the harvest never sent forth His labourers to work in any field, where He had no corn to get."[17] On the other hand, it was "a fearful sign of reprobation, when God giving to a man the means of grace, denies him a heart

---

13. Hildersham, *Lectures upon John*, 98.

14. Hildersham, *Lectures upon Psalm 51*, 132. He deals with similar fears in *The Doctrine of Fasting and Prayer, and Humiliation for Sin* (London, 1633), 130–43.

15. Hildersham, *Lectures upon Psalm 51*, 132.

16. Hildersham, *Lectures upon John*, 324.

17. Hildersham, *Lectures upon Psalm 51*, 506.

to profit by them."[18] However, Hildersham did not want profitless con-jecture about the mysteries of God's secret will to sidetrack his hearers. He insisted that "we may not in this case pry curiously, nor enquire into the secret counsel of God but reverently admire it.... Look thou, and enquire into the revealed will of God, and there thou shalt find enough to encourage thee to turn unto Him, and to assure thee that thou needest not doubt to find mercy, and grace with Him if thou canst now seek it."[19]

Hildersham firmly retained his belief in a limited atonement, unlike his friend John Preston and others who began to move toward a position of hypothetical universalism, which Jonathan Moore has defined as "the belief that in the will of God, Christ did not only die for the elect so as to secure infallibly their salvation, but He also died for the non-elect so as to provide for them a potential, or 'hypothetical,' salvation, condi-tional upon their believing the gospel."[20] When Hildersham expounded John 4:42 ("We...know that this is indeed the Christ, the Saviour of the world") he took care to explain that "by the world here" is "meant the elect only that are scattered throughout the world," so that the verse could have in effect read, "Christ is the Saviour of all the elect." In "many places of Scripture," Hildersham maintained, "the benefit of Christ's death is restrained and limited to a peculiar and choice company."[21]

However, Hildersham did not want his flock to get caught up in the theological controversies that were becoming especially divisive within Calvinist circles by the 1620s. He told them, "I shall not need to enter into the controversy which hath much troubled the church whether Christ died for all men." What was important to his hearers and was "agreed on by all divines" was that, in fact, all people were *not* saved by Christ's death, even if potentially they could be. Hildersham wrote, "But

---

18. Hildersham, *Lectures upon John*, 99.

19. Hildersham, *Lectures upon Psalm 51*, 132–33.

20. Jonathan Moore in personal communication with the author. For a fuller explana-tion of this definition and a detailed comparison between particularism and hypothetical universalism, see Jonathan D. Moore, "The Extent of the Atonement: English Hypotheti-cal Universalism versus Particular Redemption," in *Drawn into Controversie: Reformed Theological Diversity and Debates within Seventeenth-Century British Puritanism*, ed. Mark Jones and Michael A. G. Haykin (Gottingen: Vandenhoeck & Ruprecht, 2011), 124–61.

21. Hildersham, *Lectures upon John*, 329.

this I say (wherein we all agree, and of which there is no controversy; and which is as much as need be said for the purpose we have now in hand) that certainly all men shall not have benefit by Him, He hath not made all men's peace with God, He hath not undertaken for all men in particular nor satisfied God's justice for them, His death is not effectual for all men."[22]

Instead, Hildersham wanted his hearers to be concerned about whether they themselves were saved. He encouraged his flock to ask "whether we can find in ourselves those notes whereby Christ has marked His own sheep, and whereby He will own them for His."[23] There was a very personal application to each of his listeners: "unto thee as well as any other is He offered, and thou art commanded to believe He died for thee."[24] All to whom Christ was offered should indeed "have benefit of Christ, unless his own infidelity and rejecting of Christ do hinder him."[25] Although Scripture taught that there would be reprobates within the visible church, "yet," asserted Hildersham, "there is no particular person that lives in the church, but we are to judge and hope he is one of God's elect."[26]

Faith and Assurance

Many believers struggled with assurance of salvation at some stage or other. As a pastor, Hildersham had a burden to give biblical advice to those who suffered from a lack of assurance. The Roman Catholic Church taught that a full assurance of faith was impossible to attain, and Hildersham wanted to show that this was false. The possibility of full assurance was, he declared, a "doctrine which hath been so clearly and evidently confirmed unto you by the holy Scriptures."[27] However, he also acknowledged that all of God's people did not always live in a state of complete assurance. Even the strongest believer would have periods

---

22. Hildersham, *Lectures upon Psalm 51*, 609.
23. Hildersham, *Lectures upon Psalm 51*, 746.
24. Hildersham, *Lectures upon Psalm 51*, 133.
25. Hildersham, *Lectures upon John*, 331.
26. Hildersham, *Lectures upon John*, 331.
27. Hildersham, *Lectures upon John*, 341.

when he lost the assurance of his salvation and experienced some doubts: indeed, "he may be sure he hath no true faith, that feels not infidelity in himself" at some point.[28] And faith was not the same thing as assurance. Even those who possessed a weak faith need not despair, for "this weak, this little faith, is as true a faith, as effectual to justification and salvation (though it yield not a man that measure of certainty and comfort) as the other."[29] To help those who were unsure of their salvation, Arthur supplied four "signs and notes whereby we may know,...out of God's Word," that the Holy Spirit dwelt within. These comprised a rejection of our former lusts and affections (Gal. 5:24), a change in our way of thinking and living (2 Cor. 5:17), a willing resolve to obey Christ in everything (Heb. 4:9), and a "heart's grief and bitterness in thy soul for thy sins," which had caused "Christ to be pierced" (Zech. 12:10).[30] Ultimately, though, the roots of assurance were not subjective, but "grounded only upon the most sure and infallible testimony of God's Holy Word." And, explained Hildersham, "The Scripture expressly saith, that whosoever with an humbled soul, that despaireth of all help by any other means, believeth and putteth his affiance [trust] in Christ alone, resteth and relieth wholly upon him, shall certainly be saved."[31]

The Heart

For Hildersham, as for his fellow Puritans, all true religion was rooted in the heart. As he declared, "the chief and most proper seat of grace is the heart." Outward godly conduct was important, but it was only the natural fruit of an inner change of heart, or conversion. Heart-based, experiential religion was a major theme throughout Hildersham's preaching, but in particular lectures 79–94 of the *Lectures upon Psalm 51* and lectures 39–45 of the earlier series on John's gospel are devoted to this subject. Only if the heart was right, Hildersham stressed, was anything that a person did acceptable to God: "For the Lord is pleased

---

28. Hildersham, *Lectures upon John*, 333.
29. Hildersham, *Lectures upon John*, 333.
30. Hildersham, *Lectures upon Psalm 51*, 610–11.
31. Hildersham, *Lectures upon Psalm 51*, 622, 623.

with nothing that we do, unless it be done with a good heart."[32] Indeed, he insisted, "this is all in all with God, the only thing that He requireth of us, let our hearts be true to Him, and He hath enough."[33] If the heart was "good," then poor and imperfect services were acceptable to God, for He was concerned with the truth of our inward desires: "He is such a master as standeth not so much upon our actions in His service as upon our affections. Though we be able to do very little, yet if He discern in us an unfeigned desire to do well, He is ready to accept it."[34] This was a source of solace for Christians when every other indicator of faith seemed to have been stripped away: "Yea, this is almost all that the faithful have, many times to comfort themselves withal, that they find in themselves an unfeigned desire to please God."[35] Of course, Hildersham acknowledged that this must be a true and genuine desire, for there was a false kind of desire that did not result in eternal salvation. This false kind of desire was half-hearted, it came and went, it prevaricated, it arose only out of a slavish fear of God's wrath and a wish to avoid the consequences of sin, and it did not produce a changed lifestyle.

Hildersham also drew a contrast between true religion, which was spiritual and inwardly based, and the mere performance of certain outward actions, which was nothing but "formality" or "show," for "God delighteth much more in the inward than in the outward worship we do to Him."[36] However, we could not claim to be in a state of grace if the inner experience did not result in a visible outward change in our lives: "If the heart be upright and good, the speech will be good, and the actions also."[37] Hildersham was certainly no antinomian. But for him, the real enemy of true religion was hypocrisy, with its emphasis on head knowledge and outward observance. "Yet," Hildersham commented, "is there this defect in the goodness of the best hypocrite in the world, he doth nothing with a good heart." For, he affirmed, saving knowledge "swimmeth not nor floateth aloft in the brain only, of him that hath it,

---

32. Hildersham, *Lectures upon Psalm 51*, 696.
33. Hildersham, *Lectures upon Psalm 51*, 369.
34. Hildersham, *Lectures upon Psalm 51*, 366.
35. Hildersham, *Lectures upon John*, 8.
36. Hildersham, *Lectures upon Psalm 51*, 422.
37. Hildersham, *Lectures upon Psalm 51*, 371.

but it soaketh and sinketh down to the heart, it worketh upon the heart and affections of a man."[38]

Puritans are often caricatured as dour, loveless killjoys, obsessed with criticizing the behavior of their neighbors. The Ashby church itself contained a pair of finger stocks for those who misbehaved during services. And it is true that many so-called Puritans were eager to see moral improvement in society, with conduct reformed according to biblical standards and for God's glory. However, Hildersham's sermons show us that this was not his main priority. In the eternal perspective, moral improvement, though desirable, was not enough without a "lively faith" and a "good heart."[39] Hildersham often held up the type of the "civil" man, a good citizen whose conduct was entirely lawful and honest in an outward sense, but who in the final reckoning fell short of God's requirements. He warned that "an unblameable and a virtuous life will not serve the turn without [saving] knowledge."[40]

Roman Catholicism

One of the reasons Hildersham's sermons emphasized the need for true doctrine was the serious threat that Roman Catholicism posed. Although it was more than fifty years since the beginning of the Reformation in England, a significant number of people remained loyal to Catholicism, and many Catholic superstitions still lingered on in the general populace. For, Hildersham asserted, "a natural popery…is in every one of our hearts."[41] By this he meant that Catholicism, with its emphasis on a good-works mentality and outward observances, appealed to the carnality of the "natural" or unregenerate man, who wanted to contribute something to his own salvation. This produced a universal default tendency toward Catholicism, which needed to be countered constantly with biblical truth.

There was also a very real fear that the Roman Church might seek to reconvert or reclaim England. This fear was fostered through several

---

38. Hildersham, *Lectures upon Psalm 51*, 488, 489; see also 477.
39. Hildersham, *Lectures upon Psalm 51*, 316.
40. Hildersham, *Lectures upon Psalm 51*, 481.
41. Hildersham, *Lectures upon Psalm 51*, 434.

episodes, including the pope's excommunication of Elizabeth I in 1570, the defeat of the Spanish Armada in 1588, and the Gunpowder Plot in 1605. Especially alarming were the plans laid in the 1620s to find Prince Charles a Spanish bride and the defeat of Reformed armies on the Continent. In this context, a widespread anti-Catholicism resulted in society and church. Hildersham, as a pastor, usually steered away from the extremes of rhetoric some of his more polemical Protestant contemporaries employed. He concentrated on demonstrating the errors of Catholic beliefs from the Scriptures so that his congregation might be warned and equipped. Over a third of his lectures contain references to Catholicism. Many of these are quite brief and specific, dealing with issues such as the corporal presence in the Mass, clerical celibacy, confession to a priest, pilgrimage, images, relics, and so-called miracles. Each of these errors was refuted. Underlying the differences between Catholicism and Protestantism was an essential disagreement on the nature of authority. Hildersham declared, "The papist grounds his faith upon the testimony of the Church...yet it consisteth only of men who are subject to error.... But we ground our faith only upon the Word of God."[42] Hildersham also defended Protestantism against the common Catholic taunt that it was a "new" religion, no older than Luther. The only ancient—and therefore true—faith, he asserted, was one based upon the Scriptures, and it was the papacy that had introduced errors into the pure primitive church.

Worship

Hildersham attacked many forms and practices of Catholic worship. Indeed, he had much to say on the whole subject of worship, since getting it right was so fundamental. However, as this issue brought him into direct conflict with the church authorities, another chapter is devoted to considering the matter in some detail.

Strict observance of the Sabbath characterized Puritan piety, and Hildersham supplies a true example of a Puritan who advocated the practice. The Sabbath was a day to be devoted to the worship of God,

---

42. Hildersham, *Lectures upon John*, 348.

and anything that intruded upon this service was unacceptable. This might be sports or other worldly pursuits or an insufficiently serious and reverent approach to divine worship.

Hildersham was not a heretic or even an extremist. His biblical orthodoxy is unquestionable. He placed solid and unwavering emphasis on the Word of God, and his preaching provided both an evangelistic challenge for unbelievers and balanced teaching for the converted. This approach became more marginalized in the seventeenth century as a Laudian emphasis on ritual and ceremony became the norm. However, we must look for causes other than the doctrine Hildersham preached in order to explain the problems he had with the Church of England.

Chapter 7

Hildersham and the Church of England

"Is it right to separate from the Church of England?" This was the question "Mrs. N" posed in a letter to Hildersham in the early 1590s.[1] She was not the only one struggling with this issue: in fact, within twenty years of its foundation, many were questioning whether the Church of England could still be considered a true church. This conundrum has continued to exercise the minds of evangelical Anglicans to this day.

The Articles of the Church of England and its Prayer Book, drawn up under the hand of Thomas Cranmer, were, despite certain ambiguities and compromises, Calvinistic in their emphasis. However, with the early death of the young king Edward VI in 1553, the progress of reformation in England came to an abrupt halt. The burning of more than two hundred Protestants in Mary's reign gave the Church of England its first martyrs, prepared to die for gospel truth. With Elizabeth's accession in 1559, many, especially Protestants who had spent the Marian years at Reformed centers on the Continent, such as Geneva and Frankfurt, hoped to continue the process of reform that had been cut short in 1553. They saw the church as only "half-ly Reformed." However, they came up against the rock of the queen's intransigence. The peculiar constitution of the Church of England, a legacy of Henry VIII's break with Rome, made the monarch the supreme governor over the church. Although the

---

1. Johnson, *Treatise of the Ministry of the Church of England*. Unless otherwise stated, all quotations in this section are taken from this source.

Elizabethan settlement of the church was undoubtedly Protestant, Elizabeth had no wish for any further reformation. The Church of England was left with doctrines that were largely Calvinistic but many structures and rituals that were the same as they had been under Roman Catholicism. And although Elizabeth famously professed that she did not want to make windows into people's souls, she did expect an outward conformity to her church's institutions. From the 1580s, especially under the leadership of Archbishop Whitgift, there was a crackdown on those with presbyterian or "classical" sympathies that required them to subscribe to a set of three articles. For those who held more Reformed ideas of church organization and ceremony, this posed a problem. The Church of England was the only church allowed by law, and those who separated from it faced imprisonment and even death. The 1590s witnessed a determined campaign on behalf of the church authorities to root out and punish those who were meeting in underground separatist churches. In the spring of 1593, three separatist leaders—Henry Barrow, John Greenwood, and John Penry—were executed.

This was the background to Mrs. N's letter. We do not know anything definite about her except that she was a lady of gentle birth, who at the time of writing was imprisoned in a London jail for espousing the separatist cause. Evidence suggests that she may have been one Katherine Unwin, a thirty-five-year-old widow from Allgate, who had been arrested with a group of fifty-two others from a separatist congregation as they met secretly in the woods near Islington on March 10, 1593.[2] The pastor of this congregation was a man named Francis Johnson, a contemporary of Hildersham at Cambridge, who had moved to a separatist position after his university years. In 1592 he had read *A Plain Refutation*, written by the early separatist leader Henry Barrow, and become convinced that he could no longer remain within the established church.

Francis Johnson suggested that Mrs. N write to Hildersham, and Johnson then took up the issues that Hildersham had raised in his reply, writing his own letter to him in due course. The main contention of Johnson and Mrs. N was that the Church of England was an

---

2. See John Greenwood and Henry Barrow, *The Writings of John Greenwood and Henry Barrow 1591–1593*, ed. Leland H. Carlson (London: Routledge, 1970), 366–67.

"antichristian" church because it did not have proper scriptural discipline. According to them, the ministers and orders of the established church were not appointed or did not operate in the manner the New Testament prescribed. Thus true believers were required to separate from such a body, which was devoid of God's authority.

Johnson felt he had every reason to believe that Hildersham would leave the Church of England and come over to the separatist cause. This was no vain delusion on Johnson's part, but a realistic expectation based on a long acquaintance with Hildersham's character and convictions. "And of Mr. H," Johnson wrote, "I have this hope more specially, for the good things I know to be in him." After all, when they were at Cambridge together in the late 1570s and early 1580s, Hildersham and Johnson had shared very similar views on Cartwright's church polity, and both had already been in trouble with the authorities for their stand on the need for church reform. Johnson would have been well aware of the difficulties that Hildersham had experienced with the Church of England authorities by the early 1590s. Like Hildersham, the early separatist leaders were all university men and had come to that position through many theological exchanges with their peers. There was much debate, for example, over the interpretation of one key text, Matthew 18:17, "tell it unto the church" (*dic ecclesiae*), about where authority for discipline in the church was to be located. Johnson himself wrote a book on the subject, titled *A Short Treatise concerning the Words of Christ, "Tell the Church"* (1611). These men knew each other well, and the denominational divisions that became so apparent later were not yet in evidence.

At the heart of these debates was the way each side understood the nature of the church. Both accepted that two things were needful for a true church: the preaching of the gospel and the right administration of the sacraments (baptism and the Lord's Supper). However, the German Reformer Martin Bucer added a third mark that (he believed) characterized a true church of Christ: the proper exercise of ecclesiastical discipline, shown by organizing the church in line with New Testament patterns and appointing its ministers accordingly. For men like Hildersham, such discipline was desirable in a church, but its absence, while regrettable, did not invalidate the institution. But for Johnson and those who thought like he did, the lack of a proper church order made the

Church of England an "antichristian" body. Its structure of archbishops and bishops and its system of appointing clergy, not through congregational choice or presbytery approval but by an episcopal hierarchy, rendered even the Church of England's preaching ministry void.

In Hildersham's letter to Mrs. N we find him defending the Church of England, despite its faults. It brings us closer to understanding why he never separated from the established church despite the persecution he faced from within it. For Hildersham, as long as the Church of England preached the gospel from its pulpits and administered the sacraments in a proper manner, it was unlawful for any private individual to decide to leave it. As Hildersham rebuked Mrs. N, "If our pastors offer to lead you unto salvation through no other door than Christ, how dare you that say you are Christ's refuse to be guided by them." Later, he was to emphasize this point again to a congregation in Ashby, saying, "Those assemblies that enjoy the Word and doctrine of salvation, though they have many corruptions remaining in them are to be acknowledged the true churches of God, and such as none of the faithful may make separation from."[3] He warned that "till God hath forsaken a church, no man may forsake it." Gospel preaching was God's gift and a sign that "men may be assured to find and attain to salvation." For these reasons it was wrong for the so-called Brownists (named after Robert Browne, one of the earliest and most influential English separatists) to separate from the Church of England, and Hildersham strongly opposed such a course. Nevertheless, he showed some sympathy for the reasons behind the separatists' stance, if not for their ultimate conclusions. The Brownists had a point, Arthur admitted, about the "general increase of all filthy and abominable sins in the land" which gave "just cause of fear" that the "candlestick," the symbol of God's continuing presence in His church, represented by preaching, would be removed.[4] If this were to happen, the Church of England would cease to be a true church, and the warnings about the imminent danger of this happening grew more intense and urgent in Hildersham's work as the years went on.

---

3. Hildersham, *Lectures upon John*, 165.
4. Hildersham, *Lectures upon John*, 170.

Hildersham did not try to defend the office of bishop to Mrs. N, but he did give a personal account of "what moved me to seek a calling from them, and what persuadeth me to think that the calling I have received from them is not wicked and unlawful." His defense is a complex one involving the appointing of bishops by parliament, which, he said, represented the true church of God gathered throughout the realm. Although many of the bishops themselves were incapable of exercising the power committed to them, this did not negate the authority vested in the church itself. Hildersham probably thought it would have been better to be without bishops and have some sort of presbyterian system of church government, but he was prepared to live within a flawed organization in order to continue preaching the gospel. When hopes for further reform seemed to have been crushed in the 1590s, as long as he was able to resolve his conscience that the current system was not "unlawful," he negotiated a way to live with it. Even so, he excuses rather than advocates episcopacy, and when he speaks of being patient with those "not yet persuaded" that the "discipline" was necessary, it conveys the impression that he was personally convinced of this but was prepared to wait and work behind the scenes for a gradual ideological transformation among the ranks of his fellow ministers.

Although the divine gift of preaching was the central reason for Hildersham's advocacy of the Church of England, in his letter to Mrs. N, he also defended other aspects of its constitution and ministry. Despite the popish connotations of the title "priest," Arthur argued that the office of priesthood in the English church was in essence the same as that of "pastor" described in the Word. It differed from the Roman priesthood "as much...as light doth from darkness." He endeavored to show that, in substance, the Church of England's manner of calling ministers "agreeth with the law of God." Even if the execution of these matters left much to be desired, he conceded, "that is the fault of the men, not the calling."

The other main reason (apart from gospel preaching) that Hildersham gave Mrs. N for continuing to support the Church of England was that "the best Reformed churches" continued to recognize it as a true church. Rather than condemning the English church, those on the Continent had stretched out the hand of fellowship to their "sister." No individual or "private member" therefore had the right to judge that any church was anti-Christian. They might dislike the corruptions present in the church and refuse to subscribe to them, but they did not have the authority to account all the English churches as "heathens or publicans" as long as they had the Word and the sacraments.

When Johnson took Hildersham's letter and (without his knowledge or permission) published it along with his own reply to it, many thought Johnson had scored a goal for the opposition. For, in the opinion of John Cotton, his friend Hildersham's case was so powerful that it persuaded many against separatism, which was exactly the opposite of what Johnson had intended. Cotton wrote that the letter "hath so strongly and clearly convinced the iniquity of that way [separatism], that I could not but acknowledge in it, both the wisdom of God, and the weakness of the separatist. His wisdom, in bringing to light such a beam of the light of His truth by the hand of an adversary [Hildersham], against the author's mind: and the weakness of the other [Johnson], to advance the hand of his adversary to give himself and his cause such a deadly wound in open view, as neither himself nor all his associates can be able to heal."[5] On the basis of Hildersham's refutation of separatism, a fellow Puritan, Andrew Willet, dubbed him "the Hammer of Schismatics."

Nevertheless, Hildersham maintained amicable relationships with many "brethren of the separation." Although he disagreed with the conclusions they came to, he continued to recognize them as Christian brothers and sisters. He went on engaging in debate and conferences with them, attempting to persuade them of what he saw as their error. During John Penry's final imprisonment for separatism, Hildersham was in contact with him and even claimed that, prior to his execution on May 29, 1593, Penry had admitted his fault in dissuading people from hearing the "Word of life" preached in their parish churches.[6] John Smyth, like Hildersham, a former student of Christ's College, Cambridge, was another future separatist with whom Hildersham conversed. Later Smyth became known as the "Se-Baptist" (or self-baptizer) for his action in baptizing

---

5. Cotton, "To the Godly Reader," sig. A4r.

6. Cotton, *The Bloody Tenent, Washed* (London, 1647), 117–18; cited in Champlin Burrage, *The Early English Dissenters* (Cambridge, 1912), 150.

himself. Both Smyth and Hildersham, along with John Dod and others, participated in a private conference held in 1606 at the Coventry home of Isabel, Lady Bowes. The matter for discussion was "about withdrawing from true churches, ministers, and worship corrupted." By this point, Smyth had already separated from the established church; but, despite the differences of opinion, relationships between the participants appear to have remained cordial, with Smyth later recording, "I praised God for the quiet and peaceable conference."[7] Hildersham himself insisted in 1610 that "howsoever we cannot agree in judgment, yet should we love one another, and be glad to embrace one another's acquaintance."[8] As Clarke says of Hildersham, "such was his ingenuity and Christian charity, that he respected, esteemed, and was very familiar with those he knew to be religious and learned, though of another judgment."[9]

Hildersham also had "divers conferences and disputes" with Henry Jacob, often called a "nonseparating Congregationalist" or a "semiseparatist."[10] Jacob and Hildersham had worked together to organize the Millenary Petition, but after the perceived failure of reformist demands at the Hampton Court Conference in 1604, Jacob moved toward a more radical ecclesiological position. However, Jacob continued to converse with those who disagreed with him and was not cut off from godly fellowship. Indeed, the decision of Jacob and others to form a new covenanted congregation in Southwark in 1616 was only taken after "much conference" with leading figures in Puritan circles, such as Walter Travers, Richard Mansell, John Dod, and Hildersham himself.[11] Hildersham, it seems, opposed the move, but others were more encouraging or at least equivocal.

Hildersham loved the Church of England, even though he was all too aware of its "corruptions." It was his habit in sermons to refer to the Church of England as "our" church, and it is clear that he identified with that organization in its mission of preaching and pastoral care.

---

7. John Smyth, *Paralleles, Censures, Observations* (Middleburg, 1609), 129.

8. Hildersham, *Lectures upon John*, 302.

9. Clarke, "Life of Hildersam," 151.

10. Clarke, "Life of Hildersam," 151.

11. Cited in Stephen Brachlow, *The Communion of Saints: Radical Puritan and Separatist Ecclesiology 1570–1625* (Oxford: Oxford University Press, 1988), 139.

Ever since its foundation, Hildersham declared in 1628, the Church of England had been a Reformed, Calvinistic church, committed to proclaiming the gospel of God's free grace: "And so do I testify, and confidently avouch and protest unto you, that that doctrine and religion which hath (through the marvellous goodness of God) been taught in this famous and orthodox Church of England, now by the space of these seventy years, and in the profession whereof we all now stand, is the only true doctrine and religion of Christ. Because it only giveth the whole glory of man's salvation unto God's free grace in Christ, but it abaseth man, and giveth him no matter of boasting or glorying at all."[12]

Hildersham, then, was a strong defender of the Church of England, in much the same way that Bishop J. C. Ryle was in the different context of the nineteenth century. Such men held that it was wrong to separate from the Church of England as long as it retained a basis in true doctrine. But we have already alluded to the "corruptions" that Hildersham acknowledged within the institution, and we need to examine in greater detail what these were, for they caused many of the problems he was to have with the established church.

These mostly arose in the sphere of worship. For Hildersham, the governing principle, as in the area of church organization, was the authority of Scripture. In lecture 34 of the series on John, Hildersham articulated his own doctrinal position: God commanded us, "Do neither more nor less in my service than I have appointed. Say that we do that in his service which he hath not forbidden, yet if he hath not commanded it, we highly offend him."[13] This position later became known as the regulative principle of worship, and it stated that Christians should observe only things that God had commanded directly in the Bible. Though some things might be less important than others, nothing was "indifferent" (or "adiaphora"), as some argued. Unless the Bible actually prescribed a particular element or form of worship, then it was to be shunned as a "fancy and idol." Hildersham urged, "Count it thy wisdom to cleave so precisely to the Word as (in matters of God's service [worship]) not to do anything which thou canst not find warranted by the

---

12. Hildersham, *Lectures upon Psalm 51*, 525.
13. Hildersham, *Lectures upon John*, 161.

Word."[14] Anything else, even if Scripture did not formally forbid it, was a human invention, or "will worship."

The division between those who upheld this view—the regulative principle—and those who accepted the looser normative principle (which allowed in worship things not positively banned by the Word) became a major fault line in Protestantism and was a main reason why, in the early modern period, the stricter sort were labeled "Puritans" or "precisians" by their opponents. Hildersham's unwavering allegiance to this definitive principle of worship lay at the heart of his problems with the church. The ecclesiastical hierarchy worked on the premise that if the Scriptures were silent on particular practices, these were things indifferent, and it was legitimate for the church to decide what was appropriate. When the bishops ruled that compliance with their decisions was a condition for ministry, a clash became inevitable, for Hildersham felt unable to conform to any matter of worship unless he could satisfy his conscience that Scripture warranted it. This tension found its focus in the worship "ceremonies"—most notably, making the sign of the cross in baptism, wearing the surplice, and kneeling to receive the Lord's Supper. Those who could not agree to these ceremonies were known as "nonconformists," but it is important to remember that for the most part they remained *within* the Church of England at this period, unlike a later generation of nonconformists, who were outside the established church.

To find the clearest and most detailed explanation of Hildersham's position, it is helpful to turn to a book that thirty-two ministers of the Lincoln diocese, led by Hildersham, wrote and presented to James I at Hinchinbrooke, during the royal hunting season of 1604–1605.[15] As we will see later, the new regulations issued in the wake of the Hampton Court Conference demanded stricter enforcement of conformity and subscription and raised problems for men of Hildersham's persuasion. The *Abridgement* was a book of learned arguments explaining their position to the king, who was known to relish theological debate. The

---

14. Hildersham, *Lectures upon John*, 162.

15. *An Abridgement of that Book Which the Ministers of Lincoln Diocese Delivered to His Majesty upon the First of December 1605* (reprinted 1617). Unless stated, all quotations in this section are taken from this source.

ministers explained the difficulties they had with subscribing to the three articles that were required of them. The first article, which required acknowledgment of the king as "the only supreme governor," did not pose an obstacle. However, the second required a declaration that the Book of Common Prayer and the Ordinal "containeth in it nothing contrary to the Word of God." This was a problem because the Prayer Book schedule for public Bible reading meant that the greatest part of the canonical Scriptures was never read in church at all. Moreover, it held that the Apocrypha was canonical and to be treated with similar respect to the authentically canonical text. The authors of the *Abridgement* also told the king that they objected to the biblical translation prescribed by the Prayer Book, stating that in some places it added to the original text and at others took away from it.

The third exception brings us to the heart of the problem for Elizabethan and Jacobean nonconformists. How could these men subscribe to an article that declared that the Prayer Book ceremonies were not contrary to the Word of God, when their consciences were convinced otherwise? They rejected these ceremonies as totally unscriptural "relics of popery" that encouraged superstition and idolatry among the people. God Himself had abrogated the Old Testament ceremonies, and others of human devising should not replace them. For, the ministers explained, "the service we are to do unto God now is not mystical, ceremonial and carnal (as it was then) but plain and spiritual." Even the king, the "supreme governor in all causes," was not free to appoint what "rites and orders" he thought good, but "he is bound to observe therein those rules which God in His Word hath prescribed to His church for her direction in those matters."

The first ceremony to which the ministers objected was wearing the surplice. They regarded this loose, white, wide-sleeved liturgical garment as the iconic popish vestment, for Catholic priests were required to wear it for the saying of Mass, the supreme act of idolatry for Protestants. At a parish level, many people thought that the surplice was such a holy thing that they would receive Communion only from ministers who were wearing it. Already in Edward's and Elizabeth's reigns the surplice had caused controversy, most famously in 1550 when John Hooper had initially refused to wear it to be consecrated as bishop of Gloucester.

Refusal to wear the surplice became almost a badge of the Puritan party, although some were prepared to wear it on occasion so that they could continue to preach. Others made excuses to the church inspectors (visitors) that the surplice was in the wash, or they slipped it on and off in the vestry so that the churchwardens could report honestly that they had seen their minister wearing the surplice.

Making the sign of the cross was another ceremony that gave rise to superstition. Catholics believed in the mystical powers of this sign to drive away devils and combat diseases. Moreover, the papists' "breaden god (the greatest and most abominable idol that was ever known in Christendom)," could not be made without such a sign—in other words, according to Catholic practice, the sign of the cross was required to turn the bread into the physical body of Christ during the Mass. In a similar way, when Catholics baptized infants, the water had to be sanctified by the sign of the cross, and the child marked by it, to drive away the devil. As a consequence, the "common people" stood in "superstitious awe" of the sign and held that "their children were not rightly baptized without it." Most fundamentally, Hildersham and the other authors of the *Abridgement* told the king that the sign of the cross had not been made when Christ Himself had been baptized, neither had He given His apostles any directions to use it.

The ceremony of kneeling to receive the bread and wine in Communion attracted the most vehement and lengthy criticism in the *Abridgement*. At the most basic level, the authors objected to it because Christ and His disciples, at the first institution of the Lord's Supper, did not receive the elements kneeling. Indeed, the authors argued, there was no instruction for such a posture in the reception of any sacrament in the Scriptures nor any evidence of such an action in the primitive church. Besides, it was commanded that the sacrament be "received not worshipped." The ministers argued that the papists had long abused the gesture because it acknowledged Christ's corporeal presence in the Mass. Thus adoring and worshiping the elements was the mark of the greatest idolatry possible: "We may well conclude that of all the ceremonies that ever was used in popery, none may be so properly termed popish and antichristian as this." Even when adoration of the elements did not occur, the kneeling gave an *appearance* of "gross idolatry, even of bread worship." Outwardly there was no discernible difference between Catholics and those who rejected the repeated sacrifice of Christ on the altar during Mass. Kneeling to receive the elements allowed secret Catholics to maintain their own beliefs under cover of doing what everyone else was doing. Besides, the ministers concluded, Christ had ordained the Supper "to be a banquet and sacrament of that sweet familiarity that is between the faithful and him.... And in what nation was it ever held comely to kneel at their banquets, or to receive their food kneeling[?]"

Hildersham did not want things that were ultimately "matters of judgment" to become divisive, and he shunned such controversies in his preaching. As he told his brother ministers,

> We should avoid all bitterness of contention about these things, yet should we endeavour that the people may discern no difference, nor disagreement in doctrine amongst us. True it is, we may and ought to seek resolution for our consciences out of God's Word, even in these things, seem they never so small.... And when we have received good resolution in these things we ought to hold that fast, so far forth as God hath revealed His will unto us.... But if we dissent one from another in these things, it must be without bitterness, in a brotherly manner.... It is not to be held want of zeal or alteration in judgement, but true wisdom in a minister, to shun in his ministry and doctrine (so far as in him lieth) these points that brethren differ in, and to spend his time in such points wherein we all agree, and which are more profitable for the people to know.[16]

Although Hildersham was convinced of the error of the ceremonies, he declared, "For my part, I am fully persuaded there are godly and conscionable men on both sides, that will not stick to profess every truth God hath revealed unto them."[17] Again he pleaded for evangelical unity: "There may be difference in judgment even between godly and good men, and one may see that to be a sin which another man (every whit as good as he) cannot be persuaded to be so.... Christians may not

---

16. Hildersham, *Lectures upon John*, 301 (lecture 65, Sept. 11, 1610).
17. Hildersham, *Lectures upon John*, 303.

condemn or judge one another to be hypocrites for their difference in judgement in these smaller matters."[18]

Nevertheless, Hildersham recognized the difficult position of conscientious objectors who faced conformist ceremony in their parish church services. What were they to do when presented with a minister who wore a surplice or who made the sign of the cross in baptism, if they themselves believed these things were unscriptural? Hildersham was alarmed when this led some to absent themselves from services altogether:

> Many have made scruple to be present in our church assemblies, where the minister hath worn a surplice, or used the sign of [the] cross in baptism, because they have thought their presence hath been an approbation of these things, and so a partaking in those supposed corruptions. And some there are that do applaud these men in this, and say, they are far honester men than such as disliking these ceremonies, will yet join in God's worship with our congregations that use them. But both these are greatly deceived. For admitting these ceremonies doth use to be [are] monuments of idolatry, and as great corruptions in God's worship, as any man can imagine them to be, admit I say this, yet so long as the worship I go unto, is (for the substance of it) pure, and according to God's ordinance, and such as I am bound by the commandment of God to use, the corruptions and sins which another brings into it, cannot defile it unto me, nor shall be imputed unto me at all, so long as I show my dislike unto them so far as I may, keeping myself within the compass of my calling, and do unfainedly grieve and mourn for them.[19]

In other words, it was wrong to stay away from church even if the ceremonies were in place, provided that the preaching and the rest of the service were in line with Scripture. No one could be held responsible for another person's actions, but if anyone was unhappy about the ceremonies, he or she should explain the concern in a civil manner at an appropriate time. Interestingly, in this advice Hildersham avoids the most contentious subject of receiving the Lord's Supper. While the

---

18. Hildersham, *Lectures upon Psalm 51*, 715 (lecture 137, Jan. 5, 1630).
19. Hildersham, *Lectures upon Psalm 51*, 181.

congregation merely *witnessed* a minister's wearing of the surplice and making the sign of the cross, receiving Communion required an active physical response from them, as they had to choose whether or not to kneel. As we will see later, Hildersham was to find himself at the center of a storm on this issue in Ashby in 1614.

Hildersham was not a nonconformist by choice or natural inclination. His contention was that the church, rather than he himself, had moved the goalposts by requiring its ministers to subscribe to new tests of loyalty. As William Lilly, the famous astrologer and sometime resident of Ashby declared, Hildersham "was an excellent textuary, of exemplary life, pleasant in discourse, a strong enemy of the Brownists, and dissented not from the Church of England in any article of faith, but only about wearing the surplice, baptizing with the cross, and kneeling at the sacrament."[20] Hildersham's conscience would not allow him to assent that *nothing* done within the Church of England was contrary to the Word of God. He remained faithful and consistent to this position throughout his life: Clarke records that he was "always from his first entering into the ministry, a resolved and conscientious non-conformist...and so continued to his dying day."[21] In his will, made shortly before he died, Arthur wrote, "I do hereby declare and protest that I do continue and end my days, in the very same faith and judgment, touching all points of religion as I have ever been known to hold and profess, and which I have, both by my doctrine and practice and by my sufferings also given testimony unto."[22] To separate from the Church of England required great courage in late Elizabethan and early Stuart England, but to remain within it and take the stand that Hildersham did also demanded courage. It cost Hildersham dearly to abide by his conscience, as we will discover.

In our very different age, the issues that provoked such controversy four hundred years ago might appear relatively minor. We might wonder if it would have been better to submit to church regulations and thus be

20. William Lilly, *Mr. William Lilly's History of His Life and Times: From the Year 1602, to 1681*, 2nd ed. (London, 1715), 6.

21. Clarke, "Life of Hildersam," 151.

22. Will of Arthur Hildersham, Leicestershire Record Office, Leics. Wills, Ashby no. 77.

allowed to continue preaching the gospel. Indeed, some Puritans at the time took this view. However, Hildersham's life highlights a very important principle: in everything we do, we should seek to submit ourselves to the authority of Scripture. To do otherwise, and ignore the promptings of our God-given consciences, puts us on a slippery slope toward compromise and relativism. The Church of England might have been a very different church if it had followed the lead of men like Hildersham. But Hildersham's life also furnishes an example of dealing with those who disagree with us on lesser matters. His gracious love and acceptance of all true brethren in the gospel reminds us that unity in Christ should always be our aim.

Chapter 8

⚬

Suspensions and Sufferings
(1588–1605)

We last saw Hildersham at the beginning of 1605, vicar of Ashby-de-la-Zouch. By April 24 of that year, the bishop of Lincoln, William Chaderton, had suspended Hildersham for refusing to subscribe and conform to the new demands of the Canons of 1604. Deprived of his vicarage and banned from preaching in the Lincoln diocese, he was never again to serve his people as vicar of Ashby.

This was not the first time Hildersham had been in conflict with the church authorities. Shortly after he moved to Ashby in 1587 to commence his duties as lecturer, he was convened before the High Commission, the highest ecclesiastical court in the land, for subversive preaching without orders or license. A license from the bishop was required for any man to preach lawfully within the Church of England, and no other preaching was authorized. A formal submission, dated January 10, 1588, was prepared for Hildersham to sign:

> I confess here that I have rashly and indiscreetly taken upon me the office and function of a preacher, and preached abroad, neither being admitted into orders, neither licensed by any authority, and contrary to the orders and laws of this Church of England, contrary to the example of all antiquity in the primitive church, and contrary to the example and direction of the apostles in the Acts, and thereby have given great and just offence unto many. And this rashness I have made more grievous and offensive in that I have uttered in my foresaid sermons and preachings certain impertinent

and very unfit speeches for the auditory, as moving their minds rather to discontentment with the state, than tending to any godly edification for which my presumption and indiscreetness, I am very heartily sorry, and desire you to bear witness of this my confession and acknowledging of my said offences.[1]

It would have been impossible for Hildersham to sign the archbishop's document and retain any integrity, but it was also a courageous act for a young man barely setting out on his ministry to refuse. Because he did not sign it, he was ordered to appear again before the commissioners and was suspended in June 1590. Although he was restored in January 1592, he was barred from preaching in any place south of the River Trent, including Ashby. The High Commission subsequently removed this condition, allegedly through the intervention of the queen herself.[2] Nevertheless, even at the outset of Hildersham's ministry, it is clear that some were raising questions about his relationship with the ecclesiastical hierarchy. In a sense he was a marked man, and he continued to attract suspicion throughout the course of his career.

Obviously, at some stage Arthur was ordained and licensed or he would not have been allowed to continue as a minister, but this episode highlights the problems that Puritans could have in squaring their consciences with official requirements. We have already seen how Hildersham justified to himself his seeking ordination at the hands of a bishop, and how he did not consider this to be "unlawful." It seems there could be some flexibility in the wording of the license itself, for Hildersham corresponded with Humphrey Fenn, the old nonconformist minister of Coventry, on the subject.[3] The older man shared with his younger colleague a form of words used in his own license so that it contained "only that which agrees with the Word of God." Both men were anxious to avoid anything that smacked of popish doctrine in their licenses, and managed to come up with something that equally satisfied their consciences and the demands of the authorities. In the early

1. Peel, ed., *The Seconde Parte of a Register*, vol. 2 (Cambridge: Cambridge University Press, 1915), 259–60.

2. Benjamin Brook, *The Lives of the Puritans* (London, 1813), 381.

3. British Library Add. MS 4275, f. 223 (undated).

seventeenth century, tighter regulations forced men like Hildersham's protégé, Simeon Ashe, and his own son Samuel to try and sidestep the issue entirely by seeking ordination at the hands of Irish bishops, where subscription was not required.

It was probably Hildersham's relationship with the queen that protected him from the worst effects of the crackdown on Puritan ministers that took place in the 1590s. Under the auspices of Archbishop Whitgift and Richard Bancroft, bishop of London, a number of ministers, most notably Arthur's friend Thomas Cartwright, were brought before the courts of High Commission and Star Chamber on charges of sedition.[4] Despite the lifting of Hildersham's preaching ban in January 1592, he soon was in trouble with the authorities again. On July 20, 1596, a sermon Hildersham preached at the Leicester Assizes offended Judge Edmund Anderson, a notorious hater of Puritans. Hildersham took as his text I Kings 18:17–18, which reads, "And it came to pass, when Ahab saw Elijah, that Ahab said unto him, Art thou he that troubleth Israel? And he answered, I have not troubled Israel; but thou, and thy father's house, in that ye have forsaken the commandments of the LORD, and thou hast followed Baalim." Whether Hildersham intended this as a direct personal attack on Anderson we do not know, but Anderson certainly took it as such and threatened to storm out. He attempted to have Hildersham indicted before a grand jury for slandering his character. However, the power of Hildersham's patron, the fourth Earl of Huntingdon, who served as Lord Lieutenant of Leicestershire, as well as Hildersham's own fame as a godly preacher, meant that it would have been difficult for Anderson to find a jury in the county who would have found Hildersham guilty at that time. Having the queen, the Earl of Huntingdon, and other powerful friends at court (as well as in the privy council and in Parliament) protected Hildersham, in God's providence, from the worst dangers. Such influential forces may have been responsible for the failure of the attachment the High Commission sent out for Hildersham's arrest in 1598.

In the 1590s a controversy over Puritan exorcism blew up. Hildersham's friends John Darrell and George More were the targets of an

---

4. These events can be traced in Collinson, *Elizabethan Puritan Movement*, 403–31.

attempt by Bancroft and others to discredit the practice, and through it, Puritanism in general. Hildersham, too, was closely involved with the events and came under official scrutiny. Present-day Reformed Christians sometimes exhibit a certain ambivalence or uncertainty about the issue of demon possession. While rightly uncomfortable with liberal suggestions that instances of demon possession in the New Testament can be interpreted as mere manifestations of mental or physical illness, Reformed believers also recognize that medical advances may help to explain some cases that earlier generations would have attributed to demonic activity. We are wary, also, of some charismatic churches that see direct satanic activity in every possible occasion, performing dramatic and perhaps psychologically damaging exorcisms on unfortunate individuals, even very young children. However, we need to appreciate that our early modern forbears more generally recognized supernatural workings in the world. Hildersham was not alone in viewing outbreaks of plague and extreme weather conditions as signs of divine displeasure. He also gave credence to the story of a "groaning tree" in Brampton, Lincolnshire, in 1606, which was purported to warn the inhabitants of their need to pray.[5] William Perkins published a standard work on witchcraft, *A Discourse of the Damned Art of Witchcraft* (1608), expressing the view that its essence was a covenant with Satan and urging the execution of all witches because "they depend on him as their god."[6] Earlier, another leading Puritan, George Gifford, had issued *A Dialogue of Witches* in 1593.

It may be, of course, that the devil was more openly active at a time of great religious revival and blessing such as the Reformation and the period that followed in its wake. It is incontrovertible that especially in the 1590s, mainstream orthodox Puritans took the lead in a series of high-profile exorcisms, and their enemies used this to generate much negative propaganda against them. Ashby-de-la-Zouch was at the center of things. John Darrell, who became the leading figure in the exorcism controversy, had moved to Ashby from Mansfield in 1592, attracted by

---

5. Nathaniel Crouch [R. B.], *Admirable Curiosities, Rarities, and Wonders in England, Scotland and Ireland* (London, 1682), 137–38.

6. Cited in Keith Thomas, *Religion and the Decline of Magic* (London, 1970), 523.

the spiritual climate of the town. He was a godly, respected minister, and soon became one of Hildersham's closest friends and supporters. Hildersham baptized two of Darrell's sons, Andrew and Samuel, in the Ashby church in 1593 and 1597 respectively, and also buried the two-month-old Samuel on his death.[7] In the town itself, Darrell gained the respect of the local people. More than thirty of the chief inhabitants of the town were to declare in a testimonial that "for the space almost of six years together during which he hath dwelt here in Ashby, he hath lived among us in very good report, behaving himself every way as became his profession, and the gospel of Christ."[8] This, then, was no self-seeking charlatan, as his enemies claimed.

Through the exercise at Burton-on-Trent, where Hildersham was one of the main preachers, the case of Thomas Darling—a thirteen-year-old boy from the town who displayed strange symptoms—attracted attention in 1596. Darling's symptoms were similar to those of Katherine Wright of Lancashire, with whose dispossession Darrell had helped a decade earlier. Darrell's help was solicited again for Darling. At first Darrell was reluctant to become involved again, as he did not wish to be perceived as some kind of miracle worker. However, at an exercise in Ashby that Hildersham presided over, a group of sixteen fellow ministers agreed that Darrell and his co-worker, George More, should go to Burton to investigate. Hildersham accompanied Darrell on his first visit to the boy, addressing "some short godly speeches" to him, while the other ministers kept silent.[9] It was claimed that a local witch called Alse Gooderige had sent an evil spirit into Darling, and upon examination Darrell agreed that the boy was demon possessed. Around Darling's bedside, praying fervently, clustered a group of the Burton godly fraternity, including his uncle Jesse Bee (a saddler by trade), Thomas Saunders, and a couple whom we will hear more of later—Edward Wightman, a draper of Burton, and his wife, Frances. These individuals produced an

---

7. Leicestershire Record Office, parish register for Ashby St. Helen's.

8. John Darrell, *A Detection of that Sinful, Shameful, Lying and Ridiculous Discourse of Samuel Harsnett* (n.p., 1600), 78.

9. Samuel Harsnett, *A Discovery of the Fraudulent Practices of John Darrell* (1599). See also Jesse Bee, *The Most Wonderful and True Storie, of a Certain Witch Named Alse Gooderige*, ed. John Denison (London, 1597), 26.

eyewitness account of events, *The Most Wonderful and True Story, of a Certain Witch Named Alse Gooderige of Stapenhill* (1597), which the London Puritan minister John Denison edited, and which both Darrell and Hildersham purportedly approved prior to publication. Darling seemed to have felt a special affinity for Hildersham and exclaimed in one of his trances, "Come, Master Hildersham, let us five go to heaven." The session of fasting and prayer preceding the actual dispossession was entirely a lay affair; Darrell stayed away because he did not want anyone to think that he himself had any special power to cast out demons. In fact, he was very careful of how he operated—he did not want these dispossessions to appear like superstitious Catholic practice. In this context he stressed the distinction between *miracula* (miracles, like those Christ had performed) and what he and his fellows were part of, *miranda* (wonders), which were entirely attributable to God's power without human agency. He and the townspeople faithfully followed the biblical instruction of Matthew 17:21, that "this kind [of evil spirit] goeth not out but by prayer and fasting." However, the case of Thomas Darling came to the attention of Richard Bancroft, bishop of London, and his chaplain, Samuel Harsnett, who were keen to find anything that would discredit Puritans. Harsnett ridiculed "that corrupt and false and ridiculous treatise" written by Jesse Bee and the others, scorning the fact that tradesmen had penned it. Both sides in the controversy issued a whole series of publications, full of claims and counterclaims. Darrell's opponents seized on another dispossession case he had handled, that of William Sommers of Nottingham, as evidence that Darrell was a fraud. Under questioning, Sommers changed his original story and admitted that he had faked his symptoms, then accused Darrell of instructing him to counterfeit. Thomas Darling, however, stuck to his account. Darrell was sent to the Gatehouse prison in London, and his trial (along with George More) began in 1598 before the High Commission on charges of fraudulence. The prosecutors were determined to find Darrell and More guilty and put great pressure on the witnesses. Some claimed that Hildersham, John Ireton, and John Brinsley were forbidden from giving evidence on Darrell's behalf. Eventually, after many court sessions, and although no sentence was passed officially, Darrell and More were suspended from the ministry in late 1599. They were sent back to prison to await additional punishment, but further pronouncements from the court never came. Although Darrell and More were finally released, Darrell never accepted that a legal sentence had been passed on him. The whole proceedings were so controversial that public scrutiny was not allowed. However, the bad publicity enabled Bancroft to ensure that the new ecclesiastical regulations, known as canons, banned unauthorized exorcism in 1604. By this time, too, some on the godly side were beginning to question the theological grounds for exorcism. John Walker and John Deacon argued in print against Darrell's position, and divisions on this matter began to emerge among Puritans, to the delight of their enemies.

Up to 1603, the year Elizabeth I died, successive bishops of Lincoln were prepared, to some extent, to turn a blind eye to the non-conformity of Hildersham and others. Of course, the power of the earls of Huntingdon was a major factor, as was the need to combat Catholicism in the diocese. A bishop like William Cooper (1571–1584) valued strong doctrinal preaching that exposed the errors of the Catholic church, so he was willing to pay the price of putting up with a little ceremonial nonconformity to get it. Evangelicalism was the prevailing strain of churchmanship in the English church, so men like Hildersham did not feel out of place. But things were to change with the succession of James I to the English throne in 1603.

Initially, the Puritans had high hopes for the new reign. James, son of Mary Queen of Scots, had been taken away from his mother at an early age and brought up by Scottish Presbyterians. In the run up to his accession, James and his representatives had made all the right noises toward the Puritans, who thus felt hopeful that further reformation of the Church of England might be possible. That James was simultaneously making the same sort of noises to the Catholics, who looked for a more tolerant attitude toward their faith, should have been a warning that the future king was merely trying to keep both sides happy. Besides, James enjoyed the cut and thrust of theological debate. Upon the old queen's death, the Puritans in Parliament and the rest of the country thought it wise to bring together their main concerns in a document to present to the king, signed by as many of their number as possible, so that he would be aware of the strength of feeling that existed. They chose Stephen Egerton of Blackfriars, a London Puritan, and Hildersham as the

main managers of this petition, which became known as the Millenary
Petition because it had, supposedly, a thousand backers. In fact, there
were somewhat fewer, since the ministers had rallied support in such a
short period of time. That Hildersham was chosen for this task shows
that the Puritans recognized his leading role and organizational abilities. Sir Francis Hastings, brother to the late third Earl of Huntingdon
and a leader of the Puritan party in Parliament, probably had a hand in
Hildersham's appointment. At some point, Sir Francis and Hildersham
had a falling-out; over what is unclear. However, in 1608, the year before
his death, Sir Francis made his peace with Arthur, acknowledging that
the fault was on his side. He was known to be a man who did not like
to be crossed, although an ardent advocate for Puritanism.[10] Hildersham
must have been very busy in that summer of 1603, soliciting support
and collecting information about the state of the church. Surveys were
undertaken in many areas to assess the condition of the clergy and how
many were preachers.

The Millenary Petition was, in fact, a very moderate document, in
which the authors sought to assure the king that they spoke "neither as
factious men, affecting a popular parity in the Church, nor as schismatics, aiming at the dissolution of the state ecclesiastical."[11] There were no
demands in it for a more presbyterian form of government in the church.
There was not even a request for the abolishment of the hated *ex officio*
oath so often used to get Puritans into trouble in the church courts,
but merely a plea that it be used "more sparingly." Perhaps the very
moderation of the Millenary Petition gave James the impression that
the strength of feeling was not running very high or that the Puritans
would be easy pushovers. Certainly, when the Puritan representatives at
the ensuing Hampton Court Conference adopted a similar placatory,
low-key approach, James seemed to delight in quashing their under-
stated arguments. Hildersham was initially chosen to be one of the four
Puritan spokesmen who would have put the case to and debated before
the king, "if," at the last minute, "the king himself had not expressly

10. See Cross, ed., *The Letters of Sir Francis Hastings 1574–1609* (Frome: Somerset Record
Society, 1969).

11. Cited in Collinson, *Elizabethan Puritan Movement*, 452.

excepted against him." It seems James already believed Hildersham to be a dangerous extremist. However, Hildersham was one of the three men, along with Stephen Egerton and Edward Fleetwood, who communicated the instructions from the assembly of thirty ministers representing the counties to their spokesmen at the main conference. The king was adamant for episcopacy, as his experiences in Scotland had convinced him that this system was the best way for him to maintain control over the Church of England; as he put it in his famous dictum, "no bishops, no king." The commissioning of what became known as the Authorized or King James Bible was one notable achievement of the Hampton Court Conference, but really it marked the end of Puritan hopes that genuine reform of the English Church would take place.

In the aftermath of the Hampton Court Conference, new ecclesiastical regulations, or canons, were enacted in 1604. These included fresh requirements for subscription and conformity, even from ministers who were already serving within the church. Such requirements had existed before, of course, and caused problems for some Puritans, but now the bishops were instructed to enforce them more strictly. It is sometimes said that James I was prepared to tolerate Puritanism as long as the ministers would give some indication that, over time, they would consider conforming. However, he was less ready to grant concessions to Puritan leaders who refused to conform.

Hildersham, of course, was one of the leading lights of Puritanism by this time. Perhaps his prominent role in organizing the Millenary Petition, his part in the Hampton Court Conference, and his participation in writing the *Abridgement* caused James to fix him in his mind particularly as a troublemaker. His connection to the royal houses of Plantagenet and Tudor may also have contributed. For whatever reason, the king appeared to have conceived a special and very personal hatred of Hildersham. Archbishop Abbot warned the Earl of Huntingdon that Hildersham was "a person whom his Highness hath particularly in observation."[12] This was to have serious consequences for Hildersham,

---

12. HA2, "The Hastings Collection of Manuscripts from the Huntington Library. Part One: Correspondence 1477–1701" (microfilm).

as we will see. For as long as James I remained on the throne of England, Hildersham had little chance of getting a fair hearing.

After the new Canons of 1604 came into force, it seems Hildersham was able to stave off trouble for a short time. On October 3, 1604, ninety-three ministers from the diocese of Lincoln were cited to appear before Bishop Chaderton in the church of St. Benedict, Huntingdon, to answer articles that charged them with failing to wear the surplice and, in some cases, make the sign of the cross in baptism.[13] Hildersham was one of the twenty-eight ministers summoned from the Leicester archdeaconry. If, on that first day in court, he had uttered the words that he did six months later—that "he doth not nor can conform himself for many causes"—presumably the bishop would have had no option but to proceed immediately to deprivation, as he did on the latter occasion of April 24, 1605. However, Hildersham was less forthright on his initial court appearance; along with seventeen other ministers, they "confessed that the article was true and craved time to deliberate about their conformity." According to the unwritten rules of engagement for such a procedure, a properly deferential admission of fault, combined with a request for extra time to consider their position, was sufficient to get these ministers off with an episcopal admonishment and a demand for conformity by the end of October. By going through the accepted motions and offering additional reflection on the issue of conformity, yet without any promise of future change, the defendants gained nearly a month of breathing space. At their next appearance, on October 31, 1604, the ministers used the same set plea, that they "craved time to deliberate afresh," combining their inability to "conform themselves according to the monition" with the crucial prefix "as yet." This critical phrase was full of ambiguity, allowing the ministers to hold out the possibility of future persuasion without compromising their consciences by any definite commitment. The formulation "craved time to deliberate" achieved a further month's grace, and then was deployed again by certain

---

13. The history of proceedings against the nonconformists can be traced in C. W. Foster, *The State of the Church in the Reigns of Elizabeth and James I as Illustrated by Documents Relating to the Diocese of Lincoln* (Lincoln Record Society, 1926). All quotations here, unless stated, are from this source.

men, including Hildersham, on November 14 and 22, January 30, and April 10, 1605.

By playing the system and remembering Christ's injunction to be "as wise as serpents," Hildersham was able to extend his ministry in Ashby for a precious six months, in which he continued to preach the gospel. Lesser-known ministers in the diocese—such as David Allen, rector of Ludborough, John Jackson, vicar of Bourne, and Simon Bradstreet, vicar of Horbling—seem to have evaded deprivation entirely through their continued procrastination. They often used pleas of illness or infirmity to excuse court attendance. A shared nonconformity naturally drew these men together as they faced official persecution; the drive for conformity within the Lincoln diocese in 1604 and 1605 forged a fellowship of suffering among the men who appeared in the bishop's courts. Doubtless they met together for prayer and discussion outside of the formal proceedings, and some perhaps traveled together on the road. This solidarity was borne out by the petition (later published as the *Abridgement*) they drew up, signed, and presented to the king at Hinchinbrooke in 1604. The sense of brotherly unity in the face of official opposition must have made the later defection by one of the group, John Burgess, particularly bitter. Burgess not only went on to embrace conformity but also wrote a book defending it against those who held his former position. His protestations about his earlier participation in nonconformity felt like a betrayal of friendship as well as a misrepresentation of events to Hildersham, who, "with great regret and grief," felt the need to set the record straight, even upon his deathbed. Hildersham's written comments passed into the hands of Thomas Hooker, who subsequently published them. To his "fellow brother, Doctor Burgess," Hildersham had protested, "his conscience knows, that I know he speaks untruly."[14]

Despite Hildersham's generally nonconfrontational approach to the authorities, there were times when he felt required to take a principled stand. A memo in the bishop's court book demonstrates that Hildersham's demeanor was not always one of passive deference. Records from

---

14. Thomas Hooker, preface to *A Fresh Suit against Human Ceremonies in Gods Worship*, by William Ames (Amsterdam, 1633). Hildersham was refuting claims in Burgess's book, *An Answer Rejoyned* (London, 1631).

December 12, 1604, show that, in response to a call from the king for some of the nonconforming ministers to confer with the bishop and Dr. James Montagu, dean of the king's chapel, Hildersham replied that "they would not come to be borne down with countenance and scoffs." Montagu was a moderate Calvinist with some sympathy for the Puritans (indeed, he had preached William Perkins's funeral sermon in 1602), but he was also a conformist and a courtier. As a close friend of James I (and later bishop of Bath and Wells and then Winchester), Montagu was prepared to advocate conformity as necessary for a strong Anglicanism. He had taken the king's part at the Hampton Court Conference. When Chaderton finally pronounced a sentence that deprived Hildersham of his benefice on April 24, 1605, Hildersham dissented in no uncertain terms, "protesting that it was of no effect, and appealing to the archbishop of Canterbury in his court of arches." This move may have been another calculated attempt to buy still more time, for on June 19, 1605, it was recorded that he failed to appear in order to prosecute his appeal. Although Hildersham no longer was allowed to serve his people as minister after April 1605, he continued to live in his house in Ashby and participate in the life of the town. He was able to continue to preach at the exercises at Repton and Burton-on-Trent, since these fell under the jurisdiction of the bishop of Coventry and Lichfield, William Overton, who granted him a preaching license for his diocese. Overton was a moderate, easygoing man who liked preachers. It was said of him that he would grant a license for the gift of a brace of pheasants. The fifth Earl of Huntingdon continued to back Hildersham and did all he could on his behalf, including writing letters to those in authority. Ongoing financial support from the earl was vital for enabling Hildersham's material survival. The earl also generously subsidized the cost of Samuel Hildersham's university career at Cambridge.[15]

During these years, both Hildersham and the townspeople of Ashby may well have expected that he would be restored to his living in the not-too-distant future. This hope was surely encouraged by Richard Jardfield's appointment as replacement vicar of Ashby, since Jardfeild

---

15. Henry E. Huntington Library, HAF 6/3, 7/22, 7/3 (accounts 1606–1613).

resigned his post after only a matter of months in 1605–1606. Jardfeild made no discernible impact on Ashby (or in his subsequent parish in Icklingham) and the most plausible explanation for his appointment is that he was merely a stop-gap candidate, meant to fill the breach until Hildersham's reinstatement. However, in the providence of God, things did not work out that way.

FAMILY TREE OF ARTHUR HILDERSHAM

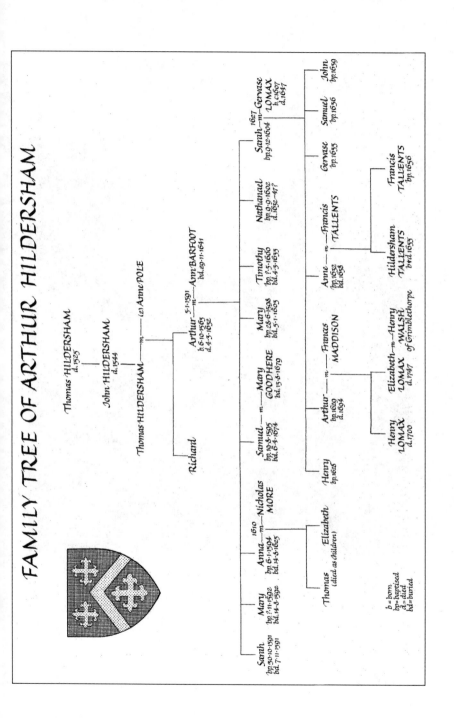

Thomas HILDERSHAM
d.1525

John HILDERSHAM
d.1544

Thomas HILDERSHAM — m — (1) Anne POLE

Richard

Arthur — 5·1·1591 m — Ann·BARFOOT
b.6·10·1563
d.4·3·1632
bd.29·11·1641

Sarah
bp.30·10·1591
bd.7·11·1591

Mary
bp.?·11·1592
bd.14·8·1592

Anna — m — Nicholas
bp.6·1·1594 1610 MORE
bd.14·8·1625

Samuel — m — Mary
bp.19·8·1595 GOODHERE
bd.8·4·1674 bd.13·8·1679

Mary
bp.28·6·1598
bd.5·1·1603

Timothy
bp.?·5·1600
d.4·3·1635

Nathanael
bp.9·9·1602
d.1632–4??

Sarah — m — Gervase
bp.9·12·1604 1627 LOMAX
b.c1607
d.1647

Thomas
(died as children)

Elizabeth

Henry
bp.1625

Arthur — m — Francis
bp.1629 MADDISON
d.1694

Anne — m — Francis
bp.1632 TALLENTS
bd.1658

Gervase
bp.1655

Samuel
bp.1656

John
bp.1659

Henry
LOMAX
d.1700

Elizabeth — m — Henry
LOMAX WALSH
d.1747 of Grimblethorpe

Hildersham
TALLENTS
brd.1655

Francis
TALLENTS
bp.1656

b = born
bp = baptised
d = died
bd = buried

St. Peter's Church, Stetchworth

Hildersham's birthplace, Patmers manor,
was sited beyond the parish church.

St. Mary the Virgin Church, Saffron Walden

Hildersham attended Saffron Walden School, adjacent to
the parish church. The church spire is a later addition.

Christ's College, Cambridge

Hildersham became a student here in 1576. The college entrance bears
the coat of arms of its benefactor, Queen Margaret of Anjou.

Ashby Castel

The seat and main residence of the Earls of Huntingdon, Hildersham's patrons and relatives. The castle was ruined during the English Civil War.

Ashby Castel (chapel)

Private chapel of the Hastings family, where
Hildersham would have preached on many occasions.

Henry Hastings, Third Earl of Huntington

"The Puritan Earl," Hildersham's cousin and patron.

CONNECTIONS BETWEEN ARTHUR HILDERSHAM, THE EARLS OF HUNTINGDON AND THE ENGLISH THRONE.

Richard, Duke of York
k.1460

EDWARD IV

George, Duke of Clarence
ex.1478

RICHARD III
k.1485

EDWARD V
k.1485
(the Princes in the Tower)

Richard
k.1485

Elizabeth — m — HENRY VII
d.1509

Margaret, Queen of Scots
d.1541

Arthur

HENRY VIII
d.1547

Mary, Queen of France
& Duchess of Suffolk

James V
k.1542

EDWARD VI
d.1553

MARY I
d.1558

ELIZABETH I
d.1603

Frances — m — Henry Grey, Duke of Suffolk
ex.1554

Mary, Queen of Scots
ex.1587

JANE
ex.1554
(Lady Jane Grey)

Katherine

Mary

JAMES I & VI
d.1625

Edward, Earl of Warwick
ex.1499

Margaret — m — Sir Richard Pole
Countess of Salisbury
ex.1541

Henry, Lord Montague
ex.1538

Reginald
Cardinal Pole
d.1558

Geoffrey Pole
d.1558

— m — Constance Pakenham
d.c.1570

Katherine Pole
m. Francis, 2nd
Earl of Huntingdon
d.1560

Winifred Pole
m.(2) Sir Thomas
Barrington

Anne Pole — m — Thomas Hildersham

Henry, 3rd
Earl of Huntingdon
d.1595

George, 4th
Earl of Huntingdon
d.1604

Arthur Hildersham
1563–1632

Francis
d.1595

Henry, 5th
Earl of Huntingdon
d.1643

d = died
k = killed
ex = executed
CAPITALS = King Queen
of England.

**St. Helen's Church,
Ashby-de-la-Zouch
(exterior)**

The parish church of Ashby,
where Hildersham preached
throughout his ministerial
career as lecturer and vicar.

**St. Helen's Church
(interior)**

Since Hildersham's time,
side aisles have been added
and the pews replaced.
Hildersham is buried in the
chancel, toward the top
of the photograph.

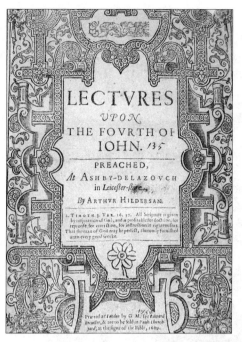

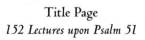

Title Page
Lectures upon the Fourth of John

Hildersham delivered these 108 lectures in Ashby between 1609 and 1611. They were first published in 1629.

Title Page
152 Lectures upon Psalm 51

Hildersham preached these lectures in Ashby between 1625 and 1631, and they were published posthumously in 1635.

Hildersham Memorial

Originally located in the chancel of St Helen's Church, Ashby,
near to Hildersham's burial site, the memorial tablet was later
moved to the southeast corner of the nave. It was erected by
Samuel Hildersham after his father's death in 1632.

Chapter 9

The Interrupted Years
(1606–1614)

Although Hildersham was no longer vicar of Ashby after 1605, he and his young family continued to live in the town. After Richard Jardfeild's brief ministry, the Hildershams witnessed the appointment of another replacement, William Darling, who entered the vicarage in October 1606. It must have been a daunting prospect for this young man of twenty-six to succeed the renowned Hildersham in the pulpit, knowing that the people expected their former minister to be reinstated soon and with Hildersham himself sitting in his congregation each Sunday. However, Darling was to stay in the post for four years, and during that time he got on well with his predecessor.

Darling had been born at nearby Clifton in Staffordshire in 1580, and was a graduate of Emmanuel College, Cambridge.[1] It is possible that he was related to Thomas Darling, the young man from Burton-on-Trent who had been at the center of the exorcism controversy. Ashby was Darling's first pastorate after his ordination. We do not know whether he already held nonconformist views at the time of his induction or whether conversations with Hildersham caused him to adopt a similar position during his sojourn in Ashby, but within three years Darling was in trouble with the church authorities. In 1609 he was reported for failing to wear the surplice and, at the next visitation in 1610, for the full range of nonconformist faults: "That he hath not worn the surplice nor

---

1. Venn and Venn, *Alumni Cantabrigienses Part 1*, 2:11.

used the cross in baptism nor the ring in marriage nor buried the dead nor churched women nor read divine service in such form as in such terms of laws he is commanded."[2] The fifth earl acted swiftly to protect Darling from further trouble with the diocesan authorities and moved him to the less prominent Hastings benefice of Packington, some two miles distant. Darling occupied that position until his death two years later in 1612.

Hildersham had been allowed to preach in Ashby as lecturer again in January 1609. Immediately after his suspension was lifted, he commenced his great series of 108 lectures on the fourth chapter of John's gospel. These ran from Tuesday, January 31, 1609, to Tuesday, November 12, 1611, and in chapter 6 we looked at some of the major themes the series treated. The fifth earl's regular attendance was a great encouragement to Hildersham. Although the lectures were not published until 1628, they obviously circulated in manuscript form in the intervening years. John Preston had received a copy and perused it carefully before urging Hildersham to seek publication, in a letter of November 28, 1615. Preston declared that Hildersham would deprive "God's church of a very great benefit, if you should refuse." Preston also observed that the whole series contained "a continued strength...without any failing or deficiency, without any inequality, unevenness of deformity of some parts with the rest." Preston candidly admitted that the book was "large," but he praised it as being "succinct...the things choice and pertinent, and thoroughly depending each on another. In brief," Preston told Hildersham, "there is nothing that need be added and *nihil quod amputem* [nothing that need be removed]."[3]

Hildersham's friend John Cotton, of Boston, Lincolnshire (and later Massachusetts), wrote the preface to the lectures, heartily recommending the book to ministers and other Christians. Undoubtedly, these lectures represent the mature Hildersham at the full height of his powers as a preacher and expositor, and over the years they have proved a source of great blessing and help to many.

---

2. Leicestershire Record Office ID41/13/33 f. 26r; ID41/13/34 f. 60r.
3. Clarke, "Life of Hildersam," 152–53.

But even during this brief yet fruitful interlude, the storm clouds were continuing to gather above Hildersham. Once again he was stopped in his tracks and his preaching interrupted. He became embroiled in another controversy, although it was later conclusively proved that he was innocent of any blame. This controversy involved the infamous figure of Edward Wightman of Burton-on-Trent.[4]

Hildersham had continued to preach at the weekly exercises at Burton-on-Trent, even when he was prohibited from preaching in Ashby itself. This was possible because Burton lay over the boundary in Staffordshire and fell within the diocese of Coventry and Lichfield. The long-established exercise in St. Modwen's church, Burton, was well attended, and a source of blessing to those in the town and surrounding district. We have already heard about the exorcism controversy that had affected the godly community in Burton in the 1590s; a decade later, another difficult situation arose that was not entirely unconnected with it. Many who had been involved with the events surrounding Thomas Darling's dispossession were tradesmen of the town who had responded positively to the gospel preaching they heard from men like Hildersham, William Bradshaw, Peter Eccleshall, and others. One of these was Edward Wightman, a draper by trade, who had helped to write the account of what had happened to Darling. He had gone with others to interview the alleged witch, and his wife was among those who prayed fervently at Darling's bedside for the young man's deliverance. He was deeply involved with the godly brethren in Burton, but as the years progressed he became a source of extreme embarrassment and anxiety to them as he moved further and further away from the truth and into heresy of a most serious nature. Hildersham became implicated, because at one point Wightman accused him of being the source of these questionable ideas.

What sort of man was Wightman? How could such preposterous allegations have been made against the orthodox and learned

---

4. Most of the following information on Wightman's story comes from research conducted in the archives for a chapter of my PhD thesis, which contains full details of the sources consulted. I have also drawn upon an article by Ian Atherton and David Como, "The Burning of Edward Wightman: Puritanism, Prelacy and the Politics of Heresy in Early Modern England," *English Historical Review* 120, no. 489 (2005): 1215–50. Clarke, in his "Life of Hildersam," devotes several pages to the Wightman episode.

Hildersham—and, worse, how could so many have believed them to be true? We need to examine Wightman's history in a bit more detail to find the answer to these questions. Wightman was baptized in the parish of Burbage, Leicestershire, on December 22, 1566, but the family moved to Burton when his father became master of the local grammar school. The young Wightman had a good education and then was apprenticed to the trade of drapery, this being the occupation of his mother's family. He was sent to Shrewsbury to serve his apprenticeship with the Drapers' Company there in the 1580s, at a time when the charismatic civic preacher, John Tomkys, was having a great impact on the town and the company.[5] Undoubtedly Wightman would have heard zealous gospel preaching while in Shrewsbury, and perhaps he started to favor this sort of teaching from then on. When he returned to Burton at the end of his apprenticeship, he found that the town had been set alight by the fervent preaching of Hildersham and others, and Wightman lost no time in attaching himself to the godly group, sitting under Hildersham's ministry in the weekday lectures for many years.

The 1590s were a difficult time economically, and Wightman began to experience a downturn in business. To help make ends meet, he opened an alehouse in Burton for a dozen years or so, probably sometime between 1590 and 1610. Many people who liked to debate religious ideas, some of them quite radical, used to frequent Wightman's house, and he loved nothing more than to get involved in discussions about the Scriptures. It was a popular pastime at his alehouse to gamble over cards and dice, so perhaps Wightman subtly was being drawn into a more worldly culture.

The first indication of a problem surfaced in 1608, when Henry Aberly, the parish minister of Burton, became aware of Wightman's irregular views on the subject of "soul sleeping" or "mortalism." Although Luther and some other early Reformers had believed that the soul and the body slept until the future day of resurrection, this position quickly was rejected in favor of Calvin and Bullinger's Reformed teaching that the

---

5. For more on Tomkys and Shrewsbury, see Patrick Collinson, "The Shearmen's Tree: The Strange Death of Merry England in Shrewsbury and Beyond," in *The Reformation in English Towns 1500–1640*, ed. Collinson and John Craig (Basingstoke: Macmillan, 1998), 205–20.

souls of believers went immediately to be with God upon death, awaiting the final reunion with their resurrected bodies. However, many early
Anabaptists continued to hold the soul sleeping position, which led to
suspicions that Wightman had become one of that number. Wightman's
mortalist opinions grieved Aberly, and he publicly reproved Wightman
in 1608. As a result, Wightman turned on his minister and told Aberly
in no uncertain terms what he thought of him. He then absented himself from the Burton church whenever Aberly was preaching, choosing
to attend services at other local churches when it pleased him. Wightman had been a prominent member of the godly community in Burton,
and this split so distressed Aberly that he called in two other pastors
in the hope of achieving a reconciliation between himself and Wightman. One of these ministers was Simon Presse, of Egginton, Derbyshire,
and the other was Hildersham himself. Hildersham was renowned for his
peacemaking skills and knowledge of Christian doctrine. Also, his long
acquaintance with Wightman stretched back to the early 1590s.

The ensuing meeting was partially successful on a personal level,
which likely testifies to Hildersham's efforts as a mediator. It was reported
that to a certain extent "they did pacify him [Wightman] towards Mr.
Aberly but touching his opinion they could nothing prevail with him."[6]
In other words, Wightman clung stubbornly to his soul sleeping heresy,
despite the best endeavors of Presse and Hildersham to show him from
the Scriptures the error of his views. Hildersham pointed Wightman to
Luke 16:22–23 (the account of the rich man and Lazarus), Luke 23:43
(the account of the dying thief), and Philippians 1:23, the classic proof
texts used to argue the case against soul sleeping. Calvin had referred to
all of them in his standard work on the subject, which had been translated into English as *An Excellent Treatise of the Immortality of the Soul* in 1581.

Shortly after this meeting, on March 10, 1609, Hildersham received
a letter from Wightman that reiterated his opinions even more strongly.
Hildersham became concerned about rumors that others, too, were

---

6. Lincolnshire Archives Office, D+C ciij (1), "The Report of Francis Lynton and
Thomas Hafter Churchwardens Made Unto the Right Reverend Father in God, Rich[ard]
Bishop of Coventry and Lich[field] concerning Edward Wightman according to His Letters
Charge and Command Imposed upon Them" (May 1611).

being infected by Wightman's doctrines. He decided to make it quite clear in public what the Scriptures taught about the soul after death, so that Wightman would not lead astray others. At the next public exercise in Burton on March 15, 1609, Hildersham took the opportunity to refute the mortalist heresy. The text, which had been fixed in advance, was Hebrews 9:27 ("And as it is appointed unto men once to die, but after this the judgment"), which provided scope for explaining the whole sequence of death and judgment. Wightman was in the congregation and did not like what he heard, for on April 21 he wrote another letter to Hildersham, reviling Hildersham for what he had said. By this point, after an interchange of letters that had gone on for some time, it was becoming increasingly clear to Hildersham that he was getting nowhere in his efforts to persuade Wightman of the error of his ways. So, somewhere around the middle of 1609, Hildersham left Wightman to himself and stopped answering his letters. It says much about Wightman's state of mind that he took this as a triumph, boasting to his friends that his opinions were "invincible and not to be confuted."[7] This seems to mark the end of any direct contact between the two men, although there were reports of a disturbance during Lent in 1611: Wightman loudly interrupted an exercise in the Burton church where the ministers were discussing a passage of Scripture, demanding the right to express his own views. However, we do not know if Hildersham was one of the ministers involved on that occasion.

Within days of this uproar, Wightman was presented at the bishop's visitation by the minister and churchwardens of Burton. Things were obviously getting out of hand and all local efforts to reclaim Wightman had proved fruitless. Shortly afterward, a bitter and excluded Wightman petitioned the king, sending him a book he had written setting out his views. Wightman also contacted the London Puritan minister Anthony Wotton. If he had been less eager to air his opinions in public, and especially to the king, Wightman might have escaped more lightly. As it was, with the attention of the bishop and the ecclesiastical courts now drawn to his irregular ideas and disruptive activities, Wightman was in

---

7. Lincolnshire Archives Office, D+C ciij (1), "Report of Lynton and Hafter."

very serious trouble. The bishop in question was Richard Neile, a hater of Puritans only too keen to look for any hint of radicalism or disorder in their ranks. This deepened the gravity of Wightman's situation. The king, too, urged Neile to make a full investigation, which he did with the help of his chaplain William Laud (later to be such a thorn in the side of God's people). When Neile asked the Burton churchwardens to report what they knew of Wightman, they stressed that they were ill-fitted to provide the bishop with much information, "by reason there has been no society or familiarity between him and us, but rather we have opposed ourselves against him for many lewd misdemeanours of his which have made us to estrange ourselves one toward another."[8] This was strictly true, in that for two years Wightman had been excluded from fellowship with local believers, but despite this, and despite Wightman's public declarations against infant baptism, his children continued to be baptized in St. Modwen's, the youngest in August 1611. But the godly folk of Burton grieved because Wightman had been one of their own, and they were reluctant to denounce him to the authorities; at the same time, they wanted to make it clear that they were not responsible for the errors he had recently expounded so publicly. The churchwardens were in an invidious position, for they recognized that Wightman was a dangerous loose cannon, a weapon that the enemies of God's people were only too ready to use against them.

Wightman was committed to prison, first at the Gatehouse in London and then locally, where a series of questions were put to him. This resulted in fourteen separate charges of heresy being brought against him. It was clear that by this stage he had gone much further than the original opinions he had held on soul sleeping and infant baptism, for he now admitted to a whole raft of antitrinitarian and christological heresies and also advocated the abolition of Communion by bread and wine. Perhaps even more damagingly, Wightman confessed, "I...have affirmed myself to be that prophet promised in the 18 of Deuteronomy and that Elijah in the 4th of Malachi promised to be sent before the great

---

8. Lincolnshire Archives Office, D+C ciij (1), "Report of Lynton and Hafter."

and fearful day of the Lord, and that comforter in the 16 of John who should convict the world of sin, of righteousness and of judgment."[9]

Such blasphemous delusions could not be ignored. Wightman appeared before a special consistory court at Lichfield Cathedral under Bishop Neile on November 19, 1611. A crowd gathered, wanting to hear the proceedings, and caused the trial to be moved on the second and third days from the intimate surroundings of the upstairs courtroom to the expansive and echoing space of the Chapel of the Blessed Virgin, part of the main cathedral itself. Samuel Clarke gives a detailed account of Hildersham's part in that trial. He writes that on the second day of proceedings, November 26, 1611, Wightman complained in front of more than five hundred hearers that Neile had been spreading the rumor that he had learned his heretical opinions from Hildersham. In fact, declared Wightman, quite the opposite was true, for Hildersham had turned even his friends against him by condemning his views. However, on the next day of the trial, whether out of craft or confusion, Wightman appeared to change his story. With Hildersham sitting in the court before him, and in front of the bishop, Wightman now avouched that at the conference he had held with Hildersham in 1609, Hildersham had admitted that the whole drift of Scripture supported the idea of soul sleeping, but that the church had judged otherwise.

Called to answer this charge, Hildersham vehemently protested that he never said, or even thought, such a thing. He offered to swear an oath, or use any other means that would satisfy the court, to affirm that he had always held that soul sleeping was contrary to Scripture and "a most detestable heresy." When Henry Aberly, curate of Burton, who had been present at the meeting between Hildersham and Wightman, gave testimony supporting Hildersham's version of events, Hildersham was vindicated and completely cleared of any blame. Even Bishop Neile, who had previously given out "that Wightman learned his opinions (at least that of the soul's sleeping) of the Puritans, and at the aforesaid exercises, and that of Master Hildersam by name," was forced to admit openly that Wightman had "greatly wronged" Hildersham in what he had said about

---

9. Lincolnshire Archives Office, D+C ciij (2), Edward Wightman, "His Prophecy of the Great Day of the L[ord] before Allhallows Day" (Sept. 3, 1611).

him. "Thus," concludes Clarke triumphantly, "was Master Hildersam's innocency cleared in a public audience, during the time of Wightman's trial at Lichfield."[10] It almost seemed as if Hildersham, as well as Wightman, had been on trial in the cathedral; but, despite successfully clearing his name, some of the mud his enemies threw at him continued to stick, as we will see.

There was little doubt that the court would find Wightman guilty, since he brazenly clung to his heterodox opinions. On March 20, 1612, he was brought to the stake at Lichfield, but, feeling the flames start to scorch him, he cried out that he would recant. Some of the onlookers risked their own lives by running into the fire and dragging him out. Before being unchained from the stake, Wightman signed a recantation; but two or three weeks later, on cooler reflection, he "blasphemed more audaciously than before" when he was again brought before the Consistory Court.[11] The writ for the burning of heretics was therefore renewed, and Wightman went to the stake for the second time on Easter Saturday, April 11, 1612. In Neile's words, "he died blaspheming."[12] The last person to be burned at Smithfield, another heretic, Bartholomew Legate, had perished at the stake on March 18, 1612, but it is Wightman, dying a month later, who holds the dubious distinction of being the last person to be burned for heresy in England.

The modern mind recoils in horror at the thought of people being burned to death, and it is impossible not to pity the profoundly deluded Wightman, despite his arrogance. Many Christians would generally regard some of his opinions, like his opposition to infant baptism, as acceptable alternative interpretations of Scripture, and many churches (both orthodox and mainstream) now practice believers' baptism. However, Wightman's self-application of several biblical prophecies still has the power to shock us with its presumption and blasphemous implications. For Hildersham and the godly brethren in Burton, the repercussions of the affair did not die with Wightman on that sad day in April 1612. Suspicion still clung to them like a cloud of smoke. Bishop

10. Clarke, "Life of Hildersam," 148.
11. *Calendar of State Papers, Domestic, 1639–40*, 85.
12. *Calendar of State Papers, Domestic, 1639–40*, 85.

Neile, "the man whom all the pious…misdoubted would do the most mischief," used the bad publicity the episode had generated as an excuse to suppress not only the lectures at Burton but also those at Repton. As a result of events, Henry Aberly, the curate of Burton, left the town and sought refuge in Ashby, remaining closely associated with Hildersham for the rest of his life. Despite Hildersham's formal exoneration in the consistory court, the preaching ban Neile had imposed earlier remained in force, and, in fact, suspension by the High Commission followed on April 22, 1613. It looks likely that the king's personal animosity toward Hildersham had something to do with this, for in the very month of Wightman's trial, Archbishop Abbot warned the bishop of Peterborough that Hildersham had angered James by (reportedly) preaching in the Lincoln diocese.

The king's approval of Richard Neile was apparent when Neile was promoted to the larger bishopric of Lincoln in 1614. In this post Neile showed a similar desire to enforce conformity—bad news for men like Hildersham, whom the bishop already had identified as a troublemaker. Neile's attitudes and orders probably influenced William Darling's successor as vicar of Ashby, Thomas Hacket, who had moved to the town in 1611.[13] Initially it might have appeared that Hacket possessed the right credentials to carry on the godly tradition prevailing in Ashby, which allowed conformity to be a matter of individual conscience. Like his predecessor, he was a graduate of the impeccably Puritan Emmanuel College. This young man, ordained in December 1607, was in his first incumbency and lacked experience, but apparently had a point to prove. At the beginning of Hacket's time in Ashby, there is evidence that Hildersham did his best to work with him, in the interests of the flock; for instance, in 1612, both men acted jointly as the witnesses to the will of one William Rise, an Ashby parishioner.[14] Hacket's small, neat handwriting in the parish registers shows that he was a stickler for detail, keen that everything should be done properly and according to the rules. At first there was little change in the types of offenses that Hacket reported to the bishop, but even from 1611 there is a small hint of the style that

---

13. Venn and Venn, *Alumni Cantabrigienses Part 1*, 2:279.

14. Leicestershire Record Office, Leicester Wills, Ashby no. 82.

Hacket favored, when the lack of Jewell's *Works* was recorded at the visitation.[15] By 1612, Hacket's more confrontational approach and his desire to achieve conformity, probably under orders from above, was becoming clear. Significantly, the churchwardens' accounts for 1614 record the purchase of two yards of Holland cloth at nine shillings and two pence to make surplice sleeves.[16] How resolutely his predecessors, Hildersham and Darling, had refused to wear the hated popish surplice!

Instead of achieving unity and conformity, all Hacket's approach achieved was deep and bitter religious division in Ashby. Hildersham had tried to resolve or contain differences by informal means and a measure of coexistence had been established, to a large extent maintained by the high personal respect in which people of all shades of spiritual opinion held him. Unfortunately, discontent with Hacket soon started to surface. He had difficulty collecting some of his tithes from parishioners and had to take them to court.[17] He also managed to annoy the inhabitants of Blackfordby, home to a dependent chapelry of the Ashby church. There had been a longstanding dispute between Ashby and Blackfordby over the provision of pastoral services and the payment of dues, and in 1615 the residents complained in the archdeaconry court that "they have no minister nor have had any service for the space of half a year last past," by reason of the neglect of "Mr. Hacket."[18]

These tensions came to a head in 1615, when, famously, nearly one hundred parishioners—including Hildersham, Brinsley (the schoolmaster and former curate), Henry Aberly (the ex-minister of Burton), and William Cox (churchwarden and locksmith), along with their wives— all were presented to the bishop for failing to receive Communion in a kneeling posture the previous Easter. The episode has been described as "an unmatched spectacle in the sheer volume of nonconformity, expressing active sympathy for their former minister."[19] However, it is

---

15. Leicestershire Record Office ID41/13/35 f. 157. John Jewel (1521–1571), Bishop of Salisbury from 1560, was a strong defender of the Settlement of the Church of England, against criticism from both Puritan and Roman Catholic attacks.

16. Historic Manuscripts Commission, *Hastings*, 1:382.

17. Leicestershire Record Office ID41/1/17 (1615), f. 7r.

18. Leicestershire Record Office ID 41/13/40 f. 20v; cited in Moxon, "Ashby," 332–33.

19. Chalmers, "Puritanism in Leicestershire," 257.

important to try to establish what actually occurred, because so much confusion surrounds not only the incident itself but also the conflicting reports of what happened.

Easter was the recognized time when the Lord's Supper was celebrated, and everyone in the parish wanted to receive Communion. There were about seven hundred communicants within the parish of Ashby, so more than one service would have been held in order to accommodate them all. In fact, it was at the Palm Sunday Communion of 1614, the week before Easter, that the difficulty arose. A man called George Reding, an apparent visitor or newcomer to Ashby, gave written evidence against Hildersham that he had approached the Communion table among the several companies waiting to receive the elements but had refused to kneel when his turn came, wishing to receive standing. "And," Reding went on, "when he could not have it so, yet [he] stood still among them that kneeled, till the Communion was done." He also informed the court that Hacket had given advance warning that he would not admit anyone to the table who did not kneel.[20]

Hildersham responded to the testimony of his accuser with a strong denial. He stated that he had been seriously ill with a fever during the spring of 1614, which had kept him bedbound in his chamber for many weeks before, during, and after the Communion service. The fever had been particularly painful and debilitating, for it had affected "the roof of his mouth, and the gristle of his nose." Evidently his life had been endangered at one stage, but "by the blessing of God, upon the care and skill of physicians and chyrurgeons [surgeons], he was recovered."[21] Everyone in Ashby knew of his sickness, Hildersham said, and the details were well attested. Hildersham then avowed, "Neither did I ever at any other time present myself in that manner to the Communion-table."[22] As we have seen, Hildersham preferred a nonconfrontational approach; knowing Hacket's views about kneeling to receive Communion, if Hildersham had not been unwell, it is likely that he would have absented himself quietly from the service and gone elsewhere, as others

---

20. Clarke, "Life of Hildersam," 148–49.
21. Clarke, "Life of Hildersam," 150.
22. Clarke, "Life of Hildersam," 150.

in fact did. Of George Reding, who had testified against him, Hildersham was very dismissive, asserting that "this fellow that hath devised this against me (whereof there was no colour at all of truth) would in all likelihood have sworn anything that might have done me hurt, if he had been required to do it."[23] Hildersham obviously believed that someone else, perhaps Hacket or Bishop Neile, had set Reding up to get Hildersham into trouble.

Although it is clear that Hildersham did not lead a protest of nonconformists at the Communion service of 1614, it is also clear that such a revolt did take place. The list of those who refused to kneel is a confusing document, with names crossed out and others erroneously included.[24] Henry Aberly, for example, had attempted to avoid confrontation by ensuring his absence on that occasion, but his name still appears on the offenders list. Others of Hildersham's most faithful supporters, like John Brinsley and William Cox, do not appear to have denied their offense. Strangely, George Reding's name also occurs, with a note beside it stating, "He appeared and confessed [the] things objected against him...to be true." Some of those reported had a long history of nonconformity, while others seem to have conformed after this. Perhaps it was true that a number refused to kneel purely out of sympathy with Hildersham, even though he would not have encouraged their actions. Many undoubtedly followed their consciences and remained standing at the Communion table, as they had been allowed to do by a succession of godly ministers from at least Thomas Widdowes onward.

Thomas Hacket was at the root of much of this trouble in Ashby. Clarke calls him "the principal accuser and informer of the court against them [the nonconformists]" and asserts that he especially and many of the other deponents were "professed adversaries" of Hildersham and the godly brethren.[25] That the issue of conformity was brought to a head at Easter 1614 is hardly surprising, for this was the first large-scale Communion to be administered since Neile's appointment as the local bishop. Neile's campaign against nonconformity in his diocese, and against

23. Clarke, "Life of Hildersam," 150.
24. Leicestershire Record Office ID41/13/39 fos. 99r–101v.
25. Clarke, "Life of Hildersam," 149.

Hildersham in particular, was gaining momentum. And, since Hildersham had been silenced again by the High Commission in 1613, he was denied the opportunity of any public defense of his stance in the pulpit. Backed by Bishop Neile, Hacket must have felt in a strong position, but he underestimated the strength of local opinion. Not only did the tradition of nonconformity in Ashby go back for more than forty years, but Hildersham himself had been living in the town for twenty-seven years and was known to be a man of great integrity and faithfulness. In contrast, Hacket had only been around for three years and was viewed as an outsider, unfamiliar or unsympathetic to local ways of doing things. Clarke declares that "all the parish" knew the sworn depositions of witnesses "to be notoriously false" and that "all the neighbours knew" that these witnesses were "mere strangers to him."[26] Only by bringing in outsiders could evidence be compiled against Hildersham, for even those in Ashby who had no sympathy for nonconformity as a religious position had communal loyalty to Hildersham, who was a respected and integral member of local society. Hacket may have thought he had won the battle by 1616, with the bishop's backing of his hardline approach and the High Commission's crushing judgment upon Hildersham (of which we will hear more later), but he had lost the war. Not only had he alienated a significant section of his parishioners and brought about unrest, he also had not counted on the intervention of the fifth Earl of Huntingdon. As the patron of the living and Hildersham's relative, the earl replaced Hacket with a more pragmatic vicar, Thomas Pestell, in late 1616.

Hildersham had to suffer the indignity of false accusations in the Wightman episode as well as over the Easter Communion of 1614. Reviled and grossly misrepresented, he had conducted himself honorably and with great integrity throughout. With his Master's example before him, he had faced his enemies and those determined to bring him down with fortitude, dignity, and much prayer. In March 1611 he had exhorted the brethren in Ashby "to prepare for affliction, and to provide for comfort against the evil day, seeing no man may hope to be exempted from it." He had urged them to "meditate, and think oft of,

---

26. Clarke, "Life of Hildersam," 149.

and look for the evil day; resolve with thy self thou must not live always in peace, and health, and prosperity, but there will be a change, there will come a time, when thou shalt part with all thy dearest comforts, there will come a time of trouble, sickness, adversity." Referring to the ruler whose son lay dying in Capernaum (John 4:46–53), Hildersham went on to explain the benefits of affliction: "It humbled him greatly, and abated his pride,…it did drive him to seek to Christ; yea to seek earnestly and importunately for help," and then "this affliction became unto him a means and occasion of his unfained conversion." Hildersham concluded by declaring that "affliction is greatly profitable and necessary unto all the elect of God."[27] Knowing the troubles that their former pastor had already been through, his congregation would have realized that this doctrine was not just scripturally correct but was the fruit of his own experience. Hildersham needed to take to heart his own teaching as much as any of his hearers, for even more trials lay ahead of him.

---

27. Hildersham, *Lectures upon John*, 389, 394.

Chapter 10

⌐⊙¬

The Silent Years
(1613–1625)

When Hildersham appeared before the High Commission on April 22, 1613, he was "judicially admonished" and instructed that "saving the catechizing of his own family only, he should not at anytime hereafter preach, catechize, or use any part of the office, or function of a minister, either publicly or privately, until he should be lawfully restored and released of his said suspension."[1] It seems the ecclesiastical authorities had decided, quite unjustly, in the aftermath of the Wightman affair, that Hildersham was a dangerous troublemaker who associated with radicals and heretics and could not be permitted to give voice to his opinions, lest others be led astray. For a man who regarded preaching of the Word of God as his primary calling in life, it was a harsh blow. And he could not have known that it would be another twelve years before he would be allowed to preach again.

It would be understandable if, in these circumstances, Hildersham had felt demoralized and useless. With the pulpit denied to him, it appeared that his service to God was at an end. However, what Philip Henry wrote about his ejected colleague, Rowland Nevet of Oswestry (who died in 1675), could apply equally to Hildersham: "Even after he was silenced for nonconformity, he continued among his people there to his dying day, doing what he could when he might not do what he

---

1. Clarke, "Life of Hildersam," 148.

would."[2] Hildersham and his family remained in Ashby, and by his ongoing involvement in parish affairs and his relationships with local people, he managed to maintain a real witness to the gospel, even when he was silenced officially. William Lilly, who went on to become a famous astrologer, gave a glowing testimony to Hildersham's influence in the town. Lilly had been a pupil at the grammar school in Ashby between the ages of eleven and eighteen, from 1613 to 1620. Recalling his schooldays, he was later to write in his autobiography:

> In this town of Ashby de la Zouch, for many years together, Mr. Arthur Hildersham exercised his ministry at my being there; and all the while I continued at Ashby, he was silenced. This is that famous Hildersham, who left behind him a commentary on the fifty-first psalm; as also many sermons upon the fourth of John, both of which are printed: he was an excellent textuary, of exemplary life, pleasant in discourse, a strong enemy to the Brownists, and dissented not from the Church of England in any article of faith, but only about wearing the surplice, baptizing with the cross, and kneeling at the sacrament; most of the people in the town were directed by his judgment, and so continued, and yet do continue presbyterianly affected.[3]

Several things are striking about this tribute, considering that Lilly himself was no friend to presbyterianism. Lilly talks of Hildersham's powerful influence on the town—"most of the people were directed by his judgment, and so continued"—but he also informs us that for the whole seven years he was in Ashby, Hildersham was silenced. Although schoolboys of that time were expected to attend many sermons, Lilly never would have heard Hildersham preach publicly when he was living in the town. And yet he mentions that "Mr. Hildersham exercised his ministry at my being there." How, then, did Hildersham manage to achieve this continued influence when he could not preach, and what form did this "silent" ministry take? Part of the answer must surely be found in something else Lilly mentioned: Hildersham's "exemplary life" and "pleasant discourse." Living among the people, many of whom he

---

2. Diary of Philip Henry, cited in Henry, *Lives of Philip and Matthew Henry*, 271.

3. Lilly, *History of His Life and Times*, 6.

had baptized or married or whose relatives he had buried, was in itself a testimony to God's grace in a time of trial.

This chapter will look at some of the ways Hildersham managed to do "what he could" when he "could not do what he would." There were various ways in which he was able to serve the flock, some of them very humble indeed. Many of these avenues of service continued throughout the forty-two years he spent in Ashby but took on greater significance when his preaching stopped.

Personal Life

The first of these ways involves Hildersham's personal life. We have already heard about the large house that he rented from the grammar school endowment and its prominent location in the town. By 1613, everyone in Ashby would have known where "Mr. Hildersham's house" was, and the very fact that he continued to live among them spoke volumes about his commitment to the townsfolk. As the public functions of preaching and other clerical duties were closed to him, his home became increasingly important as the place where he could exercise a different kind of ministry. Here he could continue his habitual practice of hospitality and household religion. Clarke tells us, "In all places where he did reside...he was always helpful in family-prayers, in expounding the Scriptures read, and in the repetition of the sermons preached in the public congregation."[4] Strictly speaking, these devotions were for the family and servants, but visitors to the home often were included. Even Hildersham's "secret prayer" was not always private but was regularly overheard by "some godly friends, whose occasions brought them often near to the place where he studied" because he was so "frequent in holy ejaculations audibly expressed."[5] Hildersham continued with his normal routine of reading a chapter of the Bible each morning and walking alone for about an hour to meditate on what he had read. He kept a commonplace book, in which he wrote notes and observations on his reading, adding quotations from other books he had found useful in his studies. It was also reported that "Mr. Hildersam used to preach in

---

4. Clarke, "Life of Hildersam," 153.
5. Clarke, "Life of Hildersam," 153.

his own house, when silenced: and two or three families came to hear him."[6] This example of a congregation within a household was to provide a model for the later nonconformists after the Great Ejection of 1662. But it is important to remember that Hildersham always encouraged people to attend services at the local parish church, even when the minister used the ceremonies, for if "the worship I go unto is (for the substance of it) pure, and according to God's ordinance...the corruptions and sins which another brings into it cannot defile it unto me."[7] He himself was "always a diligent frequenter of the public assemblies" wherever he was living, taking careful notes of the sermons. The ministry of the Word was so precious to him that he would often say that he "never heard any godly minister preach, though but of weak parts, but he got some benefit by him."[8]

Parishioners and others continued to seek him out for counsel, perhaps in increasing numbers when his public teaching was denied to them. He was "willing by private conference to instruct the ignorant, to satisfy the doubtful, to settle the wavering, to comfort the dejected, and to encourage all sorts in the exercises of religion."[9] So, by informal and unofficial means, Hildersham was able to sustain a powerful spiritual ministry among his neighbors. He also used his house as a headquarters for involvement in other local secular and quasi-religious activities such as letter writing, supplying testimonials for prospective marriage partners, and charitable business. Little of Hildersham's correspondence survives, but we know that Humphrey Fenn, John Preston, John Cotton, Walter Travers, and Robert Bolton were among those who wrote to him.

Hildersham's personal accessibility, both in terms of local geography and his approachable disposition, ensured that the public silencing did not end his influence in Ashby, as Lilly observed. Hildersham's example is helpful for those today who live in places where it is illegal to worship or share the gospel publicly. Living a holy life among people and

---

6. Vincent Alsop, *A Reply to the Reverend Dean of St. Paul's Reflections* (London, 1681), 11.

7. Hildersham, *Lectures upon Psalm 51*, 181.

8. Clarke, "Life of Hildersam," 153.

9. Clarke, "Life of Hildersam," 153.

demonstrating a love and commitment to them, for Christ's sake, can have a profound effect upon the community, as Hildersham demonstrated.

The Grammar School Feoffees

Education was another sphere in which Hildersham was able to exercise unbroken influence in the town. The third Earl of Huntingdon had founded the grammar school in Ashby, and the fact that both Anthony Gilby and Thomas Widdowes were among the signatories to the original enfeoffment of the school (the charter of foundation) on August 10, 1567, testifies to the godly intentions behind the establishment.[10] The foundation deed made provision for "a suitable master, pedagogue or instructor to instruct, teach and inform youths, children and little ones in good manners, learning, knowledge and virtue." The statutes and orders for the government of the school, set down in 1575, made attendance at public prayers, sermons, and catechizing (specifically mentioning Calvin's and Nowell's catechisms) obligatory for the pupils. Additionally, the boys were expected to take notes on sermons, memorize the catechism, and receive instruction in Greek and Latin.

The surviving school accounts, which give details of business and lists of feoffees (or trustees), do not begin until 1594, and the first list of feoffees appears in 1606, so it is impossible to say when Hildersham was officially appointed.[11] However, it is likely that he became a feoffee soon after his induction as vicar in 1593, and he quickly came to be regarded by his fellow feoffees as the most significant and respected member of their body. This was due in part to his social status and his position as vicar, but his learning, wisdom, and godliness also contributed. The other feoffees, leading inhabitants of the town, seem to have recognized Hildersham's authority in their decision making. Hildersham frequently appears as the first signatory to memoranda recorded in the accounts, and he may well have been the one who suggested and framed the business at hand. Although there were several other vicars

---

10. Unless stated, information on the school is taken from Fox, *Country Grammar School*.

11. Leicestershire Record Office ES/AB/9/1, the Feoffees Book of Accounts 1594–1768. This has been transcribed, with some omissions, in Fox, *Country Grammar School*, appendix 5, 132–76.

in Ashby during Hildersham's residence there, no other clergyman was appointed to the feoffees during Hildersham's lifetime—a sure testimony to his unrivalled preeminence in this arena. Even during the years when he was suspended, Hildersham continued attending meetings of the feoffees and making a full contribution to affairs.[12] Despite periods of enforced absence from the town after 1616, the school accounts reveal that Hildersham maintained his household in Ashby throughout and that he made regular visits for meetings of the feoffees as required. After 1616 the feoffees were obliged to be present in Ashby on at least three formal occasions annually. Hildersham also served as collector of the school rents (on properties belonging to the school's endowment, leased out to provide an income for the school, including the house he lived in) and was responsible for making the accounts in 1615–1616, again in 1623–1624, and finally in 1628–1629. The first occasion, though, was during Hildersham's enforced absence from the town, so Samuel Adams was appointed to make the accounts on his behalf. However, in 1623–1624, when Hildersham was still suspended from the ministry, it looks as if he carried out these duties personally, for no proxy is mentioned.

This close involvement with school affairs meant that Hildersham had a real influence on generations of Ashby schoolboys and their education. He obviously made a deep impact on many, like Joseph Hall and William Bradshaw, as well as the young William Lilly. He was able to ensure that godly masters were appointed, such as John Brinsley in 1599. In addition, Hildersham's service as a feoffee meant that he was working alongside other leading and influential men of Ashby, not all of whom shared his nonconformist opinions. Of the twelve feoffees listed in the accounts of 1606, only four, apart from Hildersham, were presented for nonconformity in 1615 or subsequently: Thomas Dighton, Robert Newton, Robert Clark, and John Ash. Thomas Dighton was a leading nonconformist who was fined and imprisoned by the High Commission on November 21, 1616.[13] As a result, he ceased to serve as a feoffee. The most senior member of the feoffees after Hildersham was Robert Bainbrigg, the earl's bailiff and a "gentleman." Although he seems to

---

12. For example, on October 30, 1606, and April 30, 1616.
13. Clarke, "Life of Hildersam," 149.

have been a religious conformist, this does not appear to have caused a problem, as both he and Hildersham worked harmoniously together for the good of the school. Bainbrigg seems to have deferred to Hildersham in school matters, usually signing his name immediately below that of the minister when both were present at meetings. Other feoffees who were religious conformists included Thomas Sherwood, a yeoman blacksmith with beautiful handwriting, often called upon to act as witness or appraiser to the wills and inventories of his neighbors, and another yeoman, Nicholas Haskie. Haskie is an interesting figure, illustrating that, in Ashby, conformists and nonconformists generally worked in cooperation with each other, and also that religious conformity did not stop someone from being a true believer. For, on his death in 1626, Haskie named his kinsman Joseph Hatterly as his "heir and lawful executor." Hatterly had a record of nonconformity and worked very closely with Hildersham. Moreover, Haskie's will shows a particular awareness of the language of godly piety and even mentions being one of the elect: "I offer and bequeath my soul into the hands of Almighty God my Creator, trusting only through faith in the merits, death and obedience of Jesus Christ my only Saviour and Redeemer to be saved from His wrath. And to be one of His elect at the last general…judgment day."[14] It is appropriate to be cautious when interpreting wills, of course; but could Haskie have been one of the godly conformists whom Hildersham counted as brethren and with whom he had no quarrel? Without further evidence it is impossible to say, but at the very least, Haskie's pious will warns us of the danger of automatically labeling "conformists" as nonbelievers.

Town Business

It is a testimony to Hildersham's gracious spirit, and the universal respect in which he was held, that men of differing religious views were able to work together under his leadership to promote the interests of the school and town, with no apparent disharmony. As a prominent inhabitant of Ashby, Hildersham collaborated with other leading men, irrespective of their spiritual positions, in matters relating to the town's

---

14. Leicestershire Record Office MF/660, 1626 (10–13).

welfare. This is particularly well illustrated by events during the plague summer of 1625, just before Hildersham returned to his post as lecturer in Ashby. Apparently rumors had begun to circulate in the county that plague was rife in Ashby and that many people had died. These reports were having an alarmingly detrimental effect on local trade and markets, as people stayed away for fear of catching the infection. Seeking to set the record straight and to reassure people that "since the 25th of March last there have not died in this town above 15 persons in all" and that these deaths were attributable to causes other than the plague, a group of local worthies penned a letter on June 1, 1625, to the mayor and corporation of Leicester. Hildersham heads the list of signatories— which once again underlines his status in the town and the value of his reputation for probity—followed by the vicar, Anthony Watson. The names of the other eight contributors, obviously leading men in Ashby society, included a complete mix of conformists and nonconformists: Henry Aberly, Robert Bainbrigg, Robert Newton, Nicholas Haskie, John Armeston and Joseph Tomlinson (the churchwardens), William Taylor (the constable), and Thomas Sherwood.[15] They were united in a common concern for the economic survival of their community, which was so dependent on outside trade. This sort of action may have been what Samuel Hildersham had in mind when he praised his father's "singular wisdom in settling peace, advising in secular affairs...with...love and reverence of all sorts."[16] As Clarke puts it, "He was a friend to everyone in a good cause, and it was his unwearied delight to be Christianly serviceable in any kind."[17] Hildersham did not make the mistake of thinking that only "spiritual" affairs were worth bothering with, and his concern extended to every area of life.

Charity

If Hildersham's endeavors in the area of education show him working with that body of solid, respectable men of the middling sort, who

---

15. Leicestershire Record Office BR 11/18/15, f. 586, Leicester Borough Minute Book, 1623–1625.

16. Memorial to Hildersham in St. Helen's Church, Ashby.

17. Clarke, "Life of Hildersam," 153.

formed the backbone of the town's ruling class, Hildersham's involvement with the poor demonstrates his care for the lowest in society.[18] Some twentieth-century commentators have argued that Puritanism, with its emphasis on the written Word and moral respectability, was a type of religion that appealed largely to the elite and middling classes.[19] Hildersham has even been cited to support this argument when he expressed the view that "the poor in all places are for the most part the most devoid of grace." However, Hildersham's words here have been taken completely out of context; in fact, they form part of a caution qualifying his main argument that "we must not content ourselves to pity the poor, but we must also relieve them, and be ready to do them good."[20] But the poor were not merely objects of charity; they could equally be recipients of God's grace. Hildersham reminds his hearers that the poor "may belong to God's election for aught thou knowest."[21] The leveling effect of the gospel was such that "all men claim a common interest in God, and therefore it concerneth one as well as another (the tradesman as well as the preacher, the ploughman as well as the gentleman, the poorest beggar as well as the greatest prince) to know Him."[22] Even the common, uneducated people, insisted Hildersham, were able to understand the plain truths of God's Word.[23]

In early modern England, there was no welfare state to provide benefits for the poor. The Elizabethan poor laws laid the responsibility for caring for the neediest people squarely on the parish in which they lived. This very basic provision had to be paid for by a parish rate, levied on those earning more than a certain amount, and voluntary contributions. Each parish had to appoint overseers of the poor to collect the annual rate and ensure a proper distribution of funds to those considered eligible. Care was taken to distinguish between the "deserving" and the "undeserving" poor. In times of economic depression and harvest failure,

---

18. The "middling sort" was roughly equivalent to our modern-day "middle class."

19. This has been argued by historians such as Christopher Hill, William Hunt, and Keith Wrightson.

20. Hildersham, *Lectures upon Psalm 51*, 116–18.

21. Hildersham, *Lectures upon Psalm 51*, 119.

22. Hildersham, *Lectures upon Psalm 51*, 492.

23. Hildersham, *Lectures upon Psalm 51*, 513, 768.

needs were especially acute and local provision was badly stretched. It was said of Hildersham that "he was very charitable to the poor himself, and in exciting of his auditors to contribute towards their relief." Clarke calls him "the patron of the poor."[24] In his will, Hildersham left forty shillings to the poor of Ashby, as well as several individual bequests to poor parishioners.[25]

By examining the accounts of the overseers of the poor in Ashby, we can see just how involved Hildersham was in the day-to-day arrangements of caring for the needy in his town. Although the accounts that survive cover only the period of 1623 to February 1638, it is very likely that Hildersham was involved in a similar way for many years previously and that this sort of service supplied a measure of continuity during his silent years as well. In the accounts, Hildersham's name occurs at regular intervals, giving approval for payments, encouraging collections, and providing advice. Everyone, including the earl, the overseers, and the vicar, clearly regarded charity as Hildersham's special preserve. For example, the will of John Collins, clerk, who died on May 31, 1627, left forty shillings to the poor of Ashby, with the instructions that it "be distributed by Mr. Hildersham and the churchwardens."[26] Joseph Hatterley, who had been a nonconformist in the great presentation of 1615 after the Easter Communion, was one of the overseers for 1626–1627, and he clearly deferred to Hildersham's authority in matters of poor relief. He records delivering ten shillings to Thomas Bammford in the summer of 1626, "with Mr. Hildersam's consent." On July 11 of that same year, Hatterly recorded the receipt of one pound, sixteen shillings, and eleven pence "by a collection for the poor moved by Mr. Hildersam" and on August 2 a further two pounds and sixteen shillings "by a collection at the Fast."[27] Hildersham audited Hatterly's accounts and authorized them in his own hand at the end, as the following entry indicates: "All

---

24. Clarke, "Life of Hildersam," 154.

25. About 180 pounds in 2010 values, according to the National Archives Currency Converter.

26. Public Record Office, Prob/ 11/151. Will of John Collins, October 28, 1626.

27. About 165 and 250 pounds in 2010 values.

Joseph Hatterly's accounts for the year were cleared and discharged April 9 1627 Arth; Hildersam."[28]

A further demonstration of Hildersham's involvement with the intimate mechanics of poor relief comes in 1630–1631, during the tenure of his friend and fellow nonconformist William Cox, the locksmith, as overseer. On May 1, 1631, Joan Ball was allocated one shilling for the care of Ruth Farmer's illegitimate child, in what was obviously to become a weekly allowance.[29] In the margin beside this entry, Cox noted, "Mr. Hildersam is to have Joan Ball's money." This arrangement whereby Hildersham appears to have held the money in trust for Joan Ball until she was able to collect it continued through to June 12, 1631, when Cox indicates that "Mr. Hildersam for Joan Ball here endeth." The story of Ruth Farmer, the baby's mother, was a sad one. Hildersham had baptized Ruth on August 24, 1595. Two days later, Hildersham had buried Ruth's mother, the wife of Edward Farmer, who served on the school feoffees with him. The circumstances in which Ruth became pregnant are not known, but the overseers tried unsuccessfully to trace the reputed father, William Allen, who was thought to have fled to Bosworth. Ruth died shortly after giving birth, and two local women were paid four pence for sitting up with her on the night she died. She was buried in December 1629 at the age of thirty-four. The illegitimate infant, a girl, thus became the responsibility of the parish, with Ralph Narborow receiving an allowance for her in January and February 1630 and Joan Ball taking over the care in May 1631. This was not required for long, for the child died the following spring, and her entry in the burial register immediately precedes that of Hildersham's himself in March 1632. The whole episode encapsulates Hildersham's engagement with the parish, for nothing was too small or humble to receive his attention.

Strictly speaking, at this point, we should not count the influence of Hildersham's preaching on charitable giving in Ashby, but it does give a fuller indication of his involvement in the lives of the poor. Clarke tells us that "in few country-congregations in England the collections for the

---

28. Leicestershire Record Office MF/5, Overseers accounts (unpaginated).
29. About five pounds in 2010 values.

poor were so large as at the quarter-days at his lectures."[30] The institution of such collections can be found at the end of Hildersham's lecture 22 on Psalm 51, delivered on April 18, 1626, when he exhorts his hearers:

> I speak the more of it at this time, to shew your compassion, and extend your liberality toward the poor of this town. I have long thought it a shame unto us, that such an assembly as this is, should so often meet together to serve God, and no collection made in it in all this time for the poor. I could allege the example of other Reformed churches, to provoke us to this, and name to you congregations in our own land, where collections are made for the poor, every month once, upon the lecture day. But I pray you rather consider the equity of that law of God, *Deuterono. 16:16, 17:5.*... If it were for nothing else, even to profess our homage to God, it is fit in our church-assemblies, we should sometimes give somewhat to the poor. I have hitherto forborne to do it, because of that willingness many of you shewed in your weekly contributions, while the fast continued. Now I hope it will not offend any of you...if once a quarter I crave this of you, that as you are made here partakers of our spiritual things, so you will be content to minister unto our poor, in these carnal things. *Romans 15:27.*[31]

Judging by the generous response, his hearers were not offended. Collections continued on the quarter days, with the largest amounts being recorded when Hildersham himself was preaching; for example, five pounds, five shillings, eleven pence on August 2, 1631.[32]

The poor accounts also demonstrate the involvement of not only Hildersham but his wider family within the community. On August 28, 1631, we find one pound, three shillings, and four pence being paid to Hildersham's youngest son, Nathanael, to cover the money he had laid out in London seeking treatment for a lame girl, Ann Sansom from Ashby.[33] After Hildersham's death, the receipt of five pounds is

---

30. Clarke, "Life of Hildersam," 155.
31. Hildersham, *Lectures upon Psalm 51,* 121.
32. Nearly five hundred pounds in 2010 values.
33. About 105 pounds in 2010 values.

recorded on April 24, 1632, for Samuel Hildersham, his eldest son.[34] The record does not specify the purpose for this sum, but it most likely was a contribution toward the cost of the memorial to his father that Samuel had erected in the parish church. This would surely be a tangible means for the churchwardens and overseers to demonstrate the esteem in which the town of Ashby had held Arthur Hildersham. And we have already noticed the remarkable gift of sixpence for Timothy, Hildersham's thought-to-be disabled son, on December 24, 1629.[35] Such a gift may have been only a gesture, but on behalf of the whole community, the overseers were thus able to demonstrate that they shared a sense of mutual responsibility for Timothy's welfare. It was a way of giving something back, however symbolically, to the minister who had labored for the good of Ashby's needy for so many years.

The years between 1613 and 1625, then, were difficult years for Hildersham, and undoubtedly he suffered much because he could no longer preach God's Word to his congregation. However, by the time of Hildersham's suspension as vicar in 1605, he had already delivered hundreds of lectures and sermons in the town, and the townspeople had not forgotten the truths he had proclaimed. He had earned the love and respect of his parishioners and, by performing the daily functions of his ministerial office—baptizing, marrying, burying, praying, catechizing—for twelve years, he had become part of the very fabric of society. In the minds of many, and not only those who shared his religious opinions, he remained their *de facto* pastor, and his successors were regarded in some sense as merely temporary appointments, keeping the place warm until he could be reinstated. But it was the ordinary details of his personal life and devotions, his "secular" activities and the relationships he fostered with his neighbors, that God used to sustain his extraordinary influence in Ashby even when he was silenced. Hildersham's life teaches us not to despise the ability of small and quiet things like daily routines, domestic duties, service to our neighbors, and a faithful personal witness over many years to produce fruit for God's kingdom and glory to His name.

---

34. About 450 pounds in 2010 values.
35. See chapter 4. This was about 2.23 pounds in 2010 values.

Chapter 11

"The Evil Day"
(1615–1625)

While Hildersham was attempting to carry on peaceably with his quiet service of the local people in Ashby, more troubles were brewing after 1613. The repercussions of the 1614 Easter Communion did not end with the visitation of 1615. In the Easter term of that year, Hildersham was again summoned to appear before the High Commission in London. Because he refused to swear the *ex officio* oath (as many Puritans did, for it was used to trap them into incriminating themselves), he was sent to the Fleet prison, where he remained for several weeks until he was transferred to the King's Bench prison. The Fleet was a notorious prison on the east bank of the Fleet River, built in 1197. The King's Bench was situated in Southwark, south of the Thames. Both prisons were dirty, overcrowded, and prone to outbreaks of infectious diseases. Hildersham was imprisoned for three months before being released on license to appear again before the High Commission Court. However, a serious sickness prevented this court appearance in the Michaelmas Term of 1615, and the court received a sworn affidavit to this purpose.

In the following autumn, the High Commissioners—led by Dr. Lamb, Mr. Owen, and Mr. Middleton—traveled to Ashby. There, on September 4, 5, and 6 of 1616, they heard witnesses giving evidence against Hildersham, Thomas Dighton, and John Holt. The three men were charged with espousing nonconformist views and holding conventicles.[1] We have already heard how the vicar of Ashby, Thomas Hacket, was their principal adversary and how outsiders like George Reding were drafted in to give false evidence against Hildersham. In the next legal term, the cause was heard and sentenced in London. Dighton and Holt appeared first to learn their sentence on November 21, 1616. It was a punitive one; they were to be sent back to prison, where they were to remain until they conformed. In addition, the High Commission ordered that they be fined 1,500 pounds each, excommunicated, and publicly denounced.[2] To be reinstated, they would have to make their submissions by reading a prepared form of words in three separate public places. They would also have to pay all the legal costs and expenses of the case.

When Hildersham heard of Dighton's and Holt's sentence, he went into hiding and did not appear at the court on the day when his own sentence was due to be pronounced. Eight days before that date, he sent a written copy of his answers to the points made against him to his advocate, Dr. Hussey. On November 28, 1616, the court pronounced the following judgment on Hildersham in his absence: he was "a man refractory and disobedient to the orders, rites and ceremonies of the Church of England," and since he refused to submit himself and join in "the administration of public prayer and divine service and sacraments as they are here administered" he was deemed "a schismatical person and a schismatic, and thought well worthy of severe punishment." As "the prime ring-leader of all the schismatical persons in that country [county or locality], both of the clergy and the laity," the commissioners had decided to make a public example of him. He was fined two thousand pounds (for "his Majesty's use"), and, like Dighton and Holt, it was ordered that he be excommunicated and publicly denounced.[3] It was also ordered that Hildersham be committed to prison and brought

---

1. Dr. Williams's Library, Morrice MSS, LMN, 8, "Proceedings against Arthur Hildersham, Thomas Dighton and John Holt" before the High Commission, including "2. Copy of the [blank] against Dighton and Holt, for holding conventicles etc at Ashby-de-la-Zouch (21 Nov. 1616)," f. 2a.

2. According to the currency converter of the National Archives, this would be about 144,000 pounds in 2010 values.

3. About 192,000 pounds in 2010 values.

before the commissioners to be degraded from the ministry and to make a verbal submission.[4]

Hildersham was a wanted man. From November 1616, he had to conceal himself from the authorities and keep moving from place to place in case he was apprehended. Clarke tells us that "God sheltered him under the shadow of His wings that his adversaries could not meet with him."[5] In the providence of God, Arthur had many friends and supporters throughout the country who were glad to provide refuge in their homes, particularly in London, where many were sympathetic to the Puritan cause and underground networks of supporters existed. With its system of lectureships established in many areas and connections to its political supporters in Parliament and at court, London remained the epicenter of a national Puritan brotherhood. Stephen Egerton, the co-organizer of the Millenary Petition, was a close friend of his and one of the leading Puritan ministers in the city. His parish of St. Anne's, Blackfriars, was famed for its support of Puritanism and had a succession of godly ministers. Egerton, who had been at Blackfriars since 1583, gave up his lectureship there in 1607 due to his nonconformity but continued as curate until his death in 1622. It was Hildersham, in conversation with some of the leading inhabitants of the parish in 1608, who recommended the services of William Gouge, "whom he judged to be very fit for them," as a preaching minister.[6] Gouge, a more moderate nonconformist, remained at Blackfriars until 1653.

This episode demonstrates Hildersham's familiarity with affairs in London as well as his wide network of contacts, which included the circle around Prince Henry, son of James I and heir to the throne. This young man took a serious interest in the things of God and for a brief time offered hope for the future before his untimely death in 1612 at the age of eighteen. One of the links here was Sir Robert Darcy, a knight from Kent who had married Alexander Rediche's elder daughter, Grace. Darcy, who was renowned for his piety and extensive library of theological works, was in great favor with the prince. On hearing Thomas Gataker, a young

---

4. Clarke, "Life of Hildersam," 150.
5. Clarke, "Life of Hildersam," 150.
6. Clarke, "Life and Death of Dr. Gouge," 238.

lecturer at Lincoln's Inn, preach one day, Darcy and his friend Lord Harrington were impressed. They got hold of Gataker's sermon notes and showed them to Prince Henry, who was then keeping his court at St James's. In response, Henry invited Gataker to come and preach before him and used Gataker's "worthy friend Mr. Hildersham" to convey and press the invitation. But Gataker felt too bashful to accept.[7]

After the High Commission's judgment in 1616, Hildersham spent a lot of time sheltering in the Hampstead home of Katharine Rediche, who, with her husband, was one of Hildersham's most faithful patrons. It was probably there that the only surviving oil portrait of Hildersham was commissioned in 1619. Katharine's husband, Alexander, described by Clarke as Hildersham's "bosom friend," had died at the age of forty-nine in 1613. The main seat of the Rediche family was at Newhall in Derbyshire, just over the border from Ashby and very close to Burton-on-Trent, where Hildersham lectured, and Stapenhill, the site of one of Darrell's famous exorcisms. Alexander Rediche, from an ancient Lancashire family and born in the same month as Hildersham himself, had married Katharine Dethicke of Newhall, who had become her father's heir when her brother Francis had died without issue. Katharine's mother, Elizabeth, came from the renowned Longford family, and her elder sister Matilda (or Magdalen) had married Sir Francis Hastings in 1567. Elizabeth herself was to marry a second time after the death of Katharine's father, Humfrey Dethicke, in December 1599; her new husband was Lord Edward Ferrars. Unlike her sister and her daughter, Lady Ferrars was a staunch papist and a hater of the Puritan cause. However, her obdurate refusal to stay at her daughter's house at Newhall when William Bradshaw was lodging there was finally broken down by his "mild and moderate demeanor, and his meek, kind and lowly carriage." Eventually she became a keen hearer of his sermons.

The Rediches are usually remembered as the patrons of William Bradshaw, but Hildersham had enjoyed their favor for many years prior to this and, in fact, introduced the younger man to them. After Bradshaw's death in 1618, Hildersham continued his close friendship with

---

7. Thomas Gataker, *A Discours Apologetical* (London, 1654), 37.

Katharine Rediche. In 1632 she outlived him by only eight days, "the grief for his death hastening (as it was supposed) her end." Gataker, Bradshaw's biographer, who was aided by Bradshaw's son John and Samuel Hildersham in drawing up his account, describes Katharine as "a very tender-hearted gentlewoman, much addicted to hospitality, and of very remarkable devotion and piety, reported by those who were inwardly acquainted with her more retired courses, to have been wont constantly to spend privately twice a day, at several set times an hour at least, in meditation and prayer mixed oft with many tears." Gataker gives us a detailed picture of a godly household that organized its day around spiritual exercises at set times, including two preaching services every Sunday in the chapel, which Bradshaw conducted when he was in residence. Hildersham doubtless did the same during his frequent stays with the family. It was very useful for him to have a place of escape to which he could fly in difficult times, just over the county and diocesan boundary. Although Alexander made no bequest to Hildersham in his will, it is clear that he gave him generous financial support during his lifetime. A 1609 arrangement made through Richard Hildersham, Arthur's beloved and trusted brother (and witnessed by Ezekiel Culverwell), gave over for Arthur's benefit the lease of lands and tenements in the parish of Redich, Lancashire, valued at three hundred pounds, for sixty years. A farm in Stanton Mead, assigned to Richard and his son Thomas in Arthur's will, may also have been a gift from the Rediche family.

Hildersham, for his part, was able to offer great spiritual and practical help to the Rediche family. He was the executor of Alexander's will and offered technical and legal assistance to the widowed Katharine. In the complex arrangements surrounding the marriage of her younger daughter Sarah to Clement Coke, son of Edward Coke, the Lord Chief Justice, Hildersham acted on Katharine's behalf in the assignment of certain manors in Derbyshire, Nottinghamshire, Leicestershire, Staffordshire, and Warwickshire.[8] Wherever he stayed, Hildersham helped with household prayers and gave spiritual encouragement to his hosts, just as if he had been at home with his own family.

---

8. John Rylands University Library CRU/65, March 28, 1614.

It was at Katharine Rediche's home in London that, in August 1624, Hildersham fell seriously ill with a fever from which the physicians feared he would not recover. He himself heard the sad whispers of his impending death from those gathered around his bed. Later, however, when he thought he was alone in the room, with the curtains drawn around the bed, someone overheard him utter the words of Psalm 118:17: "I shall not die, but live, and declare the works of the LORD." At that time there seemed little prospect either of his bodily recovery or of his preaching again, but God in His mercy had obviously given him an assurance on both counts. Soon afterwards Hildersham was restored to both his health and his pulpit. During this time of concealment, around 1616, Hildersham had received overtures from the English congregation in Leiden, Holland, to become their pastor. One of the elders, John Hartly, was sent over with letters from the church to find him. Hildersham seriously considered the offer, for this would have been a way out of his difficulties in England and would have provided him the opportunity once again to exercise his calling as a preacher and pastor. The Netherlands supplied a safe haven for many English nonconformists over the years—men like William Ames and Thomas Hooker—and Hildersham had many contacts there, including Willem Teellinck. As noted previously, Clarke tells us that Hildersham would have accepted the invitation if his wife had not been so unwilling to go overseas. The whole question of whether nonconformists should stay in England and face the increasing persecution directed at them as the century progressed or flee abroad where they could worship freely according to their consciences became the subject of great debate in godly circles. We will return to it in due course.

Transactions like the one Alexander Rediche had made in 1609 through Richard Hildersham may help to explain why, when the High Commission was seeking to confiscate Hildersham's assets in pursuit of the fine imposed upon him in 1616, inquiries about his financial estate in the Leicestershire area came back with the answer that "they could find none."[9] Legally, the money was Richard's and not Arthur's, but the former was only too glad to transfer the money to Arthur when

---

9. Clarke, "Life of Hildersam," 150.

he needed it. Richard was able to act on his brother's behalf in legal and financial transactions when Arthur was persona non grata. Sometime between 1618 and 1623, Hildersham managed to obtain a discharge from his fine of two thousand pounds by coming to an arrangement with an official in the Marquis (later Duke) of Buckingham's household and with the registrars of the High Commission itself. This involved parting with "a great sum of money."[10] Clarke commented, "I suppose it will be hard to find that any man was before, or scarce has been since, in that court, so deeply fined and heavily censured, merely for his judgment and conscience, having done nothing either factiously or contemptuously against that government and those orders of the church that were then established."[11]

As we have seen, Hildersham was not absent from Ashby during all of the time from 1616 to 1625, but frequently made visits to the town, where his wife and family still had their residence. In fact, he was probably away only for the greater part of two years, from about 1616 to 1618. He was in Ashby enough to strike up some sort of relationship with Thomas Pestell, who had succeeded Thomas Hacket as vicar. Thomas Pestell was instituted as vicar in December 1616 and was completely different from the man he replaced. We may know him as the author of the Christmas hymn "Behold the Great Creator Makes Himself a House of Clay," but he was a complex and contradictory personality.[12] The historian Christopher Haigh has painted a masterful portrait of Pestell, a man he describes as "arrogant, embittered, and ill-tempered but humane, sensitive and brave."[13] To Haigh, Pestell was "a more worldly and ambitious George Herbert, with a chip on his shoulder." It is certainly difficult to categorize Pestell, for he was neither Puritan nor high church—he showed sympathies for both poles at various times. He was undoubtedly a conformist, but unlike Hacket, his approach was less confrontational and more pragmatic. He was prepared to reason with Ashby's nonconformists

---

10. Clarke, "Life of Hildersam," 150.

11. Clarke, "Life of Hildersam," 150.

12. In *Christian Hymns*, ed. Paul E. G. Cook, Graham Harrison, and Evangelical Movement of Wales (Bridgend: Evangelical Movement of Wales, 1977), no. 163.

13. Christopher Haigh, "The Troubles of Thomas Pestell: Parish Squabbles and Ecclesiastical Politics in Caroline England," *Journal of British Studies* 41 (October 2002): 403–28.

and give them time to conform themselves. Certainly, the numbers being presented for nonconformity in the annual visitations gradually decreased under his ministry, but there are other possible reasons for this in addition to his more patient handling of affairs. Some nonconformists simply stayed away from St. Helen's on occasions when the ceremonies would be used, while others played for time. Margery Burrows, wife of the earl's bailiff John Burrows, for example, was happy to engage in prolonged conference with Pestell about her nonconformity but absented herself from Communion services at Ashby, choosing to receive elsewhere so that she could remain sitting or standing.[14] John Armeson and his wife had their baby christened at the chapel in Blackfordby in 1616 in a basin by an "unconformed" minister, Mr. Hanley from Derbyshire, with no sign of the cross and no churching (a ceremony to cleanse women following childbirth) afterwards.[15] John Bentley and his wife followed a similar course with their infant, also in 1616.[16]

Pestell was moved to the earl's nearby benefice of Packington in 1622. Haigh suggests that this may have been to "facilitate Hildersham's return, to work in tandem with a vicar more willing to tolerate nonconformity than Pestell had been."[17] Whatever the case, there was still ample opportunity for the two men to become acquainted, since Packington was only a couple of miles from Ashby. Pestell's lavish poetic tribute on Hildersham's death in 1632 suggests that by this time he had come to regard Hildersham as a true friend.[18] Calling Hildersham "Ashby's lamp," Pestell praises his wisdom, holiness, nobility, and learning but especially his counseling activities, his treatment of the poor, and his capacity for friendship. Above all, the consistency of Hildersham's life, which Pestell describes in metaphorical terms as "a woven robe, without a seam," stands out from the epitaph. Although by this stage Pestell had

---

14. Leicestershire Record Office ID41/13/39–40. Haigh also discusses this case in some detail.

15. Leicestershire Record Office ID 41/13/42 f. 3r.

16. Leicestershire Record Office ID 41/13/42 f. 20r.

17. Haigh, "Troubles of Thomas Pestell," 420.

18. Thomas Pestell, "Epitaph on Mr. Hildersham 1632," from *The Poems of Thomas Pestell*, ed. H. Buchan (Oxford: Blackwell, 1940), 10. For the full text of the poem, see the appendix.

fallen out with the earl, some of his parishioners, and the new vicar of Ashby (Anthony Watson), it is significant that a measure of mutual respect, even friendship, continued to exist between him and Hildersham despite their different shades of spiritual opinion.

Anthony Watson, who replaced Pestell in 1622, was the last vicar of Ashby to serve in Hildersham's lifetime. The nonconformists regarded him as a friend because he was prepared to tolerate their position, and they certainly took his side in his disputes with Pestell. Again, it says much about Hildersham that he managed to retain the goodwill of both Pestell and Watson. We will hear more about Hildersham and Watson's relationship in due course.

During these years Hildersham suffered his most severe trials. He endured prison and critical illness, he was on the run from the authorities, and he faced economic ruination. Perhaps worst of all were the slanders against his reputation and ministry that prevented him from preaching. On a wider stage, too, these years brought many setbacks for the Puritans. The young heir to the throne, Prince Henry, who had promised so much for the future, had died in 1612. Frederick, the Protestant king of Bohemia, had been dethroned after his defeat by Catholic forces at the Battle of White Mountain on November 8, 1620. There were plans to obtain a Spanish Catholic bride for Prince Charles. The rise of a vibrant Arminianism had caused Calvinists to defend and define their position at the Synod of Dort in 1618–1619, and in England Arminians and Laudians continued to be appointed to positions of church and state authority in increasing numbers.

How did Hildersham manage to endure these dark and difficult days? We have already seen how he had exhorted his congregation to prepare themselves for affliction, and he went on to draw similar lessons in his lecture series on Psalm 51. He devoted five sermons, delivered between February 27 and April 17, 1627, to the subject of bearing trials with true patience.[19] These sermons, which are rich with scriptural examples, also give us insight into how Hildersham himself faced the troubles that befell him. His congregation would have known that his own experience

---

19. Hildersham, *Lectures upon Psalm 51*, 250–74. All the following quotations are taken from these pages.

informed every word he spoke. Hildersham explained that true patience in affliction came from understanding that every "cross that befalleth us, is from God, that He hath a special hand and providence in it." True patience was a fruit of obedience to the divine will, which would "make a man more desirous to profit by his affliction than to be rid of it." Like Jacob in Genesis 32:26, "we should be unwilling that God, when He hath been wrestling and striving with us by His corrections, should depart from us, till He have left a blessing behind Him." For, went on Hildersham, "no wise man will desire to get from under the Surgeon's hand, till he be cured of his wound or past all danger." Understanding that God had a purpose for good, even in suffering, was "not the way to undo a man, or to make him miserable," but was "the way to lighten our crosses."

The knowledge that God was with His people was a great source of encouragement: "The Lord when He hath brought His people into the briars of affliction, leaveth them not there, but He will be sure to be with them, in all their troubles, and never showeth Himself to be more graciously present with them, than when they are in that case. *I will be with him in trouble* saith the Lord, Ps. 91:15." "And," Hildersham continued, "though God do discover [show] their weakness to them, and they feel themselves ready to faint, yet even then He will strengthen them." Indeed, this was so true that "they have been able to say they never felt His strength more in sustaining them than when they have felt themselves most weak."

Hildersham proceeded to give eight means "for obtaining this grace to bear the cross patiently, to bear all kind of affliction patiently and comfortably, whensoever God shall be pleased to exercise us by it." These means are of such practical use in facing trouble patiently that it is good to look at them in some detail:

1. "Oft think upon it and expect it, and prepare for it before it come." Hildersham advised, "God's people should in the time of their best health think oft of death, in the time of their greatest peace and prosperity think oft of trouble." For, "it would season all our pleasures and earthly contentments, so as we should not surfeit, nor take any harm by them, so much as we usually do." In addition, "it would have great force to restrain us from sin, and breed in us a care to please the Lord in all our ways."

2. Beforehand, a man must "labour to wean his heart from the love of all earthly things, and inure himself to bear patiently those ordinary losses and crosses that he is subject to in them.... If we would therefore make ourselves fit, either to die willingly, or to endure persecution and trouble patiently and comfortably, we must take heed of setting our hearts upon any earthly comfort, of admiring and affecting it too much, and labour to bring our hearts to a more mean conceit of these things, to be more indifferently affected towards them."

3. In advance a man "must acquaint himself well with the Word of God, he must be well seen and exercised in it.... And indeed," this was one of the main reasons "why the Lord hath given us His Holy Word in writing that by it He might prepare us for affliction, and breed true patience and comfort in us." In Revelation 3:10, God "giveth this title to His Holy Word, He calleth it the Word of His patience." Job had proved that "no food (no not my necessary food) did ever so sustain, and strengthen me, so refresh and revive my fainting body, as the Word of God, hath my soul in all my afflictions" (Job 23:12). Hildersham declared, "The remembrance of one sentence of Holy Scripture, will be more effectual to yield us comfort in the evil day, in the hour of temptation, will have more force to repel Satan in his fiercest assaults, than is in all the wisdom of the world, in all the counsel of our friends, that shall be then about us."

4. A man "must labour to get a true knowledge and sense of his own sins." For "poverty of spirit, sight, and sense of sin will cause mourning, and humiliation, and these two will make us as meek as lambs under the corrections of the Lord.... If we knew our sins well, and were truly humbled for them," Hildersham explained, referencing Psalm 103:10, "we would easily acknowledge that that which we endure is nothing to that we have deserved at God's hands."

5. Before the time of trial comes, a man "must get a true and lively faith, even a comfortable assurance of his reconciliation with God through Jesus Christ. This power that there is in faith, to make a man able patiently, and comfortably to bear afflictions,

of what kind or degree soever they be, is plentifully taught in
the Holy Scriptures, and confirmed to us by the experience of
the saints of God." Ephesians 6:15 means that "once we are
assured of our peace and reconciliation with God, which is
wrought by the gospel, then are we prepared to follow Christ
through thick and thin, through the most hard and stony, the
most sharp and thorny way, of any persecution, and trouble
whatsoever." The faith that the saints and martyrs "had in the
blood of Christ, which was sprinkled upon their hearts, made
them able to bear, and overcome so bitter torments as they did
endure; and so will it certainly do any of us in the like case."
Therefore, continued Hildersham, "shall we that have enjoyed
so many months, and years, of great prosperity and comfort,
think much to endure affliction and trouble for a few days?...
When we are once assured God is our Father," he declared, "we
shall be made well content to take the bitterest potion from
His hand." Faith "makes the heart that hath it, undoubtedly
certain of those promises God hath made to His people in
their afflictions," that they "shall tend to our good in the end,"
and that "He will not forsake us in them, but assist and support us." He that was sure of these promises could say with
David, "In God I have put my trust; I will not fear what flesh
can do unto me" (Ps. 56:4). Hildersham exhorted his hearers
that "seeing faith will stand us in that stead in the evil day, and
yield us that strength and comfort in all afflictions, it standeth
us upon, to get in time, and to look well to ourselves, that that
faith we think we have, be such as will abide the trial in the
furnace of affliction, such as will not deceive us in the evil day."
For "in the evil day, Satan will be apt to cast into men's souls his
darts of desperation, his fiery darts, as the apostle calleth them.
And what is it that will quench these darts? Surely nothing but
faith, as the apostle teacheth [in] Ephes. 6:16." Hildersham
spoke words to comfort "the weakest soul among you...that
because of the weakness of thy faith tremblest when thou hear-
est of the troublesome times we are to look for, tremblest when
thou thinkest of death; oh, sayest thou, I shall never be able to
endure in the evil day." To them he urged, "Be thou of good
comfort, certainly if thou hast the least measure and degree

of true faith in thee, thou shalt be able to bear troubles when they come, much more patiently and comfortably than thou thinkest." They should be assured that God would not overcharge them with things they could not bear, and in the day of trial it was only the Lord's strength, not their own, that would enable them to stand. For "the Lord delighteth to show His might most in them that are weakest in their own sense, 2 Cor. 12:19.... In the deepest sense of thine own weakness," Hildersham stressed, "learn to fly out of thyself, and to rely wholly upon the Lord, and on the power of His might."

6. We have the hope of going to heaven when we die. For "he that knoweth death is the worst that can befall him, in the most troublesome times, and that death will make him a happy man, as Pro. 23:18 [says]...that man needs be patient and comfortable in any affliction that can befall him." Hildersham asked, "What maketh God's people, not only patient, but even so comfortable, and full of joy in all tribulations? Surely the hope they have of the glory that is prepared for them, they know the end will pay for all." For "worldlings to rage and take on, when they must lose their life, or their peace, or their wealth, it is no marvel; for alas, when these things are gone, they have nothing left, they are quite undone; but a Christian that knoweth, and considereth what he is born unto, and what he shall enjoy when he comes home, so soon as he dieth, he cannot do so."

7. We "must be careful beforehand to lead a godly life, and to get a good conscience." Then "when the evil day shall come, the godly man shall find his labour hath not been in vain, he shall certainly find more strength and comfort in that day than any other man can do." Faithful preachers like Jeremiah could be assured that "God will not be a terror to such ministers, but their hope and comfort in the evil day." But Hildersham warned others, "O think of this, you that are so careless of your practice, careless of your consciences, whose religion standeth only in hearing and in a profession of the truth; certainly when the evil day shall come, you will be found to be foolish builders that have built upon the sand, when the rain shall fall, and the winds blow, and the floods beat upon you, when great troubles

and afflictions shall come upon you, you will never be able to stand out, you must needs fall, and sink under them, and your fall will be great as our Saviour speaketh there, Matt. 7:26–27."

8. Prayer strengthens us in trials. "Instant and earnest prayer and continuing in it, is the means to make us patient in tribulation" (see Rom. 12:12). It was the principle part of the armor in Ephesians 6:18, and had been proved by men like Job and David. Hildersham concluded by saying, "Let me apply this in a word or two. (1) Would you know the true cause you have so little patience, surely it is because you do pray so little. (2) Let the signs God giveth us every day of marvellous troublesome times that are at hand, make us all more frequent and fervent in prayer. (3) We should call upon and exhort God's people to fasting and prayer. Is there any such means either to stand in the gap, and keep out God's judgments, or to prepare us with patience and strength to bear them, as fasting and prayer is? Well, take this for a conclusion to your comfort which you shall read, Acts 2:20–21. When the sun shall be turned into darkness, and the moon into blood, when the darkest and saddest times shall come that can come, yet it shall come to pass, that whosoever shall call upon the name of the Lord, shall be saved. He that can pray shall do well enough."

~⊂⊙⊃~

Chapter 12

The Final Years
(1625–1632)

James I and VI, king of England and Scotland, died on March 27, 1625, and was succeeded by his son Charles I. On June 20, 1625, three months after James's death, Dr. Ridley relicensed Hildersham (now aged sixty-one) to preach in the dioceses of London, Lincoln, and Coventry and Lichfield. Ridley was Archbishop Abbot's vicar-general. Abbot himself was a moderate Calvinist but had been unable to do anything for Hildersham while the old king lived, for, as he reported to Arthur's patron, the fifth earl of Huntingdon, "he [Hildersham] is a person whom his Highness hath particularly in observation." Within a few weeks of Hildersham's relicensing, which enabled him to return to his duties as lecturer (but not vicar) of Ashby after a break of twelve years, a national fast had been proclaimed. We need to understand a bit of the background to this situation in which Hildersham found himself on his return to preaching in Ashby.

Plague Summer

During the late spring and summer of 1625, shortly after the accession of Charles I, a serious outbreak of plague occurred in London. The sickness quickly spread to all parts of the city, and by June 25, orders were given for Parliament to be suspended and moved to Oxford. Apprehension soon infected other parts of the country, too. People feared that tradesmen and refugees from London would transmit disease into outlying towns and districts. In this climate of snowballing panic came an official proclamation on July 3 from the palace at Whitehall of a "public, general and solemn fast" to be held throughout the land on Wednesday, July 20, 1625, and every Wednesday following, as long as the plague lasted.[1] To ensure that the fast was properly observed, a service book was also issued, titled *A Form of Common Prayer, Together with an Order of Fasting.*

Although we cannot imagine our government today ordering a time of fasting and prayer during a period of national crisis, in Elizabethan and Stuart England it was almost a standard reaction. Elizabeth I, for example, had commanded a national fast during an outbreak of plague in 1563, and James I had acted similarly in the plague year of 1603. In addition to this particular fast in 1625, Charles I went on to order three more fasts during the first five years of his reign. The Elizabethan *Book of Homilies,* devised by Cranmer, contained a sermon on fasting that set out the need for such a response: "When God shall afflict a whole region or country with wars, with famine, with pestilence, with strange diseases and unknown sicknesses, and other such like calamities: then is it time for all states and sorts of people, high and low, men, women, and children, to humble themselves by fasting, and bewail their sinful living before God, and pray with one common voice."[2] Society as a whole held that natural disasters and wars were to be regarded as a sign of God's judgments upon a sinful land. This idea was reinforced from the pulpit, where preachers used Old Testament examples to show that such heavy providences could be averted, or at least ameliorated, by a corporate demonstration of repentance and humiliation during a period of national fasting. As in the case of King Ahab, the demonstration might induce God "to alter the thing which He had purposed concerning him" by way of punishment.[3] Hildersham, too, used Ahab's example to explain that "the prayers of the people...have even overcome Him to change His mind, and put up His sword."[4] King David, in 2 Samuel 24:17, was often

---

1. *Calendar of State Papers, Domestic Series, Charles I 1625–1626* (London: Her Majesty's Stationery Office, 1858), 48. For the full text of the proclamation, see J. F. Larkin, ed., *Stuart Royal Proclamations* (Oxford, 1983), 2:46–48.

2. *Sermons or Homilies to Be Read in Churches in the Time of Queen Elizabeth* (London, 1817), 268.

3. *Homilies,* 269.

4. Hildersham, *Fasting and Prayer,* 32.

cited as the prime model for penitence: "So King David in the time of plague and pestilence which ensued upon his vain numbering of the people prayed unto God with wonderful fervency, confessing his fault, desiring God to spare the people, and rather to turn His ire to himward, who had chiefly offended in that transgression."[5]

Although there was general agreement that a fast was necessary to turn away God's wrath, not everyone had the same ideas about what constituted true fasting. Many saw fasting as something that occurred on set days in the church calendar, notably during Lent, which required the observance of special rules, such as the abstaining from particular foods and activities for fixed periods. For the Puritans, the emphasis was less on outer ritual and more on prayer and a deep inner humiliation for sin. Puritan fasts became times for assembling to hear God's Word preached and seek His face together in an atmosphere of mourning and prayerfulness. Days of fasting were very special to the Puritans, but the authorities were increasingly suspicious of such gatherings, particularly when they became associated with exorcism in the 1590s. The great era of public godly fasting was thus brought to an end when unauthorized fasting was outlawed in the canons of 1604. There is evidence that the godly did not abandon communal fasting completely after this, with or without the licensing of a sympathetic bishop. However, it tended to be in smaller groups, and less frequently, so as not to attract the attention of the authorities.

In the 1620s, the godly Calvinists in the Church of England faced increasing tension. With the rising influence in both church and state of Arminians and Laudians, who favored ceremony and ritual, many Puritans were feeling marginalized and defensive. In addition to rejecting the Puritans' type of spirituality, their opponents also implicitly challenged their loyalty to the Crown and the Church of England. However, the godly were eager to demonstrate their allegiance and support for both institutions. The declaration of a national fast, then, at the beginning of a new reign, provided an ideal opportunity for the Puritans to show their wholehearted support of the king's actions in an exercise of which they

---

5. Preface to *A Form of Common Prayer*.

entirely approved. But they had to be careful: if they went too far or did not follow the rules, they were in danger of being branded as radicals, out of step with the national consensus.

For Hildersham, this balance between opportunity and trial was especially delicate. When he stepped into the pulpit in St. Helen's Church, Ashby, on the fast day of Wednesday, August 3, 1625, all eyes were upon him. They would have seen a rather gaunt, thin-faced man, with close-cropped greying hair and a neat beard, dressed in sober black clothes. No doubt the church was full, despite its being a weekday morning, with people eager to hear this great man preach again after so many years of silence. Attendance at the fast was obligatory by law for everyone, except those who could not be excused from their necessary duties. For his text, Hildersham chose not one, but two, psalms of David for his preaching material at the fast. The first was Psalm 35:13 ("But as for me, when they were sick, my clothing was sackcloth: I humbled myself with fasting; and my prayer returned into mine own bosom"). Although this particular psalm was not listed in the fast's official schedule of Bible passages and thus seems to have been Hildersham's personal selection, its relevance to fasting is obvious. Hildersham delivered eight lectures on this verse between August 3, 1625, and August 2, 1626, and his son Samuel eventually published the series posthumously in 1633 under the title *The Doctrine of Fasting and Prayer, and Humiliation for Sin.* Interestingly, in this verse David was not fasting because of his own sins but those of his enemies, which had caused them to be struck down with sickness. And so Hildersham, in the introductory part of his first sermon, cites David not as a model of repentance but as a "type of Christ," praying for his enemies.

Hildersham used the example of David's fasting and praying for his enemies as a means to engage his congregation in the national fast. From this first sermon, it is obvious that many in Ashby felt that a plague raging in London had very little to do with them. Although nearby Leicester was badly affected, Ashby seems to have remained largely plague-free, at least in the early summer of 1625. (Indeed, as we have seen, Hildersham, along with other leading citizens of Ashby, had written to the mayor of Leicester to assure him of that fact in June 1625.) The distance of Ashby from London, the apparent lack of plague in Ashby itself, and a reliance on human precautions lulled many into a sense of personal security, as they argued: "I am far enough from London; I dwell in a good air, and we have taken good order to prevent all danger of this infectious disease; no carriers shall come from thence to us, no Londoners shall lodge amongst us."[6] But the example of David, who was affected by the sickness of his enemies, allowed Hildersham to declare this doctrine to his hearers: "God's people ought to take to heart the miseries and calamities of others, the judgments of God that do befall others."[7] For, said Hildersham, these plague victims in London were not their enemies, even, but their fellow countrymen and, in many instances, their own flesh and blood. If David could pray for his enemies, surely they should be interceding for their brethren. Besides, they, too, could be struck down by plague. Hildersham warned his listeners against complacency; he drew a sobering picture of the sudden onset, the effects, and the unpredictable nature of the sickness, of people "dying in the streets and high-ways" with friends afraid to attend them. Those suffering were not greater sinners than the folk in Ashby, he went on, and besides, God sometimes afflicted some to warn all of impending judgment.

Hildersham was aware that many unconverted people who were not often in church were in the congregation on the occasion of the fast, so he was determined to challenge them. He observed, "Many have joined with us, whose persons God never yet accepted."[8] Later he asserted, "Many of you never yet had any comfort in God, in the assurance of the pardon of your sins, never found sweetnesses in Christ nor in God's promises."[9] In an evangelistic thrust that took in all of his hearers, Hildersham declared that no one should think he could fly from God's judgment if he had not removed the cause of it, namely sin, from his own life. "It behooves us," urged Hildersham, "without delay…by all means to make our peace with God, and to seek reconciliation with Him. This and this only is the way unto true safety and comfort." And, he continued, "Now is the time to do it, if ever we will do it, now that His hand is so stretched out against us." Hildersham then proceeded to

6. Hildersham, *Fasting and Prayer*, 11.

7. Hildersham, *Fasting and Prayer*, 2.

8. Hildersham, *Fasting and Prayer*, 43–44.

9. Hildersham, *Fasting and Prayer*, 93.

explain the three things that must be done to achieve that peace with God: a full and free confession of sin, an unfeigned resolution to forsake sin, and a striving "by a living faith...to lay hold on God's mercy in Christ, and to get His blood sprinkled upon thy heart."[10]

Repentance was needed both on an individual and a corporate level, for the judgment of God was upon the entire nation: "He is angry, and not with the Londoners only, but with us, with the whole land... it may be more with us than them."[11] Having examined the particular sins for which the Israelites were punished by plague throughout the Old Testament, Hildersham concluded, "It is evident that we and our nation are guilty of all these sins." The catalogue includes ingratitude for past mercies, especially for "our deliverance out of that spiritual Egypt" (by which he meant Catholicism, and England's turning from it at the time of the Reformation); contempt for the ministry of the Word; sexual immorality, which "doth everywhere so increase and abound in our land"; reliance on human strength; indiscriminate reception of the Lord's Supper; neglect of public worship; and hearts that had become hardened against previous judgments. It is sobering to reflect on how much more abundant all these sins are in the present day; we can only continue to plead for God's mercy on our nations.

Some of the godly brethren who usually frequented Hildersham's lectures and attended fast days felt uncomfortable that "many of these lewd men that are guilty of these foul sins, intrude themselves into our assemblies, and join with us in these holy duties."[12] "And," Hildersham agreed, "we know that the sacrifice of the wicked is an abomination unto the Lord."[13] However, he explained to these unhappy believers that although the unconverted should not attempt private fasting, in "public and general calamities they may be enjoined to keep a fast that have no measure of grace in them."[14] Indeed, he goes on, "It hath greatly furthered the efficacy of the prayers of God's own people, when all have

---

10. Hildersham, *Fasting and Prayer*, 21–22.
11. Hildersham, *Fasting and Prayer*, 15.
12. Hildersham, *Fasting and Prayer*, 47.
13. Hildersham, *Fasting and Prayer*, 47.
14. Hildersham, *Fasting and Prayer*, 56.

come (tag and rag, as we may say) to join with them in this service."[15] For although the fullest spiritual blessings were reserved for believers, in a limited and temporal way "God hath oft had respect to the cries even of such as have no truth or grace." Taking to heart God's judgments, professing their humility, and obeying the commandment of the temporal authorities to attend the fast were all "good things" that demonstrated the "remainder of God's image" even in the ungodly—something God loved to see. Besides, as we have noted, Hildersham's desire was that the ungodly and hypocritical people present would be converted. At times of divine "grievous visitation," he explained, "we find by experience that…a faithful minister may much better work upon the hearts of men to bring them to repentance than at another time." People should learn to interpret the signs aright, for "every judgment of God hath a voice, and is a real sermon of repentance." Indeed, Hildersham concluded, "Certainly if in such a time the Word do not work upon men's hearts, it will never do them good."[16]

Hildersham admonished his hearers that a failure to heed the current warning of plague could result in England's receiving the greater judgment from which it had so far been spared—"I mean war."[17] Failing to deal with sin was the offense of Achan, which resulted in the whole community remaining under God's wrath until the offenses were discovered and punished (as in Joshua 7:1–26). However, this communal repentance could only be achieved if every individual searched his own conscience before God: "We know not the meaning of plague, nor make right use of it, unless everyone of us enters into his own heart, and says, what have I done?"[18]

Having engaged his listeners with the current situation and demonstrated the need for each one to be involved, Hildersham moved on after the first couple of sermons to a detailed explanation of what true repentance and prayer entails. Even the bodily exercise of fasting, defined and described in sermons 3 and 4, was shown merely to be a means to the

---

15. Hildersham, *Fasting and Prayer*, 63.
16. Hildersham, *Fasting and Prayer*, 6, 117.
17. Hildersham, *Fasting and Prayer*, 14.
18. Hildersham, *Fasting and Prayer*, 5.

end of genuine humiliation for sin. What this unfeigned mourning for sin consists of is outlined in sermon 4, and the motives and means to attain it in sermons 5, 6, and 7. Preached some months later, sermon 8 supplied guidelines for each listener to evaluate how far a state of being rightly humbled before God had been achieved in his own life.

After four sermons on Psalm 35:13, while the national fast was still in operation, Hildersham commenced his exposition of Psalm 51:1–7 on Wednesday, September 28, 1625. The two series alternated until Wednesday, December 21, by which time he had delivered seven sermons on Psalm 35 and nine on Psalm 51. By then, it safely could be said that the plague was over, and Hildersham reverted to the normal lecture day of Tuesday for the remainder of the series on Psalm 51. But the genesis of this great series was to be found in the plague of 1625. Hildersham expounded the same themes of heartfelt repentance and mourning over sin from both texts. At the beginning of the lectures on Psalm 51, Hildersham explained why he had chosen this passage: "This psalm is commonly called (and so it is indeed) a psalm of repentance; expressing the repentance of David, who (of all other men we read of in Holy Scripture) is propounded to us for the most lively pattern and example of a truly repentant sinner. And I have therefore made choice to intreat of it in these times wherein the Lord doth so many ways, call us unto repentance."[19] The choice of Psalm 51 had much to commend it. As one of the "seven penitential psalms," it was listed in the schedule of Bible passages in the *Order of the Fast* to be read at morning prayer. It was regularly recited as an act of penitence in the Church of England's liturgy, and notably just before death. Lady Jane Grey is recorded as having repeated it on the scaffold in 1554, and John Foxe tells us that John Rogers, the first Protestant to reach the Marian stake, recited it on his way to martyrdom in 1555. Psalm 51:1 became known as the "neck verse," since it was the required reading test for those hoping to escape execution by pleading benefit of clergy (originally only the clergy, who were protected from execution, could read, so if a convicted felon proved he could read, he would be spared death). Thus the words

---

19. Hildersham, *Lectures upon Psalm 51*, 1.

of the psalm would have been very familiar and richly resonant to an early modern audience.

Hildersham went on to preach 152 sermons on the first seven verses of Psalm 51, of which we will hear more in the next chapter. The first nine lectures, delivered as fast sermons, were devoted entirely to the title of the psalm: "To the chief musician. A Psalm of David, when Nathan the Prophet came unto him, after he had gone in to Bathsheba." It is a reminder not to neglect the titles of psalms, for God can have much to say to us from this source.

Unfortunately, we know very little of the impact these sermons at the fast had on the people of Ashby, although many pressed for them to be published. We do know, however, that Hildersham emerged from this initial test of his restored preaching career with flying colors. He had been very careful to do everything by the book, literally—the *Order for the Fast*. He had preached on the correct days, kept to the length of an hour that the *Order* prescribed for fast sermons, and concluded the fast on the given date. Elsewhere in Leicestershire a godly minister, St. John Burrowes of nearby Thornton, found himself in trouble with the ecclesiastical authorities for allowing too many overlong sermons to be delivered and for continuing public fasting after the official announcement of its end.[20] In Hildersham's fast sermons, too, there is evidence of his desire to demonstrate his loyalty and support for the national leadership. He praises the sovereign and the state for ordering the fast and setting an example to the people, calling their action "a thing highly pleasing to God...[that] will much further the success of our prayers."[21] He also commends the king and government for making "good laws against idolatry, swearing, profanation of the Sabbath, murder and drunkenness," although, sadly, magistrates had failed to enforce them.[22] Like most Puritans, Hildersham valued extempore prayer, but he gave an unequivocal endorsement of the liturgy issued for the fast, calling it "a book of prayers, as ample, holy, effectual and fit for the present occasion,

---

20. Leicestershire Record Office ID41/13/58 f. 262. See also Tom Webster, *Godly Clergy in Early Stuart England* (Cambridge: Cambridge University Press, 1997), 70.

21. Hildersham, *Fasting and Prayer*, 42.

22. Hildersham, *Fasting and Prayer*, 46.

as ever were in any liturgy that I have seen."[23] He urged his congregation to join together, to "make their prayers and supplications with one accord, as they did [in] Acts 1:14."[24]

Hildersham's own prayer before the lecture is recorded for us at the beginning of the *Fasting and Prayer* series, and it is worth reproducing in full. It is the only one of his we have, and shows us his heart for his people before God:

> Thy Word (O Lord) is holy and pure, as is Thine own majesty, and being sincerely preached, worketh either to the salvation or the condemnation of the hearers. And we all that are here assembled before Thee at this time, are of uncircumcised hearts and ears: utterly unworthy by reason of that sin, wherein we were conceived and born, and of those actual transgressions that we have multiplied against Thy majesty, in thought, word and deed, from our first being, until this present hour; once to set foot into Thy temple or to hear Thy Word at all. Utterly unfit and unable by reason of our custom in sin, and the hardness of our hearts to profit by it, when as we hear it. So that (Lord) we are at this time in danger, to be unprofitable hearers of Thy Holy Word, and by being unprofitable hearers of the same, we are in danger of Thy heavy displeasure. Yet forasmuch as it hath pleased Thee in mercy to command us this exercise, to appoint it to be the only ordinary means, whereby Thou wilt work faith and repentance in Thy children, and the principle means whereby Thou wilt increase them, to promise also graciously that Thou wilt accompany the outward ministry of Thy Word, with the inward grace and blessing of Thy Spirit, in the hearts of them that shall be reverently and faithfully exercised in the same: We therefore in humble obedience, to this Thy holy commandment, and in full affiance [trust] and confidence in this Thy gracious promise, are bold to present ourselves before Thee at this time: Beseeching Thee in Thy son's blood to wash away all our sins, so as they may never be laid to our charge again, either in the world to come to our condemnation, or at this time to bring a curse upon this our exercise. Good Lord so sprinkle that blood

---

23. Hildersham, *Fasting and Prayer*, 37.
24. Hildersham, *Fasting and Prayer*, 65.

of Thy Son upon our consciences, that we may be assured of Thy love and favour towards us in Him. By it sanctify us at this time, and Thy Word to our uses, opening and enlightening our understanding so as we may be able to understand and conceive of Thy Word aright, strengthening our memories so as we may be able to remember it, softening our hard and stony hearts, so as we may be able to believe it, to yield unto it, to apply it to our own souls, to meditate and confer thereupon, to practice it in our lives, and conversations, to stir up one another to the obedience thereof. That this our exercise may tend to the increase of our knowledge, and of our obedience, of our faith, and of repentance, the glory of Thy blessed name, and the everlasting comfort of our own souls. Hear us (O Lord) in these our requests, in what else soever thou knowest good for us, or any of Thy Church: for Jesus Christ His sake our Lord and only Saviour. In whose name we continue our prayers unto Thee, as He Himself hath taught us, saying, Our Father which art in heaven.[25]

Hildersham's return to the pulpit after twelve long years can best be described as bittersweet. The circumstances of that plague summer of 1625, of a nation under God's judgment, were sobering. To this was added bitter personal grief. In August 1625, the same month that Hildersham recommenced preaching in Ashby, his beloved elder daughter Anna was buried in the churchyard there. We do not know if Anna, a young mother and wife, aged thirty-one, died of plague or other causes, but her death was shortly followed by the deaths of her two children, Elizabeth and Thomas. Aside from this tragedy, these were sweet days for Hildersham—the fulfillment of the promise given to him by God a year earlier that he would live to declare His name again, though at the age of sixty-one, it would be natural for Hildersham to think that his most productive years lay behind him. However, we are told that even in his old age, though weakened by the efforts required in preaching, his powers were not diminished: Samuel Clarke records that "this happiness God vouchsafed to him, which was more than ordinary, that he outlived not his parts, but as his graces increased towards his end, so his abilities

---

25. Hildersham, *Fasting and Prayer*, inserted before sermon 1.

of invention, judgment, memory, elocution decayed not in his age."[26] God had much still to do through His aged servant before he could depart in peace.

Journey's End

By the time Hildersham resumed preaching again in August 1625, he was recognized both locally and nationally as a patriarchal figure. Locally, as we have seen, he had continued to live among his people and serve them in a variety of ways. When Anthony Watson was appointed vicar of Ashby after the departure of Thomas Pestell in 1622, he was quick to recognize Hildersham's seniority and did not attempt to upstage the older man. In this he was wise, for Ashby's inhabitants so respected and loved Hildersham that to do anything else but defer would have been foolish. Hildersham continued to take the main part in charitable and educational work and remained the town's leading spokesman. Watson remains something of an enigma: though he graduated from Pembroke College, Cambridge, in 1611, he was not ordained as a priest until 1620, at the age of twenty-eight. During Hildersham's lifetime Watson was considered sympathetic to the Puritan cause and was even presented to the authorities in 1629 for administering Communion to a parishioner who was standing instead of kneeling.[27] However, Watson's excuse for not wearing the surplice sounds like weak temporizing rather than a matter of principle; he said that he had not worn it when it could not be found or when it was being washed.[28] In 1636 he protested his conformity to a commission of enquiry. He certainly engaged in some unseemly legal wrangling with his predecessor, Pestell, and had appeared in court over allegations of sexual impropriety with servant girls. Whatever the truth may have been, Hildersham was very supportive of his younger colleague, and perhaps his kindness and loyalty helped to shield Watson from even greater criticism. The two men worked very closely

---

26. Clarke, "Life of Hildersam," 156.

27. Leicestershire Record Office ID41/13/59 f. 219r.

28. Kenneth Hillier, *The Book of Ashby-de-la-Zouch* (Buckingham: Barracuda Books, 1984), 23.

together, and Watson, along with William Cox, was one of the two signatories on Hildersham's will. Watson also participated in taking the inventory of Hildersham's goods after his death.

Within Leicestershire as a whole, Hildersham was by this stage revered and respected, with many seeking him out for advice and counsel. Francis Higginson, who, as the young rector of Claybrooke in 1615, had been persuaded to become a nonconformist after discussing the matter with Hildersham, now sought his advice on the issue of emigration. This was becoming a hot topic among nonconformists in the late 1620s as they faced increased persecution. Should they remain and fight for their cause or flee to somewhere they could worship God freely, according to their consciences? This was the dilemma in which Higginson found himself in early 1629: he had fled to London from his post as lecturer at St. Nicholas's Church in Leicester under imminent threat of imprisonment for his nonconformity. He asked Hildersham what he should do. "Were I a younger man and under your case and call, I would think I had a plain invitation of heaven unto the voyage," came Hildersham's reply.[29] Higginson obviously took this advice, for he accepted the invitation of the governors of the Massachusetts Bay Company to act as their chaplain and sailed for the New World in that same year. William Morton, another Leicester lecturer who at one time lodged with a pupil of Higginson, even dreamed of Hildersham. He recounted a vivid dream of May 19, 1630, in which he and John Bryan, another Leicester preacher, were arrested for murder. "Within a while," related Morton, "came Mr. Brettaine of our college to visit me and tells me that Mr. Hildersham the elder had been labouring what he can for me."[30] We do not know if Morton had even met Hildersham in real life, but by this stage everyone knew of him and his reputation for helping others.

Some people wrote to Hildersham asking for assistance with proposed marriage arrangements. Robert Bolton, himself a renowned

---

29. Cotton Mather, *Magnalia Christi Americana*, cited in Sidney Perley, *The History of Salem, Massachusetts* (Salem, Mass.: S. Perley, 1924), 1:108.

30. Public Record Office, SP 16, 540 (iv), 446, cited in C. E. Welch, "Early Nonconformity in Leicestershire," *Transactions of the Leicestershire Archaeological and Historical Society* (1961), 37:39.

Puritan preacher and writer, had never had the opportunity to meet Hildersham but still felt able to approach him on a matrimonial matter. He began his letter of April 10, 1628, with "Though I be not known unto you, yet I love and reverence your blessed and worthy parts." Bolton was seeking a testimonial regarding the spiritual and material estate of a Mr. Sleigh (probably Gervaise Sleigh of Ashe, Sutton-in-the-Field, Derbyshire, whose father was well known to Hildersham) on behalf of a young woman whose hand Sleigh sought in marriage.[31] John Cotton wrote to Hildersham around the same time, thanking him and his wife for recent hospitality and enclosing the preface Cotton had written for the *Lectures upon John.* The bearer of this letter was named as "Mr. Winter," and Cotton used the opportunity to solicit Hildersham's assistance in promoting Winter's marriage hopes with a "Mrs. Martha Temple, so far as you shall see God's hand making way for him." Cotton then proceeded to supply a generous testimonial to Winter's learning and piety.[32]

Hildersham, with his practical wisdom and extensive knowledge of the Puritan brotherhood, was an obvious choice when John Swayne was looking to appoint an executor for his will of 1623. Swayne, one of the Rediche family tenants at Newhall, Staffordshire, left fifty pounds for the "relief of poor ministers and preachers of the gospel."[33] He knew that Hildersham could be trusted to dispose of this bequest where it was most needed. A letter from Walter Travers (one of the leading lights of Elizabethan Presbyterianism) to Hildersham in March of 1625 thanked him for sending five pounds "as part of the legacy which the lately deceased Mr. John Swayne gave to be bestowed upon poor ministers."[34] Doubtless many other impoverished ministers also had reason to be similarly grateful for the generosity of this brother. Ashby's church records regularly noted gifts for the relief of needy ministers, which Hildersham recommended.

---

31. British Library Add. MS 4275 f. 48.

32. British Library Add. MS 4275 f. 154. This letter is also reproduced in *The Correspondence of John Cotton*, ed. Sargent Bush Jr. (Chapel Hill: University of North Carolina Press, 2001), 124–25. Bush tells us that Winter's suit was not successful, for he went on to marry Anne Beeston of Boston, and then Elizabeth Weaver.

33. Public Record Office Prob/11/141 f. 143.

34. British Library Add. MS 4276 f. 157. Five pounds was about 450 pounds in 2011 values.

For example, on May 3, 1629, it was recorded, "to a minister, his wife and 3 children, [one shilling and sixpence]," and on July 5, 1629, "to a poor minister's wife, [two shillings]." Collections were also made in the town to help specific causes. For example, on July 8, 1631, the following was recorded: "collected for Amos Bedford, minister in the County of Lincs., the sum of thirteen shillings and nine pence."[35]

A national scheme for the advancement of godly pastors also received Hildersham's full endorsement in the pulpit and outside.[36] In the 1620s a group of Puritan ministers, merchants, and lawyers set up the "Feoffees for the Impropriations" movement. Their aim was to raise money to buy back impropriated church tithes that had fallen into the hands of wealthy laymen more concerned with their own interests than the spiritual welfare of the parishes they controlled. The reacquired impropriations were then used to hire preachers in the parishes. William Gouge, Richard Sibbes, and John White of Dorchester were among those serving as feoffees (trustees). This scheme operated very successfully until the feoffees were dissolved after a court case against them in 1632–1633. William Laud, the prime opponent of the Puritan cause, recorded in his diary that the feoffees "were the main instrument for the Puritan faction to undo the church." He also noted that "most of the men they put in [as parish ministers] were persons disaffected to the discipline, if not the doctrine, too, of the Church of England."[37] Laud's vehement attack on the scheme is perhaps the best testimonial to the good it achieved.

As we have seen, Hildersham's return to preaching came in the plague summer of 1625, and unsurprisingly, themes of repentance, sin, and judgment dominated those lectures in the early months. However, Hildersham continued with his series on Psalm 51 for six years, and, indeed, it was unfinished at the time of his death. He had only got as far as verse 7 in lecture 152, but there are clear signs from within the text that he had planned to go further before illness intervened. This

---

35. Leicestershire Record Office MF/5 Ashby Overseers' Accounts.

36. Hildersham, *Lectures upon Psalm 51*, 359, 479.

37. Cited in Nicholas Tyacke, *Aspects of English Protestantism c. 1520–1700* (Manchester, UK: Manchester University Press, 2001), 121.

series plainly shows that Hildersham's powers had not diminished with age. The sermons contain all his old forensic skills of dissecting and analyzing the Word in great detail, dealing with any possible objections to his arguments, and supplying suitable applications for his different hearers. Hildersham's allegiance to the foundational doctrines of the Reformation, to grace alone through faith alone, remained unwavering. The sermons once again rehearsed those great biblical themes that he had expounded in his earlier series on John 4—faith, assurance, heart-religion, conversion, the ministry of the Word, worship, and the errors of Roman Catholic doctrine.

Hildersham's exposition of original sin and conversion in these lectures is based on his interpretation of the second part of verse 6 of the psalm. The translators of the Authorized Version rendered this as "in the hidden part thou *shalt* make me to know wisdom," that is, it puts God's actions in a future tense. However, Hildersham and other preachers, mostly Puritans, who wished to stress the importance of conversion, preferred an older, alternative reading such as that of the Geneva Bible, which translated the verb as "hadst" or "hast." This version meant that David was already converted, looking back to an earlier time when God had imparted saving wisdom to him. The whole area of sin in the regenerate thus became an important topic for consideration. Although this might seem a very fine point, it does reveal a glimpse of Hildersham's scholarship—which he normally concealed beneath a careful and deliberate "plainness"—as well as his allegiance to Calvin and the Geneva translators.

Concern for the proper observance of the Lord's Day character-ized Puritan piety, and Hildersham was no exception. This theme ran throughout his preaching, but he dealt with it specifically and directly in lecture 136 of the series on Psalm 51, delivered on December 29, 1629. Over many years he had witnessed the people of Ashby's failure to honor God properly on His day, and now he took them to task. Although the church was always full on Sundays and the gospel faithfully preached, Hildersham identified a general failure to "keep His [God's] rest and perform the duties of His worship that day cheerfully and reverently and spiritually." People habitually came to church late, left before the service was finished, or fell asleep in the sermons. Hildersham also targeted those who spent the hours of public worship in the alehouse rather than the church and the rowdy and unrestrained behavior of children both in the services and the streets. Even a congregation that was renowned as a "light to all the country" had its problems, apparently.[38]

Despite an overriding sense of continuity throughout Hildersham's preaching career, it is possible to trace some changes in emphasis in these later sermons and some new themes that became important. In Hildersham's preaching there had always been a strain of warning about impending judgment upon the nation and its church unless it heeded God's warnings, but this prophetic element became much more urgent in later years. Hildersham could see the Church of England drifting from its biblical roots as its Calvinist heritage was increasingly threatened by the infiltration of ritualism, ceremonialism, and Arminianism. These years also witnessed the rise and toleration of a resurgent Catholicism in England, in the wake of the Counter-Reformation and Jesuit missionary efforts. Hildersham's response was to warn about the imminent "removal of the candlestick," symbolizing the presence of God in the Church of England through the continued gift of His preached Word. Hildersham increasingly referenced the Marian martyrs, seeking to remind his hearers of the foundation stones of their truly Protestant heritage and the likelihood of future persecution. John Bradford (whom Hildersham mentioned three times) was a particular favorite because of his humility, strength of faith in adversity, and acknowledgment of his own hypocrisy.[39] John Foxe's description of Bradford's ministry might well have served as a model to which Hildersham aspired: "In this preaching office, by the space of three years, how faithfully Bradford walked, how diligently he laboured, many parts of England can testify. Sharply he opened and reproved sin, sweetly he preached Christ crucified, pithily he impugned heresies and errors, earnestly he persuaded to godly life."[40]

---

38. Hildersham, *Lectures upon Psalm 51*, 708.

39. For references to the Marian martyrs, see Hildersham, *Lectures upon Psalm 51*, 142, 152, 255, 267, 325, 461, 468, 495, 495, 686, 773, 792.

40. John Foxe, *Acts and Monuments* (1583), 1603, cited in *The Writings of John Bradford*, ed. Aubrey Townsend (Cambridge: Parker Society, 1853), xxvi.

Hildersham, like other Calvinists in England, felt intimately connected with his brethren in Europe. The Reformation and its aftermath had forged links between Protestants throughout the Continent; the flight of Marian refugees to cities like Frankfurt and Geneva, the preaching and writings of the Reformers, and the presence of "Stranger" churches in London all had helped to cement the bond. Now, with the Thirty Years War in progress, the afflictions of believers in Bohemia, the Palatinate, Germany, and France became a major burden of Hildersham's preaching. Reformed armies were suffering heavy defeats at the hands of Counter-Reformation forces in the 1620s, which left Protestant believers feeling confused and demoralized. Hildersham thought his congregation should be more affected than they were about the sufferings of their brethren in Europe and should be praying earnestly for them. He was also at pains to deliver a warning that events in Europe could presage a similar judgment to come for England. Although the nation had "enjoyed a long summer's day of light, of peace, and prosperity," its "great sins" meant that evil times could be anticipated: "Certainly our sky is now red and louring," Hildersham declared, "and he is a senseless and secure hypocrite that doth not expect some great storm and tempest."[41] On February 27, 1627, he warned his hearers that "it will be hard for such as we are, that have enjoyed so long peace, and ease and prosperity to endure any sharp affliction, such as our poor brethren in the Palatinate, Bohemia, Germany and France have done."[42] It was only because of God's mercy that England had thus far been spared, although many warnings had been given. God's people in England should not be complacent and think that those abroad were worse sinners than themselves but should realize that their time for judgment could be next: "God hath set a time for Bohemia and for Germany and for the Palatinate, and so He hath set a time for England also certain."[43] Hildersham had surely read the signs of the times correctly, for just over ten years later the bloody English Civil War broke out.

Two sermons in particular, lectures 112 (March 3, 1629) and 113 (March 17, 1629) are devoted to explaining "God's marvellous

---

41. Hildersham, *Lectures upon Psalm 51*, 250.
42. Hildersham, *Lectures upon Psalm 51*, 250.
43. Hildersham, *Lectures upon Psalm 51*, 345.

severity…of late showed towards" His people on the Continent.[44] By this time the Bohemian revolt had been brutally crushed, and the population was in the process of being forcibly re-Catholicized. La Rochelle, one of the few remaining Protestant strongholds in France, had fallen to the French Crown on All Saints' Day, 1628. This followed a fourteen-month siege after the disastrous intervention by the Duke of Buckingham and the English fleet on July 20, 1627. People were asking why God was allowing the seeming extinction of the gospel in so many places. Was it a direct result of the sins of these churches? Hildersham faced up to these difficult questions but knew there was no simple answer. His initial response was to declare God's sovereignty over the catastrophes happening in Europe. God alone, not "chance" or "policy of man," determined the giving and taking away of the ministry of His Word in any particular place.

The natural response was to suppose that those abroad were greater sinners: "We are apt to think that rare and extraordinary judgments do always argue rare and extraordinary sins in them, on whom God inflicteth them." Hildersham deplored the fact that "the examples of God's severity," instead of humbling those in England, had only served to make them more secure and to "think better of ourselves than we did before," to conclude that "the Lord loveth and liketh much better of us than He did of them, or else He would not have kept us so free from all the miseries that have been on them." Hildersham's main argument in these two sermons was that it was "unlawful" to think that these judgments were due to the particular sinfulness of these churches. "O take heed therefore," he stressed, "of judging of those poor churches that have so strangely perished, or of any other persons to have been hypocrites, and void of true grace, or to have been greater sinners, either than ourselves, because of the miseries they have endured." It was wrong to make a direct correlation between sin and affliction. For, Hildersham pointed out, using the example of Job, "the holiest of all God's servants have been most sharply afflicted." He explained that God did not always afflict His children to correct them for sin, "but He doth it sometimes

---

44. Hildersham, *Lectures upon Psalm 51*, 557–68, from which the following quotes are taken, unless otherwise stated.

only to try their faith and patience, to make them examples of faith and patience to others." The ultimate explanation for affliction was God's glory, and the workings of this were not always comprehensible to man: "Sometimes He doth it for other causes, which He keepeth secret unto Himself, and which the wisest and holiest men under heaven have not been able to conceive…but have been constrained in holy reverence and admiration to cry out, as [in] Isaiah 45:15, Verily thou art a God that hidest thyself."

On the other hand, Hildersham did concede that in one sense it was legitimate "to judge every man to be a sinner whom we see to be in any affliction," for everyone was a sinner and thus deserved divine punishment. Where "gross sins" had been made manifest, it was not unlawful to attribute God's judgment to that wickedness. Insomuch as these foreign churches had been known to profane the Sabbath, show contempt for the ministry, and live lives of drunkenness and immorality under the guise of an outward profession of religion, "it is not unlawful for us to impute all this marvellous severity of God towards them unto these sins." As usual, Hildersham's arguments are carefully nuanced and consider all possible perspectives. News of events abroad had reached him through the currantoes (forerunners of newspapers) that everyone seemed to be reading, letters from pastors like Samuel Loumeau in La Rochelle, and from English soldiers who had fought in Bohemia. These soldiers, many maimed and wounded, were straggling back home with their sorry stories. Grants to ex-soldiers were regularly recorded in the Ashby church records between 1628 and 1631.

Hildersham continued delivering these lectures on a Tuesday morning until the early spring of 1630, when John Williams, the bishop of Lincoln, issued another silencing order. Up to this point, lecturers had been exempt from the rules governing parish ministers, which required them to preach wearing the surplice and hood. Now this loophole was closed and the regulations extended to lecturers as well. Of course, Hildersham was not going to change his consistent objection to wearing the hated garment, and he was barred from the pulpit for eighteen months, between March 25, 1630, and August 2, 1631. During this final suspension, Hildersham wrote to his relative Lady Barrington at Hatfield Broad Oak, expressing his frustration that "now is the time come wherein not myself only but all of my judgment are cast out as men utterly unprofitable and unfit to [give] any further service in his church."[45] He also explained that he had been so busy with the duties of his calling for the past five years that he had been unable to visit her. Now he expressed the hope that this period of forced inactivity would enable him to make the trip to Essex. His son, Nathanael, was the carrier of this letter. We do not know for certain if Hildersham was able to execute his wish to see her and the family, but it seems very likely that he did so. His dear brother, Richard, was steward of the Barrington estates, and Lady Barrington had been a devoted supporter of Hildersham for many years, sending him gifts like the silver bowl for which he thanked her in his letter of March 1630. She, for her part, bought several copies of his *Lectures upon John* in addition to the volume he had sent to her as a present.[46]

Just before this final suspension, Hildersham was able to do a service for another of his patrons, the fifth Earl of Huntingdon. Lady Sarah, Henry Hastings's elderly mother, had died, and the mourning family gathered to hear a sermon Hildersham preached in their private chapel in Ashby Castle on October 4, 1629. Although this was not officially a funeral sermon (Hildersham did not approve of funeral sermons, for they gave glory to man, not God), he delivered it the day after her burial in the family vault in St. Helen's Church. He took as his text Ecclesiastes 11:8, "But if a man live many years, and rejoice in them all, yet let him remember the days of darkness, for they shall be many. All that cometh is vanity."[47] Hildersham's theme was how to make a good death. By this stage he would have been very aware that his own journey to what he called his "long home" was not far off.

When Hildersham resumed preaching again after his suspension on August 2, 1631, there is no reference in the printed text to any interruption. The lectures carry on as if there had been no break. Only the dates at the beginning of each lecture reveal that there had been an

---

45. British Library Egerton MS 2645 f. 156. This letter, the only one surviving in Hildersham's own handwriting, is also reprinted in *Barrington Family Letters*, ed. Arthur Searle (London: Royal Historical Society, 1983), 61–62.

46. Essex Record Office D/DBa A15, Account Book of Lady Barrington.

47. This sermon was published in the same volume as the series on *Fasting and Prayer* in 1633.

eighteen-month gap between lecture 143 and lecture 144. Of course, we do not know if Hildersham mentioned anything about this when he actually delivered the latter sermon. One of the major themes of lectures 144–152 was the urgent need to continue gospel preaching and to support it. Constancy in religion was another important subject. Hildersham himself was only able to fulfill his task for another four months, and on December 27, 1631, he preached his final sermon. His concluding words to his congregation, though he and they did not know it at the time, concerned preaching: "The elect of God are made the better, and the rest the worse by it, and God will be glorified in them both."[48] How fitting that God's glory was the last thing on his lips in the pulpit.

Shortly after this, Hildersham fell ill and had to take to his bed. Although at first the nature of the sickness was not diagnosed, Hildersham realized the seriousness of his condition and sent for his eldest son, Samuel. At this time Samuel was serving as the rector of West Felton in Shropshire, about fifty miles from Ashby. As soon as they got the message, Samuel and his wife, Mary, hurried over to Ashby, arriving on January 13, 1632. They stayed with Hildersham until his death nearly two months later, providing him with great comfort. Of his daughter-in-law Mary (the daughter and coheir of Sir Henry Goodhere of Polesworth, Warwickshire), whom Hildersham himself had chosen as a fit wife for Samuel and in whom he had always taken much delight, he was heard to say affectionately, "Never man had a kinder daughter-in-law."[49]

Arthur's illness was diagnosed as scorbutic fever, associated with scurvy—a condition now almost unheard of, but then very common. Due to a lack of vitamin C, it is thought that cold and damp conditions, a diet short of fresh vegetables, impure drinking fluids, fatigue, or a sedentary lifestyle may have contributed to its onset. Hildersham may well have been weakened by his previous bouts of serious fever in 1614 and 1624. Whatever the case, it was a debilitating and painful disease, with

---

48. Hildersham, *Lectures upon Psalm 51*, 815.

49. These quotes, unless otherwise stated, and the account of Hildersham's death are to be found in Clarke, "Life of Hildersam," 154–55. Clarke says that Samuel Hildersham helped him in compiling his account.

swelling of the lower limbs, suppurating skin and gum ulcers, and a corresponding mental affliction. Hildersham's condition did not predispose him to speak much, but Samuel reported that he "showed wonderful patience through his whole sickness." Because Hildersham was so beloved and honored, many people came to visit him and hear the "heavenly and holy expressions" he uttered. One who demonstrated her concern was Lady Katharine Hastings, Countess of Chesterfield, sister of the fifth Earl of Huntingdon. Samuel never forgot her kindness and dedicated his father's *Lectures upon Psalm 51* to her when they were published, "in testimony of his humble and thankful acknowledgment of her noble favour and respect showed to the author both living and dying."

Hildersham wanted to ensure that his house was in order before he departed this life, and to leave no unfinished business. We have already heard how he felt the need to set the record straight about John Burgess's recently published book on conformity. It was Thomas Hooker who made public Hildersham's notes on Burgess, but whether he was one of those attending the deathbed or was passed the notes by another, we do not know. As a pastor, Hildersham's overriding concern was for his people once he had gone, especially with the false teaching that was infiltrating the church. To some dear friends he confided his fears that "wolves would ere long come in among them, and thereupon earnestly exhorted them to continue steadfast in the truth, which they had received." When the words of I Timothy 3:5, "How shall he take care of the church of God?" were mentioned, Hildersham looked at Samuel and said, "O son, son, that care of the flock is the main thing."

Many of the godly people in and around Ashby had either been converted under Hildersham's ministry or "edified and confirmed in grace" by it. They realized what a great loss Hildersham's death would be to them, and indeed to the whole church. So together they resolved to set apart a day for public prayer and fasting on Hildersham's behalf. On this day they were led both morning and evening by Simeon Ashe, a Puritan minister, "who did more owe himself unto Master Hildersham, than to any man, having been first placed in the university, under the tuition of famous Master Thomas Hooker, fellow of Emmanuel College, and afterwards directed and encouraged in his ministry by his great care and love."

On the Lord's Day, March 4, 1632, Arthur grew very weak. He was prayed for in both the morning and evening services at St. Helen's Church. By his bedside, Samuel Hildersham prayed with his father constantly. Between nine and ten o'clock that night, when Samuel was praying for the last time, Arthur "departed and slept in the Lord." Clarke comments, "Thus he who had diligently heretofore kept the holy rest of the Sabbath, did in the close of the Sabbath rest from his labours; and having glorified God often both in public and private on that day before, was at last on that day received into glory." He was sixty-eight years and five months old.

Knowing his days to be numbered and the times uncertain, Hildersham had made his final will in October 1630.[50] In it he bequeathed his soul into the hands of "Almighty God my heavenly Father." He expressed a "full assurance of faith that, of His infinite mercy" he would be saved "through the merits of the blood of Jesus Christ my blessed Saviour." His sure hope was that he would be found in "His heavenly kingdom among them that are sanctified by faith in Christ Jesus." "And," Hildersham went on, "I do hereby declare and protest that I do continue and end my days in the very same faith and judgment touching all points of religion, as I have ever been known to hold and profess, and which I have, both by my doctrine and practice, and by my sufferings also given testimony unto."

Hildersham gave clear instructions in his will that his body should be "buried in a decent and comely manner, yet without a funeral sermon or any other religious form." Accordingly, his dear friend Julines Herring, formerly of Calke and now at Coventry, was sent for, and he hurried over the day after Hildersham's death. It was Herring who addressed the sorrowing congregation gathered in Ashby church on Tuesday morning, March 6, at the normal lecture time. It was reported that Herring spoke in much the same manner as Hildersham had done, "holily, discreetly, learnedly, and affectionately, concerning the loss that that congregation, the country and whole church had sustained by the death of him that was lately dead." That afternoon Hildersham's body was carried to the

---

50. Leicestershire Record Office, Leicestershire Wills, Ashby no. 77.

grave by a group of neighboring ministers, followed by "a great multitude both of ministers and others, who expressed much sorrow and lamentation." The poor folk especially mourned his death, for his kindness and care for them had been notable. He was buried in the chancel of the church, a place reserved for those of high standing, near to the graves of his relatives, the Hastings family. The parish register for March 6, 1632, records that "Mr. Arthur Hildersham—a worthy and faithful servant of God—a famous divine and a painful preacher, the comfort of God's people in his time departed this life the 4 of March and was interred in the chancel of our parish church in Ashby the sixth of March 1631."[51] Beside the entry is written simply "Minister of Ashby." It was how the people thought of Arthur Hildersham, and surely how he would want to be remembered.

---

51. In the modern calendar, this is actually 1632.

Chapter 13

Hildersham's Legacy

Samuel Clarke, writing almost thirty years after Hildersham's death, attempted to sum up the lasting legacy of his ministry. Of Hildersham, Clarke declared that

> he left a precious memory behind him; had letters of commendation written in the hearts of many, of which some live here, some in glory. His books will prove more durable monuments of his name, than that his son erected for him in Ashby Church. And yet his name, with the lively picture of his person, lives in his worthy son, Master Samuel Hildersham, whose learning Cambridge knew…and whose present ministerial labours and pious conversation…do perpetuate the honour of his Reverend Father whose very memory he doth much reverence, and whose rich virtues, both personal and ministerial, he doth happily imitate.[1]

For Clarke, Hildersham's memorials were of three different kinds: physical (the monument in Ashby church), personal (the people he influenced directly, in particular his son Samuel), and literary (his books). This chapter will consider these three categories and attempt to assess the legacy Hildersham left.

---

1. Clarke, "Life of Hildersam," 156.

The Legacy in Ashby

If you visit Ashby today you will find a place much changed from Hildersham's day. Ringed by a modern road system, housing, and industrial estates, its development has been shaped by mining and a brief flowering as a spa town.[2] However, much that was familiar to Hildersham endures: the main street and market place contain several historic inns, the great castle (now ruined) still dominates the town, and next to it the old gray stone church of St. Helen's remains. Hildersham's house in Wood Street, a very visible reminder of his presence, was pulled down in 1643, during the Civil War. However, until at least 1668, thirty-six years after his death, the access from this land to the Near Commons continued to be referred to as "Mr. Hildersham's gate." Today, an imposing eighteenth-century property known as Lorne House stands on the spot, but even in the early twentieth century a general folk memory in Ashby seemed to recall the Tudor mansion that once stood there.

St. Helen's Church is not unchanged from the years when Hildersham preached from its pulpit. Building work in the nineteenth century replaced the old pews and floors, and two side aisles were added. Further alterations and repairs have been carried out subsequently. In the chancel you can see the Hastings Chapel (with its burial vault below) and near the steps, the earthly resting place of Selina, ninth Countess of Huntingdon. To the left of the tower entrance stands the "finger pillory," used to detain ill-doers in a slightly less degrading fashion than the stocks. The public memorial to Hildersham, mentioned by Clarke, was moved during the Victorian alterations from its original prominent place in the chancel where he was buried to an insignificant location high up in the Lady Chapel, in the southeast corner of the nave. Once an impressive reminder of the famous minister and preacher, the condition of the memorial has deteriorated over the years and now is difficult to read. In its original spelling it states:

> Neere to this place lieth interred the bodie of Arthur Hildersam, honourably descended from Sr. Richard Poole, by his wife Margaret, Countesse of Salisbury, but more honoured for his sweet and

---

2. For an introduction to the history of Ashby, see Hillier, *Book of Ashby-de-la-Zouch.*

ingenuous disposition, his singular wisdome in settling peace, advising in secular affaires, and satisfying doubts, his abundant charitie, and especially for his extraordinary knowledge and judgment in the holy scriptures, his painfull and zealous preaching, together with his firme and lasting constancie in the truth he professed, he lived in this place for the most part of 43 yeares and 6 moneths, with great successe in his ministery, love and reverence of all sorts, and died with much honour and lamentation March the 4th 1631.

So much for the physical reminders of Hildersham in Ashby—but what became of the spiritual condition of the townspeople after his death? Was there any enduring legacy of his preaching and life? This is not an easy task to assess, for a variety of complex factors combined to impact the religious scene in Ashby. Hildersham's death had severed the personal family links and loyalty with the earls of Huntingdon, and the successors of the fifth earl were of a more conformist bent, as was clear from the type of ministers they presented to the vicarage. The earls retained the controlling influence over the church, even when the main family seat was moved from Ashby to Donington Park after the Civil War. The war itself had a great effect on Ashby—it was at the center of fighting between royalist and parliamentary forces, after the earl's second son, Lord Loughborough, had become a royalist commander and garrisoned the castle for the king. The godly townsfolk of Ashby were much offended by the drinking, swearing, and taunting of the Irish Catholic troops brought in to defend the castle for the royalist cause during the siege. This began in November 1644 and went on until the surrender to parliamentary forces at the end of February 1646. During this time Ashby became a haven for royalist ministers from Leicestershire and the surrounding areas, whom the war had pushed out of their parishes. Some were reputedly pious, but others were reported to carouse and swear along with the troops. That some of the parishioners were disgusted by their behavior indicates that Hildersham's teaching had not been entirely forgotten. Indeed, as William Lilly described, many continued to retain an allegiance to presbyterianism during the Civil War period.

Anthony Watson, vicar of Ashby since Hildersham's time, remained in office until his death in 1644. However, without the fatherly guidance and support of Hildersham, his troubles multiplied. His doctrinal position was always somewhat equivocal, and he became rather high-handed with his parishioners. Several successive churchwardens fell out with Watson over matters in which he had failed to consult them. Eventually it seems that he managed to alienate most of his flock and became almost a figure of ridicule, wearing a scarlet cap to keep his head warm in church. When he was buried in 1644, his death went unlamented: the parish register contains no eulogy like the one penned for Hildersham, merely a brief record of the event.[3] Nevertheless, although Watson's behavior did not serve to bolster the godly cause in Ashby, several of Hildersham's closest friends and supporters continued to be influential in the town during the 1630s and 1640s. Undoubtedly they helped to ensure that the legacy of godly spirituality continued in Ashby. Foremost among these was the locksmith William Cox, who, with his wife, had a long history of nonconformity, but who had also served as church warden in 1613 and again in 1631. In 1633, he was described as "a notorious nonconformitant," and in 1636 was presented for conventicling. It was Cox who was paid one shilling for making a superscription on the dictionary presented to the school after Hildersham's death. Another friend was Henry Aberly, who had been curate of Burton during the Wightman incident, but had then moved to Ashby, certainly by 1614, probably encouraged by Hildersham. He was presented for nonconformity, along with Hildersham, on several occasions, and also served as a school feoffee, acting as collector of the school rents in 1640 to 1641. Aberly was still active in Ashby in 1647, serving as a charity trustee. Others who had been closely associated with Hildersham, such as Joseph Hatterley, Joseph Tomlinson, and Nathaniel Ash, were still around in the late 1630s and into the 1640s, occupying positions of authority as churchwardens, overseers of the poor, and school feoffees.

It has sometimes been suggested that Hildersham's death marked the end of seventy years in which Ashby had been served by a succession of Puritan ministers. However, although we cannot be sure exactly where Watson stood, some of the ministers who came after him certainly espoused the godly cause. By the time Parliament had regained control

---

3. For more on Watson's difficulties see my PhD thesis, 284–88.

of Ashby in 1646, William Coke had been appointed vicar. Little is
known about him or his relatively short-lived ministry in Ashby, except
that his ejection in about 1650 (for refusing the "Engagement"—an
oath required of all men holding office, including clergy, from January 1650 onwards; under this they promised to live quietly under the
new government) demonstrated that he was a Presbyterian and was not
prepared to acknowledge the new republican commonwealth.[4] His successor, Ithiel Smart, inducted to Ashby in 1652, was a moderate Puritan.
He had studied at Emmanuel College and previously served as vicar of
Wombourn, Staffordshire. Entries in the parish register of Wombourn
reveal Smart's reluctant conformity over the installation of altar rails in
1634 and his enthusiasm for a day of public thanksgiving in September
1641, when he and his flock covenanted together "to maintain the true
reformed Protestant religion."[5] Smart remained the vicar of Ashby until
his death in 1661. His entry in the parish register is couched in exactly
the same glowing terms as the entry that refers to Hildersham. Perhaps
his parishioners saw similarities between the ministries of the two men.
Certainly, the petition on his death, signed by thirteen leading inhabitants, asked the Countess of Huntingdon to appoint a man to the Ashby
vicarage ordained by the presbyterian classis, "Mr. Buxston," which shows
that Puritan sympathies still ran strongly in the town.[6] That the countess
turned them down is a mark of the move toward Anglican conformity
after the Restoration in 1660.

Education and charity, both works of Christian service, were
spheres where Hildersham's influence continued after his death. Generations of schoolboys would have had a very tangible reminder of their
former lecturer and minister every time they consulted the dictionary
he had presented. For some years until the right passed to the earls,
the feoffees retained the power to appoint the schoolmaster, and were
thus able to express their religious convictions through their choice.
In 1669 the feoffees appointed Samuel Shaw as master of the Ashby
grammar school. Shaw had been ordained by a classical presbytery and

---

4. A. G. Matthews, *Calamy Revised* (Oxford: Clarendon Press, 1934), 132.

5. Stebbing Shaw, *The History and Antiquities of Staffordshire* (London, 1801), 217.

6. Huntington Library HA 1028 (1661).

ejected from his living by the Act of Uniformity in 1662. The books he authored, including *Samuel in Sackcloth*, also were an indication of his nonconformist persuasion. Shaw later became a leading dissenter in Ashby and in 1689 licensed the schoolhouse as a dissenters' meeting place. An Ashby yeoman, William Langley, founded a school for the poor under the provision of his will in 1695, and his prescription that all the scholars should read Joseph Alleine's *Alarm to the Unconverted* revealed Langley's evangelical motivation.[7] A large number of charities to help the poor were founded in Hildersham's lifetime and in the years following his death, including those of Margery Wright and Simeon Ashe. It is impossible to know how much Hildersham inspired these activities, but it seems likely that he had some part in their founding.

A tradition of nonconformity persisted in Ashby after the Restoration. With no outlet for such views within the established church, it seems natural that at this time Puritan spirituality should be channeled into dissent. Two houses were licensed as nonconformist meeting places in 1672, but it appears that this was only a legalization of existing arrangements; the houses belonged to William Hood and Thomas and Samuel Doughty (a minister ejected in 1662), who had earlier been presented for holding illegal conventicles.[8] However, it is almost impossible to say how many of the population were involved in dissenting piety, let alone true believers. No generation could rest secure on the basis of its forefathers' faith. When Selina, Countess of Huntingdon (wife of the ninth earl) invited the evangelist George Whitefield to visit the town in 1750 for the first time, he did not receive a warm reception from the inhabitants. Indeed, a riot ensued, and Whitefield was moved to remark, "Ungrateful Ashby.... What avails throwing pearls before swine who only turn again and rend you?"[9] Ashby's godly past was long forgotten, it seems. Later, though, he returned and a more favorable response was reported. A chapel associated with "Lady Huntingdon's connection" subsequently opened in the town. As Hildersham surely would have

---

7. Moxon, "Ashby," 273–74, 316.

8. Moxon, "Ashby," 314–15.

9. Cited in Scott, *Ashby*, 304.

testified, the preaching of the gospel brought division: bitter opposition as well as salvation was a result.

"Letters of Commendation Written in the Hearts of Many"

Many men had reason to be grateful to God for the life of Arthur Hildersham. His personal influence on a large number of friends and disciples—including such luminaries as John Dod, John Preston, John Cotton, William Gouge, Francis Higginson, William Bradshaw, Julines Herring, and Simeon Ashe—should be fully recognized. He lived on in the memory of those who survived him as a dear friend, a godly preacher, a wise counselor, and one who remained faithful in suffering. His humility was also remembered: the church historian, Thomas Fuller, declared that Hildersham, despite his royal blood, was "not like the proud Nobles of Tecoa, who counted themselves too good to put their hands to God's work."[10] After his death, Hildersham's peers also frequently cited him as an authority on contentious points of doctrine and polity, and these endorsements in themselves created a readership for his published works.

The earliest of these testimonials came in the preface John Cotton wrote to the *Lectures upon John*, which also included a commendation by John Preston. Cotton, so influential in the Massachusetts situation, almost certainly discussed with Hildersham the validity of a move to New England, and, as we have seen, Francis Higginson relied directly on Hildersham's counsel. No doubt many others from the Leicestershire and Lincolnshire areas were also encouraged to make the voyage across the Atlantic on such advice. Higginson, like his mentor Hildersham, retained the desire for episcopal forms of worship upon his departure in 1629. The merchants, too, who constituted the Massachusetts Bay Company "had great regard for the judgment of Arthur Hildersham... in the settlement of the religious life of the colony."[11] He had advised the planters to sort out in detail their form of church government before sailing, but only a general understanding that it should be based on

---

10. Fuller, *The History of the Worthies of England* (1662), 158. The biblical reference is to Nehemiah 3:5.

11. Perley, *History of Salem*, 1:151.

the teaching of the Bible had been reached in advance. If Hildersham's counsels had been heeded, the course of New England's religious history might have been somewhat different. However, it is clear that Hildersham's opinions were highly valued by many leading players who took part in the foundational debates in the colony. Richard Mather, who emigrated to New England in 1635, referred to him as "the great Mr. Hildersham" and cited Hildersham's views to corroborate his own position on matters like admittance to Communion, funeral sermons, and attending nearby lectures.[12]

If Hildersham's influence upon the early settlers in New England was considerable, his contribution to the course of the later Dutch Reformation should not be overlooked. Willem Teellinck, who had spent time in England in 1604 and again in 1612, counted men like Dod and Hildersham as his spiritual mentors. Teellinck was responsible for "injecting Puritan colour into the Dutch Second Reformation" in the form of an emphasis on practical piety.[13] With Hildersham's reputation in Holland established by Teellinck and others, the country favorably received his writings. In 1629, John Cotton received a letter from Timothy Van Vleteren, a Dutch minister in London, who was a friend of Teellinck's son, Maximilian. In this letter, Van Vleteren explained that he had sent several copies of Hildersham's *Lectures upon John* to Holland, where Dutch pastors had read them with "great satisfaction." Indeed, it whetted their appetite for more, and through Van Vleteren they entreated Hildersham to publish his series on Psalm 51 and any other manuscripts he had written. Although initially Hildersham's books would have been read in English in Holland, after 1634 multiple editions of Dutch translations appeared.[14]

After Hildersham's death in 1632, believers in England faced a time of rapid religious change and uncertainty, as civil war loomed. During these years and the interregnum that followed, questions about the

---

12. Cotton Mather, *Magnalia Christi Americana*, 27; Richard Mather, *A Defence of the Answer and Arguments of the Synod met at Boston* (Cambridge, Mass., 1664), 30; Increase Mather, *The Life and Death of Mr. Richard Mather* (Cambridge, Mass., 1670), 9, 33.

13. See Joel R. Beeke, introduction to *The Path of True Godliness*, by Willem Teellinck, trans. Annemie Godbehere (Grand Rapids: Baker, 2003), 28.

14. For details of the Dutch translations, see my PhD thesis, 195.

nature of the worship and polity of the true church were being debated. Many looked to the "old Puritans" like Hildersham for guidance and answers. The Westminster Assembly cited Hildersham as one authority as it wrestled to produce doctrinal standards. When discussing the importance and manner of public reading of the Scriptures, Edmund Calamy was minuted as declaring that Hildersham in his *Lectures upon John* had said "the reading of it [the Bible] in the church is of more efficacy than in private."[15] Richard Baxter was another who valued Hildersham's example. Looking back rather nostalgically to what he called the "old nonconformists," Baxter frequently enlisted the backing of Hildersham for his own position against separatism. Baxter advocated a continued national church, as opposed to independency. He found inspiration in the model of this earlier generation that had rejected separatism and remained loyal to the established order despite its scruples. Baxter's preface to John Bryan's *Dwelling with God* (1670), in which he defended the author's emphasis "against separation from the public assemblies," cited the precedent of Hildersham, John Paget, Thomas Brightman, and John Ball, who had all argued against separatism. Although times had changed, Baxter tried to portray the contemporary ecclesiastical battleground as essentially parallel to that of the earlier seventeenth century. Baxter admired not only the earlier nonconformists' avowed opposition to separatism, but also what he perceived as their accompanying catholic spirit. Such a spirit made them prepared to acknowledge as brethren others who did not share their rejection of the ceremonies. He referred bitterly to those who would censure him more for "sometimes holding communion with such a conformist as Richard Sibbes" than if he had joined the Quakers.[16] Although this was perhaps a fair criticism of the factionalism of his age, it was rather paradoxical in that Baxter himself was a great controversialist. Whether orthodox Calvinists like

---

15. Minutes of the Westminster Assembly, session 87, Nov. 2, 1643, cited in Chad B. Van Dixhoorn, "Reforming the Reformation: Theological Debate at the Westminster Assembly, 1643–1652" (PhD thesis, University of Cambridge, 2004), 3:249.

16. N. H. Keeble and G. F. Nuttall, *Calendar of the Correspondence of Richard Baxter* (Oxford: Clarendon Press, 1991), 2:88.

Hildersham would have been comfortable with Baxter's Amyraldian theology is another matter.

Arthur Hildersham died long before the Civil War, of course. Most of the Puritan ministers who had admired and looked up to Hildersham sided with Parliament but recoiled from the trial and execution of the king. Such was the case with Simeon Ashe, who continued to serve in the loose Puritan church of the interregnum, despite his misgivings. Arthur's son, Samuel, followed a similar course. Samuel Hildersham not only bore an apparent striking resemblance to his father (according to Clarke, "the lively picture of his person, lives in his worthy son") but also seems to have modeled his conduct consciously upon Arthur's. Samuel was Arthur's heir, and very aware that his father's mantle had fallen on him. He endeavored to perpetuate his father's memory by his own life and by publishing Arthur's works posthumously. Clarke recognized Samuel's status as a sort of living monument, contrasting him with the physical but lifeless memorial he erected in Ashby church. In the preface to *Fasting and Prayer*, published a year after Arthur's death, Samuel wrote, "As a dutiful son, in honour of my dear father's name and memory, I strive for some place for this monument [book], which may be some means to perpetuate the same in God's church.... It no way becometh me to commend this, or any other work of his (let me rather strive to imitate him myself, than to commend him, or anything of his to others) his very name will commend them."[17]

Like his father, Samuel was a nonconformist, and he had found an Irish bishop to ordain him in order to avoid subscription (it was not required in Ireland). Archbishop James Ussher, primate of the Irish Church, and his colleague, Luke Challoner at Trinity College, Dublin, were personal friends of Arthur.[18] Samuel exercised a faithful ministry in West Felton, Shropshire, for thirty-four years until his ejection for nonconformity in August 1662, when he retired to Erdington in Birmingham, living quietly until his death in April 1674, when he was nearly eighty. Like Arthur, he requested no funeral sermon, and a simple

---

17. Samuel Hildersham, "The Epistle Dedicatory," in Hildersham, *Fasting and Prayer*.

18. James Ussher, *The Whole Works of the Most Rev. James Ussher*, ed. C. R. Elrington and J. H. Todd, (Dublin, 1829–1864), 15:74.

gravestone marked the site of his burial in the parish of Aston-juxta-Birmingham. His dear wife, Mary, so loved by Arthur, outlived him by five years and was buried in Aston on August 13, 1679.[19] Samuel's fellow ministers in Shropshire esteemed his godliness, and noted that he was "a father to the sons of the prophets" in the locality. They also described him as "learned, loving and charitable, an excellent preacher, an eminent expositor and very much a gentleman."[20] Everyone remembered Samuel as Arthur's son. Thomas Blake, for example, who dedicated to Samuel and Mary Hildersham his book *Vindiciae Foederis; or, A Treatise on the Covenant of God Entered into with Mankind* (1653), recalled Arthur in the words Joseph Hall used to describe "learned Whittaker": "Whoever saw him without reverence, or heard him without wonder?" Blake concluded by telling Samuel that "to be a follower of such a precedent, and to be found worthy of such a testimony, is a greater glory than all the noble blood that ran through the veins of the greatest of either of your ancestors." Samuel published no books of his own, but concentrated on bringing out those of his father. During the interregnum, he was named as one of the twenty ministers appointed to assist the commissioners for Shropshire, inquiring into the fitness of ministers and schoolmasters. He reaffirmed his presbyterian sympathies by signing the *Testimony of the Ministers of Salop to the Solemn League and Covenant* in 1648 and was appointed to the Westminster Assembly of Divines in 1642. However, although he never attended any meetings, he was not replaced, as was the usual practice.[21] The reason for this remains a mystery. Samuel inherited his father's papers and contributed to the drawing up of Samuel Clarke's biography of Arthur.

It seems that Samuel and Mary Hildersham did not have any children, so their branch of the family line died with them. But what of Arthur's other offspring? We have already heard how his daughter Anna and her two children predeceased him. Arthur's second son, Timothy, for whom he had such a tender concern, outlived his father by only a year

---

19. Birmingham Central Library, *Register of the Parish Church of Aston-juxta-Birmingham 1640–1697*, vols. 2 and 3.

20. Henry, *Lives of Philip and Matthew Henry*, 270–71.

21. I am grateful to Dr. Chad Van Dixhoorn for this information.

and was buried in Ashby church on March 4, 1633, aged thirty-two years. The fate of Nathanael, the youngest son, remains uncertain, but it looks as if he became a London merchant, trading with the East India Company.[22] His dealings with ships' cargoes are recorded in 1631 and 1634, but it seems likely that he was dead by 1647. In that year the silver bowl bequeathed to him by his father was listed in his brother-in-law's will. The presumption is that Nathanael had died in the interim, leaving the bowl to him. Sarah, Hildersham's youngest child, married Gervase Lomax of Thrumpton, Nottinghamshire, on April 10, 1627. Gervase was a godly man whom Arthur Hildersham highly esteemed and to whom he had bequeathed his folio Bible printed in Cambridge, his copy of Foxe's *Acts and Monuments*, and Andrew Willet's *Synopsis Papismi*. Sarah was bequeathed five shillings and a gold ring. Ann Hildersham, Arthur's widow, went to live with her daughter and son-in-law when her husband died and was buried in the parish of Thrumpton All Saints on November 29, 1641.

Gervase and Sarah Lomax had six children between 1628 and 1639. The oldest three, Henry, Arthur, and Ann, were baptized in Ashby, but the three youngest, Gervase, Samuel, and John, were born in Thrumpton, after the family had moved there. Gervase Lomax (senior) was a strong supporter of Parliament from the beginning of the Civil War. Having raised a foot company of militia in Nottingham, he led it as captain to join Oliver Cromwell and fight at Gainsborough in 1643. This was Parliament's (and Cromwell's) first significant victory. Lomax also was responsible for running the war effort in Nottinghamshire and became Deputy Governor of the garrison in Nottingham castle. A contemporary described him as "a very honest man.... He was in strength and performance of his age, a stout and understanding man, plain and blunt, but withal godly, faithful to his country, and honest to all men."[23] Sadly, Gervase died during the Civil War period, either of natural causes or as a result of the fighting, for he made his last will in 1647, when he was still in his forties. This will reveals that he was a very wealthy man with extensive property, but more

---

22. *Calendar of State Papers Colonial, East Indies and Persia*, 8:155, 158.

23. Lucy Hutchinson, *Memoirs of the Life of Colonel John Hutchinson*, ed. James Sutherland (Oxford: Oxford University Press, 1973), 73. More details of Lomax's career during the Civil War can be found in this source.

significantly shows that he was a true believer, "resting on Christ alone for salvation." He specifically requested burial according to the Directory of Worship, which came into force in 1645, and not the Prayer Book service. His great concern was for the future welfare of his young children, and his will contained a remarkable piece of spiritual advice and benediction. By "the authority of a dying father" he charged his "beloved children" to "know the God of your fathers and to serve Him with a perfect heart and willing mind, to advance what lieth in you the kingdom of the Lord Christ that redeemed you, and to approve yourselves true members of His mystical body by your faithful, holy, humble and temperate life and conversation." He also required them to be "dutiful to your mother whilst she livest," not entering into any marriages without her consent, and to be loving and kind to each other, "studying quietness."[24]

It is clear that Gervase and Sarah Lomax maintained a close relationship with Samuel and Mary Hildersham. After her father's death, Gervase and Sarah's daughter Ann went to live with her aunt and uncle at West Felton. There, in 1653, Ann Lomax married Francis Tallents, another man very much in the mold of her grandfather Hildersham. Francis was a town preacher in Shrewsbury and a close friend and ministerial associate of Samuel's in the Shropshire Puritan scene. It looks as if Samuel was responsible for arranging this marriage between a favored niece and a man he highly esteemed. For his part, Tallents reciprocated Samuel's regard, calling him "Great Hildersham" in a poem composed on the death of Rowland Nevet, another Shropshire minister.[25] Richard Baxter described Tallents as "a good scholar, a godly blameless divine...most eminent for extraordinary prudence and moderation and peaceableness towards all."[26] Francis and Ann's first child, born in April 1655, was christened Hildersham Tallents, recalling his descent from his godly great-grandfather, but sadly he died in infancy.[27] Ann herself died shortly afterward, in March 1658, and Tallents was to remarry three

---

24. Nottinghamshire Archives Office, PR/NW, Will of Gervase Lomax (1647). Full details can be found in my PhD thesis.

25. Henry, *Lives of Philip and Matthew Henry*, 459.

26. Henry, *Lives of Philip and Matthew Henry*, 489–90.

27. *Shropshire Parish Registers, Lichfield Diocese*, vol. 12, *The Register of St Mary's, Shrewsbury, 1584–1812* (transcription), 7:115–16.

times. Francis and Ann had had another son, Francis, in 1656, but he too predeceased his father, who lived until April 1708. It seems very possible, though, that Tallents senior inherited at least some of Arthur Hildersham's private papers. He is known to have supplied Philip Henry with a manuscript Arthur had written. Philip Henry, in turn, told the antiquarian collector Mr. Thoresby that Tallents had "by him many more," and that he could procure one for him.[28] However, the subsequent whereabouts of these papers is now unknown.

Of Gervase and Sarah Lomax's sons, only Arthur appears to have lived a long life; he died in 1694. He became a wealthy wholesale mercer in London and married Frances Maddison, daughter and eventual heir of Edward Maddison of Grimblethorpe, Lincolnshire. They seem to have settled in Habrough in Lincolnshire and had two children, Henry (died 1700) and Elizabeth (died 1747). Elizabeth Lomax became the ancestress of the Walsh family of Grimblethorpe through her marriage in 1695 to Henry Walsh. We know nothing of Arthur Lomax's spiritual convictions, but only that in 1684, as "Lord of the Manor," he contributed to the repair of the steeple in Habrough church.[29]

Hildersham's Printed Works

Samuel Clarke adjudged that Hildersham's writings would "prove more durable monuments of his name" than the memorial in Ashby church. His published works comprised *The Doctrine of Communicating Worthily in the Lords Supper*, which was first issued in 1609, appended to a treatise by William Bradshaw on the same subject; *Lectures upon the Fourth of John* (1629); *The Doctrine of Fasting, Prayer, and Humiliation for Sin* (1633); and *CLII Lectures upon Psalm 51* (1635). These last two works were published posthumously, as was a paraphrase of Canticles (the Song of Solomon), attributed to Hildersham, which appeared in 1674. Several editions of

---

28. Original manuscript, Feb 1, 1702/3, cited in Henry, *Lives of Philip and Matthew Henry*, 220.

29. See Melville Henry Massue Ruvigny Raineval, *The Plantagenet Roll of the Blood Royal* (London: T. C. and E. C. Jack, 1908), 570. Arthur Lomax's brother Henry was probably dead by 1659, and his brother Gervase by 1656. There is no record of his brother Samuel after his admittance to Trinity College, Cambridge, in 1653. For full details see my PhD thesis.

these works appeared in the seventeenth century, indicating a steady readership. The treatise on the Lord's Supper, a short catechism of questions and answers, proved to be the most popular and became an early-modern best seller.[30] In Holland, too, as we have seen, Hildersham's works were influential in shaping the character of the Further Reformation. For as long as Hildersham's memory lingered, it seems that people continued to read his books, spurred on by his reputation for godliness and learning. For example, an Exeter merchant, John Hayne, paid seven shillings for one copy of the *Lectures on John*, which he purchased for his future wife in 1634. Another copy of the same book, which a George Mackenzie owned in the eighteenth century, contains a handwritten summary of Hildersham's life on the endpaper: "This book is a very commendable one, it being preached by that faithfull minister of Jesus Christ, Arthur Hildersam, minister at Ashby Delazouch in Leicester Shire."[31]

However, the sheer length and price of the books on John and Psalm 51 would have put them beyond the reach of most ordinary readers. Hildersham's prose style—solid, judicious, and weighty—also posed a problem for all but the most determined student. Charles Haddon Spurgeon described the *Lectures upon Psalm 51* as "copious and discursive, we had almost said long-winded" and called the *Lectures upon John* "a mass of godly teaching; but rather heavy reading."[32] Nevertheless, he included both titles in his category of "books most heartily recommended." John Preston said that he was unable to find brief highlights of the *Lectures upon John* that he could transcribe into his commonplace book because of Hildersham's undifferentiated style. John Cotton, who wrote the preface to the *Lectures upon John*, was also unable to select the kind of punchy quotations that anthologizers so favor from Hildersham's closely argued work:

> In reading most of the best books extant, the studious reader is wont to select and transcribe the pith of such notes, as stand like lights, or goads, or nails, in the body of the discourse, and in the spirit of the writer. But in this book…I find such variety of

---

30. Ian Green, *Print and Protestantism in Early Modern England* (Oxford: Oxford University Press, 2000).

31. Author's personal copy.

32. Spurgeon, *Commenting and Commentaries*, 33, 99, 161.

choice matter running throughout every vein of each discourse herein handled, and carried along with such strength of sound and deep judgment, and with such life and power of a heavenly spirit, and withal expressed in such pithy and pregnant words of wisdom, that I knew not what to select, and what to omit, unless I should have transcribed the whole book.

As the years went by, Hildersham's writings tended to become reference works in the libraries of ministers and theological colleges. The Presbyterian minister Thomas Lye had three works by Hildersham in his library. Others also owned his volumes—for example, Edward Lewis of Chirbury (Shropshire), Clement Sankey of Whitchurch (Shropshire), Richard Waugh of Calverley, Thomas Hall of King's Norton, and Thomas Plume of Maldon (Essex). In New England, John Harvard and Peter Bulkeley had copies of Hildersham's works, as did Thomas Teackle in Virginia. In nineteenth-century England, the renowned congregational minister John Angel James had his own copy of the *Lectures upon Psalm 51*.[33] We know that seventeenth- and eighteenth-century clerical writers such as Thomas Hall, John Flavel, John Spencer, Richard Mather, Lewis Stucley, Henry Newcome, and Hezekiah Woodward esteemed Hildersham, since they all cited him in their own works. Thomas Hall, a seventeenth-century nonconformist minister from Birmingham, was probably Hildersham's most enthusiastic literary admirer, to judge by the number of times he referred to Hildersham's writings in his own works, especially on matters of practical divinity.

In the nineteenth century there was a flourishing interest in Puritan literature, especially that of John Bunyan. British publishers also brought out editions of the complete works of godly writers such as Richard Sibbes, Richard Baxter, John Owen, Thomas Manton, Thomas Brooks, John Howe, John Flavel, and William Bridge. Hildersham's writings were not among this list. Despite the revival of Reformed beliefs in the second half of the twentieth century, no editions of any of Hildersham's

---

33. I have examined thirty-nine early modern copies of works by Hildersham held in various libraries and archives (full details in my PhD thesis), perused old library catalogues, and consulted Early English Books on Line (EEBO) to compile this survey of ownership and readership.

works were reissued. Five sermons relating to the upbringing of children, taken from the *Lectures upon Psalm 51*, have appeared under the title of *Dealing with Sin in Our Children* (Soli Deo Gloria publishers), but the remainder of the five hundred folio pages of *Lectures upon John* and the 813 pages of the *Lectures upon Psalm 51*, as well as the two shorter volumes, have thus far gathered dust in university libraries and archives. However, those who have the opportunity to read Hildersham and are prepared to exercise stamina and concentration will find their labors richly rewarded.[34] Although perhaps not the best introduction to Puritan preaching, those who are already familiar with and treasure similar sermons will find them very profitable. They will discover a wealth of deeply serious, balanced, godly teaching, both doctrinal and practical, that will edify and challenge them. It would be wonderful if Clarke's prophecy did not go entirely unfulfilled in this generation, for, indeed, Hildersham's books deserve to be a lasting monument to his name.

---

34. Copies at Shropshire Archives Office; Leicestershire Record Office; Cambridge University Library; Edinburgh University Library; Dr. Williams's Library, London; Birmingham Central Library.

Chapter 14

Ten Lessons from Hildersham for Us Today

1. Never believe anyone is beyond the grace of God.

Many people would have looked upon Hildersham, with his zealous and systematic upbringing in the Roman Catholic faith, as an unlikely convert. He was submersed in all aspects of Catholicism from his earliest days and taught to be suspicious of the "new" Protestant religion. However, when God has His hand on a person, His grace is irresistible. All human barriers are broken down as Christ draws His sheep to Himself. It may not be an easy course, as the opposition from Hildersham's family demonstrated, but nothing can stand against God's purposes. We should never dismiss anyone as too difficult a case or too young to be saved, and this should encourage us to persevere in prayer for the lost.

2. Do what you can when you cannot do what you would.

Hildersham felt God's calling to preach His Word and was frustrated when prevented from exercising that calling. However, he did not despair or give up, but looked for other avenues of Christian service. God was able to use him mightily through the witness of his personal life as he continued to live among the people of Ashby. As we get older, especially, we are tempted sometimes to feel that we are no longer useful to God. Physically, our options may be limited, but as long as we live on this earth, God has some purpose for our lives. We should not give up, but continue to serve God in whatever sphere He has placed us, for His glory. For those, too, who live in circumstances where open declaration of the gospel is not possible or is fraught with danger, Hildersham's example teaches us that people can be won "without a word" by our holy conduct and patient example.

3. Follow your conscience whatever the cost.

Once Hildersham had become convinced that the Church of England's "ceremonies" were unbiblical and superstitious, he could no longer continue to countenance them. This decision proved costly, for it meant that he was banned from preaching for nearly twenty years in total. He was also labeled a radical and a troublemaker. Some suggested compromise on these "matters of judgment" so that the gospel could continue to be preached, but Hildersham was resolute. If he could not find warrant for a practice in God's Word, then there was no place for it in his life. Although Hildersham did not seek out controversy, he was prepared to face it when it came. We should pray for grace to be similarly steadfast in following our consciences, whatever the personal repercussions. In an age where God's Word and biblical standards are increasingly opposed in legislation and public life, a principled stand by Christians may well bring us into conflict with the authorities.

4. Maintain a gracious and catholic spirit.

Hildersham's opinions on some secondary matters were different from the opinions of some other believers of his day. He opposed the separatists, who felt they should leave the Church of England. He rejected the ceremonies, while others submitted to them. But still he recognized all true believers as brethren in Christ, and continued to converse with those of differing views in a gracious and generous spirit. He urged these brethren not to fall out over "matters of judgment" but to maintain unity in the bond of peace, for the sake of the gospel. Reformed evangelical Christians today may hold different positions on, for example, baptism or church government, but we should not let such things divide us or bring strife.

5. Value fellowship.

In the troubles and difficulties that Hildersham faced, he was sustained by the practical and spiritual support of other Christians. Without the generous provision of the earls of Huntingdon and the Rediche family, he would have been unable to complete university or sustain his ministerial career. Without the fellowship, prayers, and love of a host of sympathetic friends, he could have felt isolated and lonely. In turn, Hildersham extended his friendship, kindness, and advice to a number of young men hoping to enter the ministry. We, too, should value the blessing of Christian fellowship and encourage it wherever possible. Our homes, hearts, and material gifts should be open to those in need, especially those of the household of faith.

6. Care for those in need.

Like his Savior, Hildersham had great compassion for the needy. He did much to encourage his congregation to give money to help the poor and was personally very generous. In other practical ways, he helped to organize poor relief and was intimately involved with the daily lives of his humble neighbors. In an age where status was very important and Hildersham himself was of high birth, he did not stand upon his position but willingly undertook menial tasks to assist those in need. He recognized that the poor and rich equally required God's grace in salvation. We can learn much from Hildersham's example in this.

7. Leave a church only when God has left it.

Hildersham faced the difficult choice of whether to leave the Church of England or to remain within it. He recognized its flaws and corruptions but reckoned that as long as gospel preaching continued, this was a sign that God was still present in the church. His decision brought criticism from both sides: from the separatists, who argued that he lacked the courage to follow his convictions to their logical conclusion and leave an unbiblical organization, and from conformists, who regarded him as a troublemaker refusing to submit to lawful authority. Deciding to stay within the Church of England was not an easy option for Hildersham, for it brought years of suspension from ministry and suffering. Although some of the issues may be different now, evangelicals within the Church of England face a similar dilemma today. In nonconformist denominations affected by liberalism and the charismatic movement, too, believers can find themselves in the same sort of position—wondering whether to stay or leave. Hildersham shows us that these choices are not to be made lightly but through a prayerful searching of the Scriptures. Our decision may not be the same as Hildersham's, because the situation is different from that of his day, but the way in which he regarded gospel preaching as the central touchstone is very helpful.

8. Prepare for adversity.

Both Hildersham's life and his preaching remind us that trials and troubles will come to the Christian, and we should expect nothing else. By preparing our hearts in advance and not letting ourselves become too attached to the things of the world, we can be more ready to face whatever comes. We may not have to undergo trial and imprisonment for the gospel, but believers in many countries do have to suffer such things. Prayer for them, and ourselves, is the most important weapon we have. Heavy providences can be difficult to understand sometimes, but we need to exercise faith in God's sovereign purposes.

9. Heed warnings of judgment.

In his sermons, Hildersham often warned his hearers against complacency and hypocrisy. God's grace had caused the light of His gospel to shine in England for so many years, but most people neglected Him or took their privileges for granted. But sin abounded in the land, and God was warning the church that this would not go unpunished. A time was coming when the gift of preaching could be withdrawn from them. Only God's mercy had stayed His hand of judgment thus far. We, too, live in an age when God's Word is spurned and where sin abounds. God's deliverances in past wars and the peace and prosperity we enjoy are taken for granted. As a nation and as individuals we need, like Hildersham, to humble ourselves before God in repentance, pleading for divine mercy. The seriousness of sin is a lesson that we can all learn from Hildersham.

10. Do all for God's glory.

The primary motivation in Hildersham's life was that God should be glorified in everything he did. He could count his sufferings as nothing if they served this end. His preaching focused on bringing glory to God's name, and the final words he spoke in the pulpit were on this theme. Hildersham's example inspires us to keep a heavenly perspective, especially when our earthly circumstances are difficult or perplexing. His watchword was *soli Deo gloria*. Ours should be the same.

Epitaph on Mr. Hildersham 1632[1]

Whose fervent prayer, cold hearers' bosoms warmed
Whose sharp sweet strains our deafest passion charmed
From whose bright presence dark profaners fled
Wise, holy, noble Hildersam is dead
Ashby thy lamp is quenched and thou art mad
At heart, or else at heart thou wilt be sad
Where will you run to find a font so pure
That could so full and still so fresh endure
Can that fair orb whence radiant fire he threw
With glow-worms fill, or candlerush renew?
Yet all his learning was but as a limb
To the main body, as a piece of him;
Father and founder to the poor he was
The layman's counsellor, the clergy's glass
His high blood swelled him not; in wealth of wit
Excelling, he as trifles rated it.
And from full store of trials I may spend
This surplusage; he was a faithful friend.
His life a woven robe, without a seam
His heavenly temper an eternal theme
For tongues and pens, but his immortal mind

---

1. Thomas Pestell, *The Poems of Thomas Pestell*, ed. H. Buchan (Oxford: Oxford University Press, 1940), 10.

Reigns with Eli[j]ah, in a throne designed
Twixt him and Esay [Isaiah], hark celestial choirs
Prophets, apostles, strike their ivory lyres
And peals of joy resound on golden strings
While seraphims do clap their silver wings.

—Thomas Pestell

Hildersham Who's Who?
A Guide to People in the Book

(** indicates Ashby connection*)

Abbot, George (1562–1633): archbishop of Canterbury, Calvinist

*Aberly, Henry: curate of Burton-on-Trent, later resident of Ashby, friend

Anderson, Sir Edmund (c. 1530–1605): judge and anti-Puritan

*Ashe, Simeon (d. 1662): protégé of Arthur, Puritan minister

*Bainbrigg, Robert: Earl's bailiff and fellow school feoffee

Bancroft, Richard (1544–1610): bishop of London and archbishop of Canterbury, anti-Puritan

*Barfoot, Ann: wife of Arthur, married 1591

Barfoot, Edward: brother of Ann and first husband of Winifred Hildersham

Barfoot, Thomas: father-in-law of Arthur

Barlow, William (d. 1613): bishop of Lincoln and friend

Barrington family of Hatfield Broad Oak, Essex: relatives and patrons

Barrington, Lady Joan (1558–1641): godly matriarch, relative, and patron

Barrington, Sir Thomas: married Hildersham's mother's cousin, Winifred Pole

*Blithe, Hugh: rector of Appleby, benefactor of Timothy Hildersham

Bolton, Robert (1572–1631): Puritan preacher and writer, correspondent of Arthur

*Bradshaw, William (d. 1618): protégé and close friend, Puritan minister

*Brinsley, John (c. 1581–1624): schoolmaster and curate of Ashby, nonconformist

Burgess, John: fellow-nonconformist minister in 1604–1605, later turned conformist

*Burrows, John: bailiff to the earl, nonconformist

*Burrows, Margery: wife of John, nonconformist

Cartwright, Thomas (1535–1603): Puritan theologian and leader, friend

Chaderton, Laurence (c. 1536–1640): Cambridge academic, Bible translator, moderate Puritan

Chaderton, William (1540?–1608): bishop of Lincoln, 1595–1608

Cotton, John (1585–1652): friend, Puritan minister of Boston, Lincs., and New England

*Cox, William: locksmith and sometime churchwarden of Ashby, nonconformist, friend

Culverwell, Ezekiel (1560–1631): friend from Cambridge days, Essex Puritan minister

Darling, Thomas: "boy of Burton" involved in exorcism case

*Darling, William: vicar of Ashby, 1606–1611

*Darrell, John (c. 1562–c.1607): Puritan exorcist, friend

*Dighton, Thomas: school feoffee, leading nonconformist, sentenced 1616

Disborow, John (d. 1607): schoolmaster of Saffron Walden school from 1573

Dod, John (1550–1645): Puritan minister, friend

Egerton, Stephen (c. 1555–1622): Puritan minister of Blackfriars, co-organizer of Millenary Petition

*Farmer, Ruth: single mother, she and baby helped by Arthur

Fenn, Humphrey (1544–1634): nonconformist minister of Coventry, correspondent

Ferrars, Lady Elizabeth: mother of Katharine Rediche, Roman Catholic

Gataker, Thomas (1574–1654): Puritan minister, biographer of William Bradshaw, friend

*Gilby, Anthony (d. 1584): Marian exile, lecturer of Ashby from early 1560s to death

Goodhere, Lady Mary (d. 1679): from Polesworth, Warwickshire, married Samuel Hildersham

Gouge, William (1573–1653): London Puritan minister and author, friend

Greenham, Richard (d. 1594): rector of Dry Drayton, Cambridgeshire; mentor

*Hacket, Thomas: vicar of Ashby, 1611–1616; opponent of the godly
  Harsnett, Samuel: chaplain and ally of Richard Bancroft, anti-Puritan
*Hastings, Sir Francis (d. 1609): brother of third Earl, Puritan organizer
  and supporter in Parliament
*Hastings, George (d. 1604): fourth Earl of Huntingdon
*Hastings, Sir Henry (1536–1595): "the Puritan earl," third Earl of
  Huntingdon, patron
*Hastings, Sir Henry (1586–1643): great-nephew of above, fifth Earl of
  Huntingdon, patron
*Hastings, Lady Katharine: sister of fifth earl, married Earl of Chesterfield,
  patron
*Hastings, Lady Sarah (d. 1629): mother of fifth earl
  Herring, Julines (1582–1644): protégé of Hildersham; Puritan minister in
  Calke, Coventry, and in Netherlands
  Higginson, Francis (c. 1587–1630): protégé, nonconformist, emigrated
  to New England
*Hildersham, Ann (d. 1641): Arthur's wife, mother of his children
*Hildersham, Anna (1594–1625): elder surviving daughter of Arthur,
  married Nicholas More
*Hildersham, Nathanael (1602–?): youngest son of Arthur
  Hildersham, Richard: brother of Arthur, Puritan, Barrington family
  steward
*Hildersham, Samuel (1595–1674): eldest son of Arthur, Puritan minister
*Hildersham, Sarah (1604–?): youngest daughter of Arthur, married
  Gervase Lomax
  Hildersham, Thomas: father of Arthur, Roman Catholic
*Hildersham, Timothy (1600–1633): middle son of Arthur, probably
  disabled
  Hildersham, Winifred: sister or niece of Arthur, married (1) Edward
  Barfoot and (2) Ezekiel Culverwell
  Hooker, Thomas (1586–1647): nonconformist minister, friend, founder
  of New England
*Ireton, John: Cambridge friend, rector of Kegworth, Leicestershire
  Jacob, Henry (1563–1624): semi-separatist minister, friend
*Jardfeild, Richard: vicar of Ashby, 1605–1606
  Johnson, Francis (1562–1617): fellow student at Cambridge, later
  separatist minister

Laud, William (1573–1645): archbishop of Canterbury from 1633, anti-Puritan

*Lilly, William (1602–1681): pupil of Ashby school, astrologer

Lomax, Ann (1632–1658): granddaughter of Arthur, married Francis Tallents

Lomax, Arthur (1629–1694): grandson, London cloth-merchant, settled in Lincolnshire

Lomax, Gervase: son-in-law of Arthur, married his daughter Sarah

Lomax, Henry (b. 1628): grandson of Arthur

Montagu, Dr. James (c. 1568–1618): moderate Calvinist; bishop of Bath and Wells, and Winchester

*More, George: minister of Calke, exorcist with John Darrell

*More, Nicholas: son-in-law, married Anna Hildersham in 1610

Neile, Richard (1562–1640): bishop of Coventry and Lichfield, Lincoln, and then archbishop of York; anti-Puritan

Nutter, Anthony: rector of Fenny Drayton

Overton, William (c. 1525–1609): bishop of Coventry and Lichfield

Perkins, William (1558–1602): leading Puritan theologian and Cambridge minister

*Pestell, Thomas: vicar of Ashby 1616–1622, poet

Pole, Anne: Arthur's mother, of royal descent, Roman Catholic

Pole, Sir Geoffrey (d. 1558): Anne's father, Arthur's grandfather

*Pole, Katherine: cousin of Arthur's mother; married Francis, second Earl of Huntingdon

Pole, Margaret, Countess of Salisbury (1473–1541): formerly Plantagenet; daughter of George, Duke of Clarence; executed 1541 by Henry VIII; declared Catholic martyr; Arthur's great-grandmother

Pole, Cardinal Reginald (d. 1558): Arthur's great-uncle, Queen Mary's archbishop

Pole, Sir Richard (1462–c.1505): Arthur's great-grandfather; married Margaret, Countess of Salisbury

Pole, Winifred: cousin of Arthur's mother, married Sir Thomas Barrington

*Presbury, Henry: minister of Packington, near Ashby

Preston, John (1587–1628): friend, Puritan minister, Cambridge academic

Rediche, Alexander (1563–1613): close friend and patron, lived at Newhall, Staffordshire

Rediche, Grace: elder daughter of Alexander and Katharine, married Sir Robert Darcy

Rediche, Katharine (d. 1632): formerly Dethicke, wife of Alexander, friend

Rediche, Sarah: younger daughter of Alexander and Katharine, married Sir Clement Coke

*Reding, George: gave testimony against Arthur in 1615

*Rosse, Gabriel: minister of Packington, near Ashby

Smyth, John (d. 1612): separatist minister, Baptist

*Spencer, Richard (d. 1610): complained about Brinsley and Hildershams to bishop in 1606

Tallents, Francis (1619–1708): Puritan preacher of Shrewsbury, married Ann Lomax

Teellinck, Willem (1579–1629): Dutch Puritan, converted through John Dod and Arthur Hildersham

Travers, Walter (1548?–1635): Presbyterian leader and theologian, friend

Ussher, James (1581–1656): archbishop of Armagh from 1625, Calvinist, friend

Van Vleteren, Timothy (d. 1641): Dutch minister in London, reader of Arthur's books

*Watson, Anthony (d. 1644): vicar of Ashby 1622–1644

Whitgift, John (c. 1530–1604): archbishop of Canterbury from 1583, enforcer of conformity

*Widdowes, Thomas (d. 1593): vicar of Ashby, Arthur's predecessor

Wightman, Edward (1566–1612): of Burton-on-Trent, burned for heresy 1612

Willet, Andrew (1562–1621): conformist minister and anti-Papist author, friend

Bibliography

This is a select bibliography. A full bibliography can be found in my PhD thesis.

Manuscript Sources
Birmingham Central Library
Bodleian Library, Oxford
British Library, London
Cambridgeshire Record Office, Cambridge
Derbyshire Record Office, Matlock
Essex Record Office, Chelmsford
Henry E. Huntington Library, San Marino, California
John Rylands University Library, Manchester
Leicestershire Record Office, Leicester
Lichfield Record Office
Lincolnshire Archives Office, Lincoln
The National Archive, Kew
Nottinghamshire Archives Office, Nottingham
Shropshire Archive Office, Shrewsbury
Staffordshire Archive Office, Stafford
Dr. Williams's Library, London

Primary Sources

An Abridgement of that Booke which the Ministers of Lincoln Diocesse Delivered to His Majestie upon the First of December 1605. London, 1605. Reprinted in 1617.
Alsop, Vincent. *A Reply to the Reverend Dean of St. Paul's Reflections*. London, 1681.

Barrow, Henry. *The Writings of Henry Barrow 1590–1591*. Edited by Leland H. Carlson. London: Allen and Unwin, 1966.

Bee, Jesse. *The Wonderful and True Storie, of a Certaine Witch Named Alse Gooderige of Stapenhill*. Edited by John Denison. London, 1597.

Blake, Thomas. *Vindiciae Foederis: Or, A Treatise on the Covenant of God Entered into with Man-kinde*. London, 1653.

Bradford, John. *The Writings of John Bradford*. Edited by Aubrey Townsend. Cambridge: Parker Society, 1853.

Bradshaw, William. *A Direction for the Weaker Sort of Christians: Shewing in What Manner They May be Prepared to the Worthy Receiving of the Sacrament of the Bodie and Bloud of Christ*. London, 1609.

Bray, Gerald, ed. *The Anglican Canons 1529–1947*. Church of England Record Society 6. Woodbridge, UK: Boydell Press, 1998.

Brinsley, John. *Ludus Literarius: Or, The Grammar Schoole*. London, 1612.

Burne, S. A. H., ed. *Collections for a History of Staffordshire 1935: Staffordshire Quarter Sessions Rolls*. Vol. 4, *1598–1602*. William Salt Archaeological Society, Kendal, 1936.

———, ed. *Collections for a History of Staffordshire 1940: Staffordshire Quarter Sessions Rolls*. Vol. 5, *1603–1606*. William Salt Archaeological Society, Kendal, 1940.

Calendar of State Papers. Domestic Series, Charles I 1625–1626. London: Her Majesty's Stationery Office, 1858.

Calendar of State Papers. Domestic Series, Charles I 1639–1640. London: Her Majesty's Stationery Office, 1877.

Calendar of State Papers Colonial, East Indies and Persia. Edited by W. Noel Sainsbury. Vol. 8, *1630–34*. London: Her Majesty's Stationery Office, 1892.

Calvin, John. *An Excellent Treatise of the Immortalytie of the Soule*. London, 1581.

Clarke, Samuel. "The Life of Master Arthur Hildersam." In *The Lives of Two and Twenty English Divines*, 144–56. London, 1660.

———. "The Life and Death of Dr. Robert Harris." In *A Collection of the Lives of Ten Eminent Divines*, 274–329. London, 1662.

———. "The Life and Death of Doctor Gouge." In *A General Martyrologie*, 234–47. London, 1677.

Clay, John W., ed. *The Visitation of Cambridge Made in AD [1575] Continued and Enlarged with the Visitation of the Same County made by Henery St George*

Richmond—Herald, Marshall and Deputy to William Camden, Clarenceulx, in AD 1619. London, 1897.

Cotton, John. *The Correspondence of John Cotton*. Edited by Sargent Bush Jr. Chapel Hill: University of North Carolina Press, 2001.

Cross, Claire, ed. *The Letters of Sir Francis Hastings 1574–1609*. Vol. 69. Frome: Somerset Record Society, 1969.

Crouch, Nathaniel [R. B.]. *Admirable Curiosities, Rarities, and Wonders in England, Scotland and Ireland*. London, 1682.

Darrell, John. *A True Narration of the Strange and Grevous Vexation by the Devil of 7 Persons in Lancashire and William Sommers of Nottingham*. N.p., 1600.

————. *A Detection of that Sinful, Shameful, Lying and Ridiculous Discourse of Samuel Harshnet*. N.p., 1600.

Ellesmere, Francis Egerton. *The Egerton Papers*. Edited by J. Payne Collier. Camden Society First Series, 12. London, 1840.

Elrington, C. R., and J. H. Todd, eds. *The Whole Works of the Most Rev. James Ussher*. Vol. 15. Dublin: Hodges, Smith, and Co., 1829–1864.

Fincham, Kenneth, ed. *Visitation Articles and Injunctions of the Early Stuart Church*. Vol. 2. Church of England Record Society 5, Woodbridge, 1998.

A Form of Common Prayer, Together with an Order of Fasting. London, 1625.

Foster, C. W., ed. *The State of the Church in the Reigns of Elizabeth and James I as Illustrated by Documents relating to the Diocese of Lincoln*. Lincoln Record Society, 1926.

Fuller, Thomas. *The Church History of Britain: From the Birth of Jesus Christ Untill the Year M.DC.XLVIII*. London, 1655.

————. *The History of the Worthies of England*. London, 1662.

Gataker, Thomas. *A Discours Apologetical*. London, 1654.

————. "The Life and Death of Master William Bradshaw." In Samuel Clarke, *A General Martyrologie*, 25–60. London, 1677.

Greenwood, John, and Henry Barrow. *The Writings of John Greenwood and Henry Barrow 1591–1593*. Edited by Leland H. Carlson. London: Routledge, 1970.

Harsnett, Samuel. *A Discovery of the Fraudulent Practises of John Darrel*. London, 1599.

Henry, Matthew. *A Sermon Preach'd at the Funeral of the Reverend Mr Francis Tallents... With a Short Account of his Life and Death*. London, 1709.

————. *The Lives of Philip and Matthew Henry.* Edited by J. B. Williams. Edinburgh: Banner of Truth, 1974.

Hildersham, Arthur. *The Doctrine of Communicating Worthily in the Lords Supper.* London, 1609. Reprinted in 1615, 1617, 1619, 1623, 1627, 1630, 1634, 1636, and 1643.

————. *CVIII Lectures upon the Fourth of John.* London, 1629. Reprinted in 1632, 1647, and 1656.

————. *The Doctrine of Fasting and Prayer, and Humiliation for Sinne.* London, 1633. 2nd edition printed in 1636.

————. *CLII Lectures upon Psalm LI.* London, 1635. 2nd edition printed in 1642.

————. *The Canticles.* London, 1672.

————. *Dealing with Sin in Our Children.* Morgan, Pa.: Soli Deo Gloria, 2004.

Historic Manuscripts Commission, Hastings I and II. Series 78. London: His Majesty's Stationery Office, 1928 and 1930.

Hooker, Thomas. Preface to *A Fresh Suit against Human Ceremonies,* by William Ames. Amsterdam, 1633.

Hutchinson, Lucy. *Memoirs of the Life of Colonel John Hutchinson.* Edited by James Sutherland. Oxford: Oxford University Press, 1973.

Johnson, Francis. *A Treatise of the Ministery of the Church of England.* [Low Countries?], 1595.

Keeble, N. H., and Geoffrey F. Nuttall, eds. *A Calendar of the Correspondence of Richard Baxter.* 2 vols. Oxford: Clarendon Press, 1990 and 1991.

Larkin, J. F., ed. *Stuart Royal Proclamations.* Vol. 2. Oxford: Clarendon Press, 1983.

Lilly, William. *Mr William Lilly's History of His Life and Times: From the Year 1602, to 1681.* 2nd ed. London, 1715.

Mather, Cotton. *Magnalia Christi Americana.* London, 1702.

Mather, Increase. *The Life and Death of Mr Richard Mather.* Cambridge, Mass., 1670.

Mather, Richard. *A Defence of the Answer and Arguments of the Synod Met at Boston.* Cambridge, Mass., 1664.

Matthews, A. G. *Calamy Revised.* Oxford: Clarendon Press, 1934.

More, George. *A True Discourse concerning the Certaine Possession and Dispossession of 7 Persons in One Familie in Lancashire.* N.p., 1600.

Peel, Albert. "A Puritan Survey of the Church in Staffordshire in 1604." *English Historical Review* 26, no. 102 (1911): 348–52.

———, ed. *The Seconde Parte of a Register*. Vols. 1–2. Cambridge: Cambridge University Press, 1915.

———, and Leland H. Carlson, eds. *Cartwrightiana*. London: Allen & Unwin, 1951.

Pestell, Thomas. *The Poems of Thomas Pestell*. Edited by Hannah Buchan. Oxford: Blackwell, 1940.

Searle, Arthur, ed. *The Barrington Family Letters 1628–1632*. Camden Fourth Series. Vol. 28. London: Royal Historical Society, 1983.

Sermons or Homilies Appointed to be Read in Churches in the Time of Queen Elizabeth, of Famous Memory. London, 1817.

Smyth, John. *Paralleles, Censures, Observations*. Middelburg, 1609.

Teellinck, Willem. *The Path of True Godliness*. Edited by Joel R. Beeke. Translated by Annemie Godbehere. Grand Rapids: Baker, 2003.

The Triall of Maister Dorrell. Middelburg, 1599.

Willet, Andrew. *An Harmonie Upon the Second Book of Samuel*. Cambridge, 1614.

———. *Synopsis Papismi*. London, 1592.

Secondary Sources

Atherton, Ian, and David Como. "The Burning of Edward Wightman: Puritanism, Prelacy and the Politics of Heresy in Early Modern England." *English Historical Review* 120, no. 489 (2005): 1215–50.

Babbage, Stuart Barton. *Puritanism and Richard Bancroft*. London: SPCK Publishing, 1962.

Bossy, John. *The English Catholic Community 1570–1850*. London: Darton, Longman and Todd, 1975.

Brachlow, Stephen. *The Communion of Saints: Radical Puritan and Separatist Ecclesiology 1570–1625*. Oxford: Oxford University Press, 1988.

Bremer, Francis. *Congregational Communion: Clerical Friendship in the Anglo American Puritan Community, 1610–1692*. Boston: Northeastern University Press, 1994.

Brook, Benjamin. *The Lives of the Puritans*. London, 1813.

Burns, Norman T. *Christian Mortalism from Tyndale to Milton*. Cambridge, Mass.: Harvard University Press, 1972.

Burrage, Champlin. *The Early English Dissenters in the Light of Recent Research (1550–1641).* Cambridge: Cambridge University Press, 1912.

Butler, Jon. "Thomas Teackle's 333 Books: A Great Library on Virginia's Eastern Shore, 1697." *The William and Mary Quarterly.* 3rd ser., 49, no. 3 (July 1992): 449–91.

Catalogue of Books from Parochial Libraries in Shropshire. London: Mansell, 1971.

Cliffe, J. T. *The Puritan Gentry: The Great Puritan Families of Early Stuart England.* London: Routledge & Kegan, 1984.

Coffey, John, and Paul C. H. Lim, eds. *The Cambridge Companion to Puritanism.* Cambridge: Cambridge University Press, 2008.

Cogswell, Thomas. *Home Divisions: Aristocracy, the State and Provincial Conflict.* Manchester, UK: Manchester University Press, 1998.

Collinson, Patrick. *The Elizabethan Puritan Movement.* Oxford: Clarendon Press, 1967.

———. "The Shearmen's Tree and the Preacher: The Strange Death of Merry England in Shrewsbury and Beyond." In *The Reformation in English Towns 1500–1640,* edited by Patrick Collinson and John Craig, 205–20. Basingstoke: Macmillan, 1998.

Cross, Claire. *The Puritan Earl: The Life of Henry Hastings Third Earl of Huntingdon 1536–1595.* London: Macmillan, 1966.

Durston, Christopher, and Jacqueline Eales, eds. *The Culture of English Puritanism, 1560–1700.* Basingstoke: Macmillan, 1996.

Fincham, Kenneth. *Prelate as Pastor: The Episcopate of James I.* Oxford: Clarendon Press, 1990.

Fox, Levi. *A Country Grammar School: A History of Ashby-de-la-Zouch Grammar School through Four Centuries 1567 to 1967.* Oxford: Oxford University Press, 1967.

Freeman, Thomas. "Demons, Deviance and Defiance: John Darrell and the Politics of Exorcism in Late Elizabethan England." In *Conformity and Orthodoxy in the English Church c. 1560–1660,* 34–63. Edited by Peter Lake and Michael Questier. Woodbridge: Boydell Press, 2000.

Gibson, Marion. *Possession, Puritanism and Print: Darrell, Harsnett, Shakespeare and the Elizabethan Exorcism Controversy.* London: Pickering & Chatto, 2006.

Goadby, Joseph. *Memoirs of the Rev. Arthur Hildersham.* N.p., 1819.

Green, Ian. *Print and Protestantism in Early Modern England.* Oxford: Oxford University Press, 2000.

Grell, Ole Peter. *Dutch Calvinists in Early Stuart London: The Dutch Church in Austin Friars, 1603–1642.* Leiden: Brill, 1988.

Haigh, Christopher. "The Troubles of Thomas Pestell: Parish Squabbles and Ecclesiastical Politics in Caroline England." *Journal of British Studies* 41 (Oct. 2002): 403–28.

Hextall, W. and J. Hextall. *The History and Description of Ashby-de-la-Zouch with Excursions in the Neighbourhood.* London, 1852.

Hillier, Kenneth. *The Book of Ashby-de-la-Zouch.* Buckingham: Barracuda Books, 1984.

Hoskins, W. G., ed. *The Victoria County History of the County of Leicester.* Vol. 2. Oxford: Oxford University Press, 1969.

Kendall, R. T., *Calvin and English Calvinism to 1649.* Oxford: Oxford University Press, 1979.

Lake, Peter, and Michael Questier, eds. *Conformity and Orthodoxy in the English Church c. 1560–1660*: Woodbridge: Boydell Press, 2000.

Mayer, Thomas F., *Reginald Pole: Prince and Prophet.* Cambridge: Cambridge University Press, 2000.

Middleton, Erasmus. *Biographica Evangelica.* London, 1816.

Moore, Jonathan D. "The Extent of the Atonement: English Hypothetical Universalism versus Particular Redemption." In *Drawn into Controversie: Reformed Theological Diversity and Debates within Seventeenth-Century British Puritanism*, 124–61. Edited by Mark Jones & Michael A. G. Haykin. Gottingen: Vandenhoeck & Ruprecht, 2011.

Morgan, John. *Godly Learning: Puritan Attitudes towards Reason, Learning, and Education, 1560–1640.* Cambridge: Cambridge University Press, 1986.

Morgan, Victor. *A History of the University of Cambridge.* Vol. 2, 1546–1750. Cambridge: Cambridge University Press, 2004.

Neal, Daniel. *The History of the Puritans.* London, 1732.

Nichols, John. *The History and Antiquities of Leicestershire.* 4 vols. London, 1804.

Oates, J. C. T. *A Catalogue of the Fifteenth Century Printed Books in the University Library Cambridge.* Cambridge: Cambridge University Press, 1954.

Parker, Kenneth L., and Eric J. Carlson. *"Practical Divinity": The Works and Life of Revd Richard Greenham.* Aldershot, Eng.: Ashgate, 1998.

Peile, John. *Christ's College.* London, 1900.

Perley, Sidney, *A History of Salem, Massachusetts.* Vol. I, 1626–1637. Salem, Mass.: S. Perley, 1924.

Plume, Thomas. *Catalogue of the Plume Library.* Edited by S. G. Deed. Maldon, Eng.: Plume Library Trustees, 1959.

Pollard, A. W., and G. R. Redgrave. *A Short Title Catalogue of Books Printed in England, Scotland, and Ireland, 1475–1640.* 3 vols. London: London Bibliographical Society, 1986.

Powell, William R., ed. *The Victoria County History of the County of Essex.* Vol. 4.: London: Oxford University Press for the Institute of Historical Research, 1956.

Quintrell, B. W. "The Royal Hunt and the Puritans, 1604–1605." *Journal of Ecclesiastical History* 31, no. 1 (1980): 41–58.

Raineval, Melville Henry Massue Ruvigny. *The Plantagenet Roll of the Blood Royal.* London: T.C. and E.C. Jack, 1908.

Scott, W. *The Story of Ashby-de-la-Zouch.* Ashby-de-la-Zouch: George Brown, 1907.

Seaver, Paul. *The Puritan Lectureships: The Politics of Religious Dissent 1560–1662.* Stanford: Stanford University Press, 1970.

Shaw, Stebbing. *The History and Antiquities of Staffordshire.* Vol. 1. London, 1801.

A Short History of Saffron Walden School 1317–1928. Saffron Walden: Talbot Press, [1928?].

Spurgeon, Charles H. "Catalogue of Biblical Commentaries and Expositions," in *Commenting and Commentaries.* London, 1890.

Thomas, Keith. *Religion and the Decline of Magic.* London: Weidenfeld and Nicolson, 1971.

Tyacke, Nicholas. *Aspects of English Protestantism c. 1520–1700.* Manchester, UK: Manchester University Press, 2001.

Venn, John, and John Archibald Venn. *Alumni Cantabrigienses: A Biographical List of All Known Students, Graduates and Holders of Office at the University of Cambridge, Part I: From the Earliest Times to 1751.* 4 vols. Cambridge: Cambridge University Press, 1922–1927.

Webster, Tom. *Godly Clergy in Early Stuart England: The Caroline Puritan Movement c. 1620–1643.* Cambridge: Cambridge University Press, 1997.

Welch, C. E. "Early Nonconformity in Leicestershire." *Transactions of the Leicestershire Archaeological and Historical Society.* Vol. 37, 1961, 29–43.

Wing, Donald. *A Short-Title Catalogue of Books Printed in England, Scotland and Ireland, 1641–1700,* 3 vols. New York: Modern Language Association of America, 1972–1988.

Wright, A. P. M., ed. *The Victoria County History of the County of Cambridge and the Isle of Ely.* Vol. 6. Oxford: Oxford University Press, 1978.

Unpublished Papers and Theses

Chalmers, C. D. "Puritanism in Leicestershire, 1558–1663." MA thesis, University of Leeds, 1962.

Moore, Jonathan. "'Christ Is Dead for Him': John Preston (1587–1628) and English Hypothetical Universalism." PhD thesis, University of Cambridge, 2000.

Moxon, C. J. M. "Ashby-de-la-Zouch: A Social and Economic Survey of a Market Town—1570–1720." DPhil thesis, University of Oxford, 1971.

Rowe, Lesley. "Guilt by Association? Arthur Hildersham and the 'Blasphemous Heretic' Edward Wightman." MA essay, University of Warwick, 2003.

———. "The Worlds of Arthur Hildersham (1563–1632)." PhD thesis, University of Warwick, 2009.

Van Dixhoorn, Chad B., "Reforming the Reformation: Theological Debate at the Westminster Assembly, 1643–1652." PhD thesis, University of Cambridge, 2004.

Index

Map (not to scale) of
ASHBY-DE-LA-ZOUCH
at the time of
ARTHUR HILDERSHAM
showing the approximate
location of key sites.

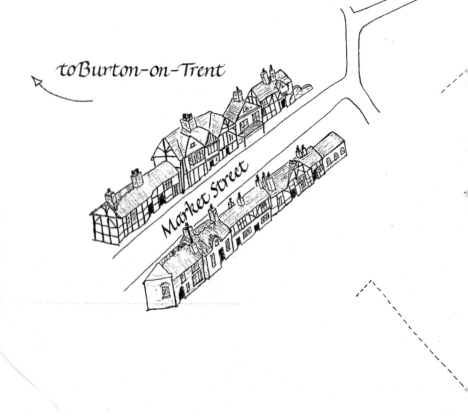

to Burton-on-Trent

Market Street